How to Understand Language

How to Understand Language

A Philosophical Inquiry

Bernhard Weiss

McGill-Queen's University Press
Montreal & Kingston • Ithaca

© Bernhard Weiss, 2010

ISBN: 978-0-7735-3734-7 (bound)
ISBN: 978-0-7735-3735-4 (pbk.)

Legal deposit first quarter 2010
Bibliothèque nationale du Québec

Published simultaneously outside North America by Acumen Publishing Limited

Library and Archives Canada Cataloguing in Publication

Weiss, Bernhard
    How to understand language : a philosophical inquiry / Bernhard Weiss.

Includes bibliographical references and index.
ISBN 978-0-7735-3734-7 (bound).--ISBN 978-0-7735-3735-4 (pbk.)

    1. Language and languages--Philosophy. I. Title.

P107.W455 2010   401   C2009-906199-6

Typeset in Minion Pro.
Printed in the UK by MPG Books Group.

Contents

Preface

The course of true argument does not always run smooth. Obviously I hope the argument presented here is close to "true" and I have done my level best in the text to keep it smooth. But I can do more: the next few pages give an overview of the argument and place each chapter in its development. This should help to set readers up for what is coming and may help them negotiate their way through some of the transitions.

I begin, in the opening chapter, by drawing out some of the reasons that language is philosophically puzzling. The chapter should not be read as cataloguing a set of questions to which we require a philosophical answer. One might well wish that the discipline were as clear-cut as that. Rather, there are a number of apparently puzzling facets of language and one might take different approaches to them. What one philosopher sees as a genuine source of puzzlement another will dismiss as some sort of confusion; where one takes a feature to stand in need of explanation another will take that same feature as fundamentally explanatory; where one proposes a certain form of explanation another will offer an alternative. So, in the face of these mysteries about language, we seek an approach. My first task thus becomes that of finding a productive approach to the philosophical understanding of language. This largely occupies the business of Chapters 2–6. Let me anticipate the upshot of that long discussion: at Chapter 6 we arrive at a claim that is motivated, although not compelled by, the previous four chapters, namely, that we should pursue the philosophy of language by considering the form that a theory of meaning for a language would take. That approach was introduced to us by Donald Davidson and receives strong support in the writings of Michael Dummett, and is, I suppose, the current orthodoxy in the field. I arrive at that Davidsonian position by first considering the approach of analysis.

Can we analyse linguistic meaning (or a cognate notion) so as to yield philosophical insight? I argue that there is a real difficulty in seeing how such an analysis should begin. Just what should we be analysing and how can we postulate a starting-point for analysis without significant philosophical reflection on the nature of language? I illustrate the difficulty of answering this question by focusing on names (Chapter 2). In fact, this discussion performs a dual role. On the one hand, it enables me to introduce some basic material in the philosophy of language, which will be drawn on later in the book, and, on the other, it seems to demonstrate that there is no philosophically uncontroversial category of names or singular terms; one's demarcation of this category of expression will be informed by significant insight into the philosophy of language.

My next port of call is Grice's analysis of sentence-meaning (Chapter 3). I raise a series of problems for Grice's account, many of which will not be news to those familiar with the field but some of which I hope are both new and worth taking seriously. But a Gricean approach will be unable to help us with our puzzlement about language unless it can feed into an account of word-meaning. I find the most hopeful development of a Gricean approach in this direction in Schiffer's writings; but conclude that the best interpretation of the proposal is as that of offering a theory of truth for the language that is constrained by the account of sentence-meaning. Since the account of sentence-meaning is fraught with difficulty, this suggests that a Davidsonian attempt to constrain such a theory by the business of interpretation might be more promising.

Our route to that Davidsonian position is, however, not yet complete. For, in thinking about the analysis of the concept of meaning, we have thus far neglected the notion of synonymy, and Quine's work is extremely helpful in focusing on just this notion. First, I suggest that we can read "Two Dogmas of Empiricism" as, in part, providing an argument that there is no informative analysis of the notion of synonymy (Chapter 4). This is not to cast any doubt on that notion – as Quine claims – but it is to place a bar on this approach to the philosophy of language. We might thus do better to approach the notion of synonymy indirectly. That is, we might try to understand it by thinking about a project that would require us to be sensitive to relations of synonymy, and thus the philosophical interest in translation and the topic for the next chapter is born. Before tackling that issue, however, I look at the pragmatic, holistic model of language that Quine espouses in the second part of that paper. I suggest that Quine's suspicions about analyticity and synonymy lie in his weddedness to that model, which is not adequately motivated. However, a possible reply to Quine's vision here is achieved only at the close of the book.

The business of radical translation now shifts into view (Chapter 5). Here I support Evans's argument that claims that the enterprise of translation is likely to be insufficiently sensitive to facts about speakers' use of language and thus that we ought instead to consider a project that will constrain itself in this way: attention thus turns to the theory of meaning. The first phase of the book is complete with the establishment of this Davidsonian approach. After a discussion of some general issues to do with the theory of meaning (Chapter 6), we begin an extended examination of Davidson's position (Chapters 7, 8 and 10).

Let us summarize Davidson's position thus: he advocates the meaning-theoretic approach to the philosophy of language and conceives of a theory of meaning as a theory of truth constructed via the business of radical interpretation. That is, we are to imagine the attempt to interpret an entirely foreign speaker by constructing a scheme of interpretation; the form of that scheme will be a systematic specification of each sentence's truth-conditions. Most of the rest of the book is concerned with levering Davidson's *conception* of the theory of meaning away from his more general *approach* and with finding a replacement for it. Two notions are crucial in that endeavour: the conception of meanings as public – the publicity of meaning – and the conception of language as normative. A notion of the publicity of meaning will already have arisen explicitly in the discussion of Quine on translation. The publicity of meaning is an insistence that the meanings a speaker attaches to her terms are *in some sense* publicly available. Of course, in just what sense meanings are publicly available is an issue that is amply worth disputing, and my concern with Davidson is that he conceives of the publicity of meaning in terms of radical interpretation; I complain that that conception is unmotivated and has some upalatable consequences (Chapter 10); that sets up the search for a motivated conception. In Chapter 11, I argue that this motivation is not to be found in semantic externalist positions. I concede that the arguments for semantic externalism require that we make room in our account for the linguistic division of labour, that is, for the idea that a speaker's use of language will, in part, depend on what other speakers are able to do, on her behalf, as it were. But none of this demonstrates that a solitary speaker *could not* do everything for herself. And thoughts about the need to explain communication are, I argue, indecisive since nothing has been said about what *other* explanatory burdens might be placed on our conception of meaning. I go on to argue that the true motivation for the publicity of meaning lies in the normativity of meaning. That, however, is a contentious notion and so I have work to do before being able to launch that argument. Davidson, in his later writings on the philosophy of language, eschews the notion. In Chapter 8, I argue that he is wrong to do so – and by "wrong" I mean wrong by his own lights. And in Chapter 9, I take on a slightly different denier of normativity. A number of writers have recently conceded that linguistic items have correctness-conditions but have denied that these entail that there are any prescriptions governing speakers' use of language. I argue that, at the very least, meanings figure in practical reasoning in a quite distinctive way, delivering prescriptions relating to use. And I take this to establish that meaning is essentially normative. So the simplest reading of these two chapters is as comprising, first, a refutation of what I take to be our best non-normative conception of meaning, and then a rebuttal of the simple rejection of normativity. Thus, having established the normativity of language (Chapters 8 and 9) and having rejected alternative sources of publicity (Chapter 11), I take myself to be motivated in searching for a basis and conception of publicity (a need established in Chapter 10) in the normativity of meaning.

Before I take up that tale I ought to react to a speculative aspect of Chapters 8 and 9. At the end of Chapter 8, I speculate that there might be a generalization of the argument that derives the normativity of meaning from *any* conception of the publicity of meaning. Since I go on to derive the publicity of meaning from the normativity of meaning, what I shall have established, if the generalization holds, is that meaning is normative if and only if it is public. One might then read the ensuing work as unpacking the conception of publicity that would go with accepting this package. But, as I said, this all lies very much in the realm of speculation.

In thinking about the normativity of language, I turn to Wittgenstein and his commentators. Chapters 12 and 13 thus constitute a sustained exposition and meditation on the impact of Wittgenstein's rule-following considerations. I draw the consequence of publicity of meaning at the start of Chapter 13 and do so from my rejection of meaning-scepticism voiced in Chapter 12. The rest of Chapter 13 attempts to come to terms with the nature of rule-following in such a way as to yield a particular conception of publicity. The conception is close to, but distinct from, one I find in the writings of Dummett.

The book closes (Chapter 14) by committing itself to a broad conception of the theory of meaning. I sympathetically present Dummett's and Brandom's objections to truth-conditional accounts of meaning and then go on to investigate ways of developing opposing use-conditional accounts. Here I argue for a view according to which meaning is characterized in terms of dual features of the use of sentences; my suggestion – that is all it is – is to account for meaning in terms of the assertion-conditions of a sentence combined with the conditions in which such an assertion is defeated. Finally I close by deploying such an account to respond to Quine's worries about analyticity and analytic sentences.

Much of the material in this book is not easy, and the course of argument (as the above paragraphs will suggest) is by no means straightforward. I have, however, attempted to give expositions of every area of the subject that features in the book and assume only some familiarity with the subject and with elementary logic. Senior undergraduates wishing to push their thinking in the subject further should be able to tackle the book, and I hope it will engage both graduate students working in the field and my academic colleagues.

Some of the writing of the book was made possible by sabbatical leave at the University of Cape Town (UCT), for which I am extremely grateful. Audiences at the Spring Colloquium at Rhodes University in 2008 and at UCT have been the source of useful feedback. I would like to thank my colleagues in the department at UCT for providing a congenial work and research environment. In particular, I would like to thank Jeremy Wanderer and Jack Ritchie for useful discussions. Two anonymous referees for Acumen provided immensely useful advice, which saved me from many embarrassments and brought about substantial and beneficial changes in the text. My thanks too to Steven Gerrard, at

Acumen, who was positive about the project from my first suggestion of it and who has been patient and supportive throughout the protracted writing of the book. Special thanks to Christine Jacobsen, who enabled the process of writing in all sorts of ways and who was my best respite from it.

This is for Chad and Pepper – my boys – neither of whom had much use for language: Chad, who was driven by both love and fear but whose love was always overpowering; and Pepper, who was gentleness incarnate – apart, that is, from his mean streak.

1. The puzzles of language

One often hears it remarked that language is a marvellous tool. The metaphor is striking and worth taking seriously, if only because it is so pregnant. In what sense is language a tool? Tools enable or facilitate us to do certain things. What sorts of things do we use language to achieve? What is it about language that, unlike most other tools, it deserves to be marvelled at? Are aspects of the marvelling distinctly philosophical?

Consider a humdrum, familiar tool: a hammer. We use a hammer to achieve a variety of things: to bang in a nail, to drive in a wooden dowel or wedge, to replace the lid on a can of paint, to make a hole in someone's skull or to manipulate a chisel and so on. One might do a huge variety of things with a hammer, many of which were not anticipated by its maker or by the inventor – if there was an inventor – of hammers. But (virtually) every use to which a hammer is put is a function of its use in banging. One might say that the basic function of hammers is to direct an impact to a desired point. Well that, anyway, is my theory of hammers. I lay no great claim to its being correct; we are not interested in hammers here; we are interested in language. What is suggestive in this example is that tools seem to have a variety of uses each of which stems from some basic function. Is this true of the tool of language? What purposes does language serve? And is there a basic function of language that underlies these purposes?

I want to begin with an attempt to come to grips with some of the philosophical puzzles about language. The puzzles are like a "checklist" for gauging the success of one or another approach to language that we shall go on to consider. But we shall not be applying them *as* a checklist since the issues are far too open-ended and complex for us to be able to do that. For instance, what one philosopher takes to be a basic riddle to be solved is taken by another to be a basic explanatory concept. However, the puzzles will inform our thinking about the different approaches we go on to consider.

1.1 The uses of language

1.1.1 Language and the world

Reference

We use language to talk about things. My head of department and I just had a discussion about the talented student in PHI 3010 and were considering ways of steering her away from postgraduate work in economics and towards a Master's degree in philosophy. What enabled us to achieve this was, in part, an ability to use words such as "the most talented student in PHI 3010" or "Nozizwe Madlala", which succeed in picking out or referring to the academically distinguished student. This is such a common occurrence that it may not seem in the least remarkable. But reflect for a moment on what is happening here. The words refer to a certain individual and, in virtue of this fact, we are able to talk about her by using those words. So at the base of this ability is a relation between the words and an individual: the relation of reference. But what sort of relation is this?

Let us not address that question right now. Our aim now is to try to clarify what is puzzling about language, so let me say a few words about why this question might well be very difficult to answer. There are two aspects to the problem: one is the range of modes of referring to an object and the other is the range of things to which we can refer.

Consider the different means that language provides for achieving reference to an object. One can pick on any object presented to one in experience and talk about it, recruiting demonstrative expressions such as "this" and "that", or complex demonstratives such as "this piece of chalk" in order to do so. Expressions of this form enable one to isolate a given object from the rest of one's experience and to single it out as an object of discussion. Indexical expressions enable one to exploit features of the context of use in order to effect a reference. Thus when I speak I can refer to the time of utterance by saying "now", refer to the place of utterance by saying "here" and refer to the utterer by saying "I". One can talk about an object by means of its properties, picking it out as *the* object that has such and such property. That is, one might refer to an object by using a definite description. And then there are names. I can name an object and then use the name at any time and at any place to refer to the object, or I can exploit names that already exist in the language. Finally, by means of anaphoric expressions I can exploit a previously successful reference. Ludwig might say to me, "I visited the Victoria Falls on my trip to Zambia" and I might respond, "Was it as beautiful as they say?" Here Ludwig refers to a particular geographical feature by means of the phrase "the Victoria Falls" and I can borrow the successful reference by means of the expression "it". Notice that the "it" here functions as a pronoun of laziness – it relieves me of the obligation of going to the trouble of repeating Ludwig's phrase "the Victoria Falls". But circumstances might be different. Nina might say to me, "I saw a lynx over at Silvermines on Sunday" and I might respond, "Was it in the woods or in the fynbos?" Here Nina has not used an expression to refer to the particular lynx that she saw. But it is understood that she saw one lynx and the anaphoric "it" enables me to refer to the lynx whose existence is responsible for the truth of her statement, without having to manufacture a definite description, for example, "the lynx that you saw".

We shall not probe these different ways of referring any further. For now, the point is simple: if reference is a relation between a word or phrase and an object, then there are many different sorts of words and phrases that refer. Or alternatively, if speakers rather than words refer, then they are enabled to do so by a variety of sorts of words and phrases.

What lies on the other side of the relation of reference? To what can we refer? The answer here appears truly bewildering. I can refer to objects in my immediate surroundings or use names and definite descriptions – among others – to refer to objects which are not now present. But since I need not be responsible for the introduction of the name into language and since I can refer by a definite description to the object that satisfies the descriptive property, whether or not I have ever come across it, I can refer to objects that are separated from me either in time – objects in the past, for example the library of Alexandria, or in the future, for example the fifth president of the democratic South Africa – or in space – objects flung to the far reaches of the universe: "the largest star in the closest galaxy to the Milky Way". I can also refer to objects that are available to me only indirectly by means of tools such as the microscope, or that are perhaps known only through their effects: theoretical entities such as electrons. It seems too that I can refer to objects that I could not possibly come across, abstract objects such as numbers, forms of government and rights. And, if that were not impressive enough, I can refer to objects that do not exist: the golden mountain, Nessie (the Loch Ness Monster) and Santa Claus. Perhaps one can refer, too, to objects that could not possibly exist: the round square, the greatest prime number, the devout heretic.

Speakers of a language thus appear to have an astonishing ability to refer to a huge range of entities. What sort of relation could it be that connects humble signs – words: marks on paper or noises – with such a mind-boggling array of things? And, more than that, with one small word one can refer to them all en masse. When I say "everything" I seem to be talking about literally and absolutely everything: everything is such that if it is a man then it is mortal. The property of being mortal, if a man, applies to absolutely everything and has been asserted so to do in my previous sentence. How wonderful!

Truth
By combining appropriate simple expressions we can form a certain sort of complex expression, declarative sentences, which have a very distinctive role: they enable us to make utterances that are either true or false. Sentences allow

3

us to represent both how the world is and how the world is not. We can represent the world accurately – truly – or inaccurately – falsely. Now the relation of reference seems puzzling, in part, because of the range of expressions that refer and the range of things that expressions, at least apparently, refer to. But sentences are puzzling in a rather different way. What is this special feature of the way signs are unified in sentences that suddenly means that the sentence does not simply relate to something in the world but is now capable of saying how the world is? Names and descriptions either refer to some object or fail to refer, but sentences relate to the world either by being true or by being false. What is responsible for bringing this *duality* of truth and falsehood into play?

Some of our (utterances of) sentences are true but might have been false. Others are true and could not have been false. Some sentences are false but might have been true. Other sentences are false and could not have been true. So we can talk about the way the world happens to be, about the way the world must be, about the way the world could be and about the way the world could not be: a truly impressive expressive ability.

1.1.2 Language and the mind

Language may well be related to the world in interesting ways. But it is also clearly related to the mind: our relation to language, as speakers, is a relation of language to the mind. We can express and convey thoughts in language; language links minds; language use is itself rational; and there is a close affinity between language and thinking: thoughts and beliefs, like sentences, are capable of being about things and of being true or false.

Language and thought
As just mentioned, we use language as a medium of thought in the sense that we can express and so convey our thoughts to one another. Language is our primary means of communicating. But, additionally, language appears to be a vehicle of thought. It is certainly true that, on occasion, we think in language. So language is, at least incidentally, a vehicle of thought: it is capable of facilitating thought even though it remains an open possibility that those thoughts could have been had independently of language. This possibility – if, indeed, it is a genuine possibility – raises the question of whether we can explain the capacity of language to express thought in terms of a relationship it bears to independently existing thoughts. Could language simply be a code for thought? Or, in contrast, might there be at least some thoughts where the relationship between the thought and language is much closer; that is, could there be thoughts for which language is not merely an incidental but an essential vehicle? The idea is nicely illustrated by an example of Wittgenstein's. Plausibly, non-linguistic creatures have thoughts; we are happy to ascribe thought, on suitable occasions, to pre-linguistic children

and to animals. So for instance we might say that the dog expects his owner to come home when, for instance, the dog sits expectantly by the front door as it did the previous night, reacting with joy and relief when its owner made it home. But, asks Wittgenstein, could we say that the dog is expecting his owner home next week? This seems to stretch things too far. There is no way we could ascribe this thought to the dog without ascribing to him advanced concepts about time that he could only show that he has by interacting with language or with calendars and the like, which themselves depend on language. (See Wittgenstein 1958: 174.) So language seems to enable certain thoughts; it is an *essential* vehicle for those thoughts.

Language and rational activity

There is a different, although clearly not unrelated, sense, in which language relates to the mind. Language use is itself minded in the sense that our uses of language are actions, deliberate intentional actions, performed with the aim of furthering purposes that are not themselves, in general, linguistic. Say I perform the speech act of asserting the sentence "There is a hideous and, doubtless, dangerous spider crawling into your boot". In most cases this sort of doing is a rational action; I intend to perform that speech act and doing so involves using a sentence with a certain meaning. Moreover, I intend to perform that speech act because, in doing so, I fulfil a goal that need not be itself essentially linguistic. Perhaps I intend to inform you of the unwelcome proximity of the spider to your person. Using language to make an assertion such as the one I made might be one way, in most cases a peculiarly efficient way, of informing you. But if you were a monolingual Shona speaker, then I, a monolingual English speaker, might resort to elaborate mimes, gestures or sketches of spiders on boots to inform you of the same. In congenial circumstances any of these methods might be successful. But maybe there is no spider and the speech act was not intended to inform; I might merely have wanted to scare you, tease you or get you to practise touching your toes. Whatever – I have my various projects and language is at my service in pursuing them. Once I have linguistic competence I can choose to perform one or another speech act as a way of furthering my goals.

Language and communication

Language is at the service of our extralinguistic goals largely, if not exclusively, because it enables communication. Sharing a language (whatever that means exactly) enables us quickly and efficiently to communicate our thoughts and desires. Sometimes, of course, it is possible to imagine doing so without the aid of language, but in many cases it is impossible to imagine that we could communicate without using language and without there being some linguistic commonality between speaker and hearer. It is a vexed question just how we understand this commonality, but no account of language can be accepted if it makes it impossible to understand this social function.

1.1.3 The basic function of language

We can use a word to talk about an entity in virtue of the word's meaning. We can say that a certain situation obtains in the world because of a sentence's meaning. I can use a sentence to formulate a given thought, again, in virtue of the sentence's meaning. I can convey the thought to another, once again, in virtue of the sentence's agreed meaning. The sentence can be used to perform a given act, can be used to further a certain purpose, in virtue of what it means. So is there a basic function of linguistic expressions that stands to language as banging stands to hammers? It seems as if we have discovered that this basic function is the expression of meaning.

In one way this is a useful result and in another it is not. It is useful because it helps focus our attention: what we are interested in is a philosophical account of linguistic meaning that enables us to account for the uses of language that we have just detailed. So our goal is an adequate philosophical account of linguistic meaning. The hammer analogy gets us this far; just as the capacity of hammers to impart an impact explains their ability to facilitate driving in nails and cracking nuts and skulls, so the meaningfulness of language explains its functions in talking about the world or in expressing thoughts, thinking and acting. However, in another way the analogy is entirely misleading. For the way we account for meaning *might* well be to focus on one of the functions of language as primary and as capable of being deployed in an explanation of the other functions: perhaps language's relation to the world is what meaning consists in and we can explain its relations with thought in terms of its relation with the world or, perhaps, just the reverse is true: language's relation to thought is primary and this explains its worldly relations. In contrast, we simply could not think of the ability of a hammer to rectify dents as explained in terms of its ability to drive in nails, or vice versa for that matter.

The sense in which the result is not useful is this. I think it is intuitively obvious that banging – applying an impact to a particular spot – is itself a fairly uniform basic function. What we are assuming is that expressing a meaning exhibits a similar uniformity. At first sight there is perhaps not much reason for thinking so and, it seems, one of the intended lessons of Wittgenstein's later work is that there is no such uniformity. So at those points when he is attracted to the tool analogy he precisely uses it, not to liken language to a single tool, but to liken it to a collection of tools: "Think of the tools in a tool-box: there is a hammer, pliers, a saw, a screw-driver, a rule, a glue-pot, glue, nails and screws. – The functions of words are as diverse as the functions of these objects" (1958: §11). And moreover, he thinks that philosophers are confused when they pretend that there is a single underlying function here since, as he continues, "Of course, what confuses us is the uniform appearance of words when we hear them spoken or meet them in script and print. For their application is not presented to us so clearly. Especially when we are doing philosophy!" (*ibid.*).

It is like looking into the cabin of a locomotive. We see handles looking more or less alike. (Naturally, since they are all supposed to be handled.) But one is the handle of a crank which can be moved continuously (it regulates the opening of a valve); another is the handle of a switch, which has only two effective positions, it is either off or on; a third is the handle of a brake-lever, the harder one pulls on it, the harder it brakes; a fourth, the handle of a pump: it has an effect only so long as it is moved to and fro. (*Ibid.*: §12)

Wittgenstein's accusation is that philosophers are deluded by superficial similarities between words into searching for an underlying unity in the way words function. But if you think about language as it actually functions you will come to see that words perform a range of roles.

To be sure, this whole discussion of the unity of the phenomenon of meaning is somewhat vague. Obviously words and expressions in different syntactic categories and in different regions of language do function quite differently. Any account of meaning must do justice to this fact. So just what sort of unity are we proposing is exhibited by meaning? Wittgenstein's interlocutor is not put off by the move to the tool-box analogy:

Imagine someone saying: "*All* tools serve to modify something. Thus the hammer modifies the position of the nail, the saw the shape of the board, and so on." – And what is modified by the rule, the glue-pot, the nails? – "Our knowledge of a thing's length, the temperature of the glue, and the solidity of the box." – Would anything be gained by this assimilation of expressions? (*Ibid.*: §14)

Of course we can find or impose a unity on the most disparate of phenomena. But what would be the point of finding this unity? In our case the question is not hard to answer. We want meaning to be unified in a robust enough and relevant way to enable us to explain the functions of language in terms of meaning. So it is the explanatory role for which we intend the notion that dictates the character of its uniformity. If you suppose that such an explanatory ambition is appropriate and potentially interesting then you will, in all likelihood, take Wittgenstein's examples as pointing to interesting difficulties that the account will have to face. But that general message is not news: no one ever thought that accounting for meaning was going to be easy. So there seems to be something else lurking in Wittgenstein's suggestion here, namely that our philosophical ambitions to explain are worthy of suspicion.

Wittgenstein has a number of reasons for suspecting the business of philosophical explanation. We cannot allow ourselves here to be diverted too far from our route into a proper discussion of these meta-philosophical issues. However, one of Wittgenstein's worries seems to be that philosophical questions are based

on confusions. Here the accusation might well be that we are confused in supposing that meaning is a sufficiently unified phenomenon. However, although
the traditional philosopher of language may be confused on this score – and
perhaps Wittgenstein himself, in his earlier writings, was – there is no reason to
suppose that she *must* be. Many investigations are premised on certain claims.
This does not discredit them, nor does it show that those intellectual explorers
are confused. We simply need to be sufficiently self-conscious to realize the
nature of the assumptions underlying our investigation and ready to realize
that the failure of the task we set ourselves, in light of this assumption, will
show that the assumption is false. The question is one of method. Are we likely
to achieve more by making the assumption and undertaking the investigation
or by rejecting the assumption and not undertaking that investigation, perhaps
replacing it with another?

We could react as Wittgenstein does, rejecting the search for a philosophical
elucidation of the phenomenon of linguistic meaning and settling for pointed
descriptions of the actual functioning of language. Or, we could insist that there
is an underlying unity to the phenomenon of meaning and insist that it will take
a great deal of philosophical excavation to reveal. But rather than plump for one
or other of these alternatives, we could adopt a more self-conscious approach
– one that, first, is aware that it makes an *assumption* in supposing that there is
sufficient unity to meaning for it to be capable of philosophical elucidation and
that, secondly, admits a tension: the account is premised on seeing some unity
to meaning but must be capable of encompassing considerable diversity within
that unity. What would drive us towards this position is a sense that there are
apparently sensible philosophical questions to be asked about the nature of language and that Wittgenstein's approach would offer us no satisfaction on these
questions. We might in the end be driven to Wittgenstein's conclusion, but as
long as there are prospects of achieving philosophical answers here we should
persevere with the attempt. So I think Wittgenstein's position here is motivated
by a much more general suspicion about philosophical explanation. He is doubtful about what purposes such explanations serve, what constitutes an adequate
explanation and whether philosophy can stand outside ordinary practices and
justify them. But these meta-philosophical issues take us a long way from our
concerns in the philosophy of language.[1] Having noted them, let us press on.

We should record another sense in which trying to understand a hammer as a
tool and trying to understand language as a tool are very different enterprises. In
the latter case we are attempting to use *language* in order to understand *language*;
so the project is inevitably self-reflective. In itself, this is not an odd phenomenon
since one often uses language to talk about language, for example my last sentence used the word "language" twice; never split an infinitive. But there may be
a sense in which using language in order to understand language leads us to presuppose certain features of the very phenomenon we are trying to explain and so
limits the sort of explanation we can give, either in terms of who can receive the

explanation, or in terms of what is explained and what is left unexplained. Quite how this self-reflective character of our investigation plays itself out is not easy to anticipate and will depend on the view we have of meaning itself; some philosophers see no, or little, problem here. Others, such as the early Wittgenstein (1922), think that this self-reflective project is fundamentally problematic. I shall be suggesting that there is an important lesson here, one that both determines who our explanation is aimed at and quite what it succeeds in explaining.

1.2 Words and meanings

In some sense, yet to be made precise, it is clear that a word, considered just as a sign, does not select its own meaning. The same word might mean different things – homonyms exist – so there is no function from the word to its meaning. Similarly, different words may have the same meaning – synonyms exist – so there is no function from a meaning to a word. Perhaps for these reasons it is intuitively plausible that the word itself, considered merely as a mark or as a sound abstracted from the language it occurs in, *as such* bears no relation to its meaning. So there is something ad hoc, some would say conventional, about linguistic meaning. Any account of language must do justice to this fact.

If it is a fact, then it entails that the word does not connect itself to what it means. So this must be achieved in some other way. And the question is: what other way? We confer meanings on words by *using* them. So how does our use of a word forge the link with its meaning? One might think that the meaning is what causes us to use the word. But then how do we confer meanings on words that refer to abstract objects and to objects that do not exist or that we happen not to be causally related to?

As remarked, it is tempting to think of the connection of word to meaning as conventional. But what sort of convention established the connections? It is surely fanciful to suppose that these conventions are, other than exceptionally, explicitly agreed. Mostly we do not deliberately act as a community to confer meanings on words and, if we did so, we would presumably need to use language in order to state and communicate the convention. So the idea sets off a vicious regress or is circular. Are these, then, implicit conventions, conventions that we do not explicitly ratify as a community but somehow succeed in establishing? This is more promising but is still a difficult approach to sustain. The idea of an implicit convention depends on us acting, that is acting deliberately, in ways that preserve the convention and avoiding actions that flout the convention. But here we seem to be appealing to actions with specific intentions and the question now is: what confers content on those intentions?

These questions will occupy much of our attention. For now let us simply note, as a constraint on the account of meaning, that there is no intrinsic connection between a sign and its meaning.

1.3 Compositionality

1.3.1 Linguistic creativity

"George Bush just absconded on the space shuttle, *Discovery*, wearing a clown suit and carrying a pet monkey called 'Tony Blair'." I suspect that you have never heard that sentence before, yet presume you had no trouble understanding it. The reason you understand it is that you understand each of the component parts of the sentence and the significance of the way they are put together to form the sentence. If we presume that understanding is knowledge of meaning, then this fact has to be reflected in the account of meaning. If knowledge of the meaning of a complex expression can be derived from knowledge of the meanings of its parts and of the way they are composed, then the meaning of the complex expression must be determined by, must be a function of, the meanings of the parts and the way they are put together.

So the supposition is that in order to explain the phenomenon of linguistic creativity – our abilities to make and understand utterances of a potential infinity of sentences – we need to suppose that meaning and understanding have a compositional structure.

1.3.2 Acquisition of language

Speakers' acquisition of language seems to be a gradual process, and there seems to be considerable and significant agreement over the pattern of learners' entry into linguistic competence. One learns the simpler regions of language first and then moves on to more complex regions. But the point is not merely a contingent one to do with regularities displayed in the patterns in which linguistic ability accrues. Rather, the point is logical. You could not learn the concept of being a prime number or the meaning of the words "prime number" if you did not have the concept of multiplication, if you did not grasp the meaning of the word "multiply" (or the meaning of one of its synonyms). You could not understand the notion of communism if you did not have the concept of government – you need the latter to explain the former. So it is a feature of language – at least apparently – that one can only acquire the ability to speak certain bits of it after one has acquired mastery of other, simpler bits of it. Language learning *must* be a stage-by-stage process; earlier stages provide a stable base for one's passage to later stages.

These are fairly intuitive ideas about the nature of language and the structure of linguistic meanings. But they are powerful. For, if we accept that meaning and understanding have a compositional structure, we have strong reason for thinking that there must be some underlying unity to meanings themselves. We cannot both think of meanings as a motley – as a thoroughly diverse range of tools, whose unity is only superficial – and think of meanings as function-ing within an organized system in which the meanings of simple signs can be brought together to determine the meanings of complex signs. It is difficult to be clear about what is involved in thinking about meanings as displaying some sort of unity. But the opposing position – language (and meaning) as a motley – entails that there cannot be a philosophical account of how a language, consid-ered as a whole, functions. The most we can offer is descriptions of the working of local regions of language. If we now wheel in the thought about meanings fitting into a compositional structure, it becomes hard to sustain the view of language as a motley. The reason for this is that the compositional view forces us to see language as forming a single system – since words can be combined with other words across different regions of language to enable the expression of novel meanings – and that requires us to think systematically about language, that is, to look for an encompassing philosophical account of how a language, any language, functions.

Arguably, some philosophers overplay the systematic unity of (natural) lan-guages. Frege, for instance, insists that the semantic role of an expression is completely determined by its logico-syntactic role. For example, he holds that if we have decided that each of two expressions functions as a name, then we must always be able to exchange the one for the other without moving from sense to non-sense. Thus, having decided that numerical terms are names he thinks we need to be able to decide whether or not Julius Caesar is a number: if "5 = 3 + 2" is meaningful, then so too must be "Julius Caesar = 3 + 2", since both "Julius Caesar" and "5" are names. But, in contrast, attempts to fragment language face serious obstacles. Expressivism in ethics can be seen as precisely running counter to the Fregean insistence on systematic unity. The expressivist holds that sentences in ethical discourse, though apparently taking the form of declarative assertions, are no such things. Rather, they are expressions of an attitude towards an actual or possible state of affairs. Thus someone who claims that taking drugs is wrong is expressing her disapproval of taking drugs. A major problem with such an account is that it cannot explain how such pseudo-assertions are taken into logically complex sentences that figure in arguments whose goodness is purely a matter of logic. The expressivist has trouble explain-ing why refusal to accept the following argument (cf. Blackburn 1984: 190) betokens irrationality rather than wickedness.

> If taking drugs is wrong, then getting one's granny to take drugs is wrong.
> Taking drugs is wrong.
> So getting one's granny to take drugs is wrong.

Although these thoughts about compositionality may seem intuitively appeal-ing, we shall see that they can be and have been challenged. But, accepting them for the moment at face value, they still require some unpacking. Crucially the motivation for compositionality supposes that, as speakers of the language, we somehow deploy information about the meanings of words and the structure of complex expressions in order to arrive at the meanings of those complexes. But, in most cases, these are processes we are unaware of and, even reflectively, may be unable to account for. So just how is this information supposed to be stored and deployed? How is the speaker supposed to use her knowledge of the meaning of a particular word: is this at all like one's knowledge that fires are hot?

Secondly, the position imposes a certain view of meanings on us. It supposes that we can have established a meaning for simple expressions that then "runs ahead" of us and determines the meanings of complexes. In other words, it supposes that the meanings of the complexes are independent of our judgements about their meanings because they are fully determined by the meanings of their components. Wittgenstein, on the supposition that meanings determine a standard for correct use, throws this whole conception into doubt. The notion of compositionality that has just been introduced seems to force a conception of meaning that is challenged by Wittgenstein's argument. But Wittgenstein's target is not compositionality itself but a consequence of it – the consequence that standards of correctness can run ahead of our verdicts. We shall explore this issue much further in the later chapters; some very preliminary remarks follow.

1.4 The normativity of meaning

In a certain sense it is a platitude to say that speakers' uses of language are subject to standards of correctness. It is correct to call something "a hadeda" only if it is indeed a hadeda and it is wrong so to call an egret. Dictionaries record standards of this sort; teachers of language attempt to impart them; and, in general, speakers intend to uphold them and will often be criticized for failing to do so. No philosopher denies any of this, but some are inclined to read into these phenomena important lessons about the very nature of language: language use, they claim, is essentially normatively constrained. Others are less impressed by the phenomena: either they are inessential products of the circumstances of our actual use of language or the sense of normativity implicated in the phenomena is very weak. Whatever view you take, you will, however, need to address the phenomena, which either require explaining or explaining away. The normative character of language will be a major theme of the book. In Chapters 8 and 9 we encounter and argue against views that either deny that normativity is essential to use of language or deny its profundity. In Chapter 12 we raise a sceptical concern about meaning that is premised on the essentially normative character of language use, and in Chapter 13 we attempt to respond to the sceptical difficulty, drawing out potentially important lessons for the character of meaning and our attempts to portray it.

So much for the problems; let us move on to attempts to address them.

2. The starting-point for analysis

Although it has a wider range of techniques available to it, analytical philosophy is closely linked with a bold, direct approach towards understanding a philosophically problematic concept: conceptual analysis. Conceptual analysis aims at revealing the nature of a complex concept by revealing how it is constituted. It proceeds by focusing on central applications of the concept and detailing necessary and sufficient conditions for the application of the concept in those circumstances. The central applications are those, if they exist, from which all other applications flow, that is, can be explained. Let us consider an example of attempted conceptual analysis, in order to bring out some general points about how the method works. We shall consider the justified, true-belief account of knowledge.[1]

2.1 Knowledge

The analysis of knowledge focuses on what confers truth on sentences of the form:

S knows that p.

In other words, it attempts to fill in the question mark in the following:

S knows that p iff ?

One, sometime popular suggestion, is the following:

S knows that p iff S believes p, S's belief in p is justified and p is true.

We shall leave it to epistemologists to decree on the adequacy of this definition: that is not our present concern. Simply note the process. We begin with ordinary sentences of English that uncontroversially involve use of the concept. These sentences can obviously be either true or false and it is the task of the analysis to say just when they are true. Other sentences that use the concept are then supposed to be explicable in terms of this analysis. For example, if we have

S knows what T knows,

we shall expand this as a generalization of

If T knows that p, then S knows that p,

and then use the analysis to explain the sub-clauses "T knows that p" and "S knows that p".

In the case of knowledge, our ordinary, uncontroversial sentences of English seem[2] to tell us quite a lot. They seem to tell us that an ascription of knowledge involves relating a subject to a proposition. We then try to spell out this relation in the analysis.

So our procedure is: we begin with ordinary sentences of the language that involve our problematic concept and claim to be able to see all uses of the concept as stemming from these.

2.2 Linguistic meaning

Can we do anything similar in the case of meaning? What are the ordinary sentences of English that centrally involve the concept of meaning? Well we are interested in linguistic meaning, that is, the meaning of a linguistic expression, e. So a seemingly natural place to start is with sentences of the form:

e means m,

where "e" stands for an expression and "m" for the sort of thing that might be its meaning.

We would then want to be able to go on to say just when such sentences are true, that is, to fill in the question mark in

e means m iff ?

But these are hardly our ordinary sentences of English. Take an expression such as "Kilimanjaro". What would be a plausible filling for "m"? Perhaps – but only "perhaps" – "the highest mountain in Africa". We shall come back to that case in a moment. What would be a plausible filling for "m" when the expression is "red"?

   (a) "red" means red
   (b) "red" means the colour red
   (c) "red" means the property of being red

Here (a) is ungrammatical. Some philosophers try to circumvent this by placing the right-hand side in inverted commas or in italics. But clearly this is a technical device: there is no progress to be made by analysing "red means *red*" and no understanding of "*red*" except as a term to refer to the meaning of "red". Use of italics or quotes is best read, in most cases, not as providing a glimmer of illumination but simply as a placeholder for an account of meaning. (In this fashion, I shall be happy to use the locution.) (b) and (c), although they have been argued to be correct by some philosophers, are distinctly controversial: other philosophers have questioned whether properties exist, others whether we can possibly give a meaning to a predicate or relation by assigning to it an entity (see Wittgenstein 1922). The reason some have held this points to another obvious failing in this whole approach: if meaning functions by assigning an entity to a term, how could we deploy this fact in explaining complex meanings? How could we explain the fact that "Fred" and "is red" can be combined meaningfully whereas "is red" and "is green" cannot be so combined? The point is not that we are condemned to silence here – one might, for instance, begin by saying that atomic sentences are formed from expressions whose meanings are individuals and others whose meanings are properties – rather the point is that these statements are clearly theoretical in nature. So our supposed starting-point of analysis cannot even be seen as a plausible starting-point unless supported by statements that belong not to our intuitive, pre-theoretical commerce with the notion of meaning, but to the business of philosophical reflection on meaning itself.

Additionally, it is hard to see how the analysis would proceed. Could we imagine a single, simple clause capable of filling the place of the question mark, no matter what syntactic or semantic category the expression "e" belongs to? We are obviously just speculating here, but if we focus on syntactic categories then it seems likely that the best we can expect is a complex disjunctive filling of the form

e means m iff e is a name and $?_n$ or e is a predicate and $?_p$ or e is a relational expression and $?_r$ or e is a sentence and $?_s$ ...

But this entails that our grasp of our starting-point sentences will vary from one syntactic category to another: the univocity of "e means m" is merely apparent. In effect we have:

e means m iff $?_n$, where e is a name

e means m iff $?_p$, where e is a predicate

e means m iff $?_r$, where e is a relational expression

e means m iff $?_s$, where e is a sentence ....

Thus our starting-point presupposes that we have already lighted on the logico-syntactic structure of language. Again, it is a huge stretch to imagine that this structure is present in the ordinary sentences we use to talk about meanings.

Despite these problems with analysis as a *general* starting-point, it is worth considering the strategy in application to two special cases: names, or, better, singular terms and sentences. So we shall assume that dissection of language thus far is acceptable. The discussion of names brings us into contact with important views of Frege, Russell and Kripke; that of sentences with those of Grice (for this see Chapter 3).

2.3 Frege's distinction between sense and reference

In the case of names there does, at first sight, seem to be a plausible starting-point for analysis:

"Kilimanjaro" means the highest mountain in Africa

is grammatical, and, just possibly, an ordinary sentence of English. In this case the analysis would be something like the following:

"Kilimanjaro" means the highest mountain in Africa iff "Kilimanjaro" refers to the highest mountain in Africa.[3]

What we shall learn in this section is that this analysis faces severe problems. These problems are sufficient to cast doubt on the original sentences as being an acceptable starting-point. These lessons are due to Frege.[4] We shall then go on to look at Russell's alternative account, which serves to show that the logico-syntactic category of singular terms is highly moot. Although we shall be looking at these questions from the point of view of giving an analysis of meaning, the discussion takes us to the heart of philosophical attempts to understand names and definite descriptions. This is scarcely surprising since the general point that we are pushing is that fixing on the starting-point for analysis already requires considerable philosophical insight into how language works.

2.3.1 Frege's argument for the notion of sense

Frege's argument focuses on identity statements (see Frege 1980b: 56–78). But this is primarily a heuristic device: he could have made the same point by focusing on elementary sentences in general. However, it is worth following through his reasoning about identity statements simply because, in doing so, we restrict our attention to the way names function.

We often assert statements of identity. For instance: "The morning star is the evening star"; "Everest is Gaurisanker"; "Clark Kent is Superman"; "Portia is Balthazar". The crucial thing to note is that these statements often carry useful information. If you remember the plot of *The Merchant of Venice* you will know that Bassanio would not have got himself in a pickle with Portia had he known that Portia and Balthazar are identical. Similarly, Lois Lane would have acted quite differently had she known that Clark Kent was Superman: that piece of knowledge would have been informative to her. So statements of identity can be informative. No account of language and, in particular, of the functioning of names can be acceptable unless it explains this fact.

Frege asks himself the question: what does the relation of identity hold between? It would seem that, on the analysis of names with which we have so far been provided, we can give only two answers. The relation either holds between the objects named by the names or it holds between the names themselves. Let us consider each suggestion in turn. Suppose that "a" and "b" are names and that "$a = b$" is true. If the relation holds between the objects denoted by the names, then "$a = b$" cannot differ from "$a = a$". For, since "$a = b$" is true, "a" and "b" name the same object. But clearly "$a = b$" and "$a = a$" differ because on many occasions (such as those above) statements of the form "$a = b$" are informative whereas those of the form "$a = a$" are uninformative since they are known *a priori* to be true.

Should we then take the identity statement to assert a relation between names? Frege says not since this can never be informative. Why so? Well, what a sign means is a matter of speakers conferring meaning on the sign. So, if identity asserts a relation between names, then either "$a = b$" is false since "a" and "b" are different names, or it registers a stipulation (which we are entirely entitled to make) that the signs "a" and "b" are to be treated as the same name. On neither reading can "$a = b$" be treated as an informative statement.

The point seems to be this. The character of a particular language is arbitrary in the sense that there is no intrinsic connection between the signs we use and what those signs refer to: whatever connections actually exist can be imagined to be quite other without supposing any difference in extralinguistic reality. But we cannot simply suppose that the link of a name to its reference is purely arbitrary – that there is no saying *how* the use or the meaning of the name establishes the link. Why not? Because then there could be no informative identity statements; these would just be the laying down of arbitrary conventions. What we need to be able to see is that there is both an element of convention or arbitrariness and an element that is non-conventional or non-arbitrary in the relation of a name to its referent. That is, we need to see the link as *mediated*: the name is conventionally or arbitrarily related to something and that thing is non-conventionally, non-arbitrarily related to the referent. Frege calls this thing "the sense of the name". How does this help with our problem?

What we wanted to be able to explain is that we can learn something when we are told that "$a = b$". Well "a" is arbitrarily related to the sense of "a" and the sense of "a" is non-arbitrarily related to the referent of "a". Likewise for "b". What we learn when we are told that "$a = b$" is that the sense of "a" and the sense of "b" are related to the same object. And, since neither of these relations is a matter of arbitrary stipulation, this is a genuine piece of knowledge: conceivably, things might have been different.

The point can be made in terms of what speakers understand when they grasp the meaning of an expression. If speakers grasped the reference of an expression, then, for those regions of language that they understood, their understanding would suffice for them to arrive at a verdict on the truth-value of an identity statement. For, in such a case, they would know the referent of each name as part of their understanding of it. They would simply need to reflect on this understanding in order to appreciate the truth or falsity of an identity statement. Clearly this misconstrues the nature of our understanding of language. So, we might say that in grasping the meaning of an expression speakers do not grasp as much as the reference of an expression.

Conversely, it is clear that speakers do not grasp as little as the reference of an expression. For, if they did, then co-referring terms (terms that refer to the same thing) would be synonymous – indeed, since Frege treats sentences as names for truth-values, all true sentences would be synonymous with one another, as would all false sentences. In this case we could not distinguish the sentences "$a = a$" and "$a = b$" in terms of meaning.

The conclusion is that the reference of a term is not an ingredient of what speakers understand when they understand the term's meaning. In short, reference is not part of meaning. What do speakers grasp when they understand a term? Among other things, they grasp its sense.

Now, if we are to explain the informativeness of "$a = b$" by saying that it informs us that the sense of "a" and the sense of "b" share a reference, then it had better be the case that "a" and "b" have different senses. So it is possible for the same referent to have many senses.

We are able now to explain or, better, to allow for the possibility of meaningful terms which do not have a reference. If we insist on thinking of the meaning of a term as what it refers to, then terms that fail to refer will fail to have a meaning. But, once we introduce the notion of sense, it may be possible for a term to have a sense, and thus to be meaningful, yet fail to have a reference.

Let us sum up so far what we have discovered about sense. (i) The sense of a term is part of what speakers understand when they understand the term's meaning. (ii) The sense is non-conventionally, non-arbitrarily related to the term's reference. (iii) The sense of the term is that ingredient of a term's meaning that determines its reference. For Frege, sense determines reference. (iv) The relation of sense to reference is many–one; that is, many senses may share the same reference. (v) In addition, a sense may fail to have a reference.

We should note also that Frege thinks that these arguments can be extended to cover all terms of the language: all expressions have a sense. The sense of a sentence is a thought.

So, according to Frege's argument, our analysis of the meaning of a name is wrong. The reasons for this relate to the information content conveyed by sentences that include names. And this is brought out by consideration of routine uses of such sentences. So the starting-point of analysis ("Kilimanjaro" means the highest mountain in Africa) itself seems threatened: such sentences, even if they are sometimes used, cannot be thought to capture the essentials of the way names mean since they are blind to the name's possession of a sense. Just to be clear, we are not saying that names have senses. Frege says this. But we want a starting-point for analysis that does not beg the question against Frege, whether or not he is right.

2.3.2 Sense and statements of belief

Consider the following argument:

Premise 1: King George doubts that Scott is the author of *Waverley*.
Premise 2: Scott is the author of *Waverley*.
Conclusion: Therefore King George doubts that Scott is Scott.

Clearly something has gone very awry here. The first premise attributes an understandable doubt to King George, who may simply be not very well informed about Scott's literary productions. The second premise states a truth. But the conclusion attributes to King George a doubt about the law of identity and clearly it is unlikely that even he was so confused: such a conclusion is surely not warranted by the premises (see Russell 1956: 39–55).

Now it is hard to explain what goes wrong here. What, in effect, premise 2 tells us is that "Scott" and "the author of *Waverley*" have the same reference. And in that case we should be able to substitute one term for the other without changing the truth-value of any sentence in which they occur. This is a consequence of Frege's compositional view of semantic value. The semantic value of a name is its referent; that of a sentence is its truth-value. According to compositionality, the semantic value of a complex expression is determined by the semantic values of its components. What seems to be our problem is that applying this principle in the context of statements about someone's beliefs, doubts, knowledge and so on, leads from plausible truths to evident untruths and absurdities.

How should we resolve the situation? We could either say that in the context of statements of belief and so on the principle of the compositionality of semantic values no longer holds. Or we could say that the semantic values of expressions in the context of statements of belief and so on change so that terms that shared a semantic value, that is, that referred to the same thing, may no longer do so. But what could the terms now refer to? Frege's answer is that the terms shift their reference from what is their usual reference to what is usually their sense. So in the context of the sentence, "King George doubts that Scott is the author of *Waverley*", the name "Scott" does not refer to Scott; it refers to the sense of "Scott". Similarly "the author of *Waverley*" no longer refers to the author of *Waverley* (i.e. to Scott); it refers to the sense of "the author of *Waverley*". Since the sense of "Scott" and the sense of "the author of *Waverley*" are different, we can no longer be assured that when we substitute "Scott" for "the author of *Waverley*" the truth-value of the containing sentence remains unchanged. Note that, as a consequence of this account, senses are in the realm of reference.

2.3.3 The objectivity of sense

Different speakers can grasp the same sense. Indeed, grasping the same sense is a condition for communication. When we communicate, one speaker uses a sentence to express a certain thought; to do so she must grasp that thought. She successfully communicates only if her audience takes the sentence she utters to express just that thought. Thus the audience must grasp that thought as the sense of that sentence. Thus communication requires that speakers share the senses of their terms. More than this, though, Frege requires, or seems to require, that not merely do speakers share senses; they can *know* that they share senses. So conceived, the requirement is often viewed as a publicity constraint on meaning: meanings are publicly available in the sense that speakers can know the meanings that other speakers attach to their terms. I shall not probe this notion of the publicity of meaning any more deeply now but its content and motivation will be a major preoccupation in later chapters, in particular Chapters 10, 11 and 13.

The sense of an expression must thus be sharply distinguished from any set of subjective impressions associated with it. Ideas, impressions and feelings are all things that are had by a certain subject: one can always ask whose idea, whose feeling and so on. Something that can be had in this way cannot be shared or, perhaps better, cannot be known to be shared. The most that we can determine is qualitative differences between different people's feelings, sensations or ideas.

We cannot determine that they are qualitatively identical since, for that, the sensations would have to be compared by a single subject. And that is clearly impossible since no subject can have another's sensations or impressions. So sensations, feelings and ideas cannot be known to be shared. Thus, since communication requires that we share and can know that we share senses, senses must be sharply distinguished from ideas. That is, senses are not part of the subjective realm and, for Frege, this means that they are objective. (Another option might be to say that they belong to the intersubjective realm, but Frege does not consider this as a possible challenge to his dichotomy of subjective and objective.) Moreover, for Frege, to say that senses are objective is to reify them: senses are objective items in the world. He thus distinguishes three realms of existents. There is the realm of the actual, which includes ordinary middle-sized objects and so on, then there is the subjective realm consisting of ideas and sense impressions and the like, and finally there is a third realm consisting of senses and abstract objects such as numbers and truth-values.

2.4 Russell's theory of descriptions

The phrases that concern Russell[5] are descriptive phrases, both definite and indefinite descriptions. For any predicate, F, Russell thinks we have five forms of associated description:

Indefinite descriptions: all Fs; any F; an F; some F
Definite descriptions: the F

We are primarily concerned with definite descriptions, since we are interested in terms that (seem to) aim to refer to a single individual.

2.4.1 Indefinite descriptions

"All men are mortal" appears to be a proposition in which "All men" occupies the subject position. In his earlier work Russell (1903: 53–6) had postulated that the term "All men" thus has a certain meaning, which he called a denoting concept, whose role was to pick out that range of things that either make the proposition true or make it false, depending on how things are with them. So the denoting concept that is the meaning of "All men" is related to the totality of men taken as a whole.

In "On Denoting" Russell rejects the theory of denoting concepts and makes the following radical suggestion: the logical form of the sentence is quite other than it appears to be: when the true logical form is exhibited there is no subject corresponding to "All men". What we get is:

"For all x, if x is a man then x is mortal"

"All men" is an *incomplete symbol*: it has a meaning in the sense that it occurs in meaningful sentences; those sentences are shown to be meaningful because each has a logical paraphrase. The paraphrase does not include a phrase that corresponds to the incomplete symbol and that could therefore be taken to give its meaning; thus there is no reason to think that the incomplete symbol has a meaning by standing for an extra-linguistic something.

2.4.2 Definite descriptions

Russell tries to apply a similar analysis to definite descriptions. So the aim is to rewrite any sentence containing a definite description in such a way that the definite description is eliminated. The definite description is meaningful because a *sentence* containing it is analysed into a meaningful sentence but we do not need to think of it as having a meaning because it stands for some entity – thus it is also an incomplete symbol. Thus:

The king of France is bald

becomes

There is one and only one king of France and that entity is bald.
That is, "There is an x such that x is a king of France and if y is a king of France then $x = y$ and x is bald."
That is, "$(\exists x)(x$ is a king of France $\bullet$ $(\forall y)(y$ is a king of France $\supset x = y)$ $\bullet$ x is bald)."

Russell argues for his analysis by showing how it solves Frege's puzzles of: (i) informative identities; (ii) empty singular terms; and (iii) substitution into propositional attitude ascriptions.

(i) Informative identities

The last one in = the first one out.

becomes

There is one and only one entity x such that x is last in and there is one and only one entity y such that y is first out and $x = y$.

Or,

$(\exists x)(Lx \bullet (\forall z)(Lz \supset x = z) \bullet (\exists y)(Fy \bullet (\forall z)(Fz \supset y = z) \bullet x = y)).$

So our identity becomes an assertion that there is a certain entity fulfilling a certain condition, here, that it is both last in and first out. There is clearly no reason at all why such assertions should not be informative.

(ii) Empty singular terms

We have already seen how to account for our understanding of "The king of France is bald". What truth-value has it? It is false since it asserts the existence of a certain entity and there is no such entity. So are we committed to "The king of France is not bald"? No, since the logical form of that is

> There is one and only one king of France and that entity is not bald.
> That is, "$(\exists x)(x$ is a king of $F \bullet (\forall y)(y$ is a king of $F \supset x = y) \bullet x$ is *not* bald)."

When we negate the false sentence "The king of France is bald", we get the true sentence:

> $\sim(\exists x)(x$ is a king of $F \bullet (\forall y)(y$ is a king of $F \supset x = y) \bullet x$ is bald)
> That is, "It is not the case that there is one and only one king of France and that entity is bald."

(iii) Propositional attitude ascription

> George IV doubts that Scott is the author of *Waverley*.
> Scott is the author of *Waverley*.
> So George IV doubts that Scott is Scott.

This becomes

> George IV doubts that there is one and only one entity that wrote *Waverley* and that entity is Scott.
> There is one and only one entity that wrote *Waverley* and that entity is Scott.

That is,

> George IV doubts that $(\exists x)(\forall y)\{(y$ wrote *Waverley* $\equiv x = y) \bullet x = $ Scott$\}$.
> $(\exists x)(\forall y)\{(y$ wrote *Waverley* $\equiv x = y) \bullet x = $ Scott$\}$.

"The author of *Waverley*" is not treated as a singular term; it is treated as a quantificational expression, so the law of identity does not apply. Or to put the point differently, since the definite description is an incomplete symbol – it is not a referring expression – it makes no sense to talk of intersubstituting it with another co-referential term.

2.4.3 A problem

What we have been given is a solution to Frege's puzzles when the singular term is a definite description, but Frege thought that the problems applied to *names* also. What can Russell say about names? Russell's answer is short and sweet, but has some far-reaching consequences. He claims that ordinary proper names are disguised definite descriptions; that is, every name can be analysed as a definite description. So his previous solution can be recycled to apply here as well.

A consequence of this view, which relates directly to the issues we have been concerned with, is this. According to Frege, the logico-syntactic category of singular terms comprises names and definite descriptions. But Russell demurs. Definite descriptions are, he considers, not singular terms at all. Rather, sentences involving definite descriptions are analysed in terms of sentences involving existential quantification and identity. So our working assumption that the category of singular terms can be determined independently of views in the philosophy of language is quite false; different philosophical positions – those of Frege and Russell – draw the line differently.

Another interesting consequence emerges when we then ask what, according to Russell, are logically proper names. Well, a logically proper name will be a name that is guaranteed a reference and there can be no informative identity statements linking logically proper names. So for Russell the only logically proper names are expressions such as "this" and "that", which one might have been disinclined to think of as names at all since they pick out different individuals on different occasions of use. But from Russell's perspective this does not matter; on each occasion such a term is guaranteed to pick out an object presented to one's senses. Note, however, that these are not ordinary objects; they must be objects that are immediately presented – objects about which one cannot be mistaken whether or not they exist, nor about their identities. A table will not do because I might well be hallucinating the table, or might not notice that the table seen from the hall is the same as the table seen from the kitchen. But even if I am hallucinating the table, I have sense impressions as of a table. So for Russell "this" and "that" name the contents of sense impressions; he calls them sense data. Sense data that I fail to distinguish are identical and those I do distinguish are distinct. A statement that appears to be about some entity that is not a sense datum must be analysed into a statement involving descriptions based on named sense data and their properties.

A different but interesting question – one discussed by Strawson (1971: essay 1, §4) – is whether one could have a language that had no logically proper names. On Russell's account this would be a language containing only predication and the apparatus of generality and identity. Quine (see 1962: §37) favours such a language but it is hard to see how such a language could connect with the particularities of experience and therefore how it could be learnable. We also seem, then, to allow for a certain kind of scepticism. If we talk about particular objects only by means of the qualitative properties, it seems that all our attempts might fail because we could never rule out the possibility that the clause claiming uniqueness is false.

2.4.4 Russell on incomplete symbols

Russell took the discovery of incomplete symbols to be a major philosophical breakthrough and, in the years following the publication of "On Denoting", we find him attempting to deploy the notion in a variety of ways dictated largely by an effort to abide by Ockham's razor: the principle not to multiply entities beyond necessity. His project to reconstruct mathematics on logical foundations was, in large part, an attempt to treat class terms – such as "the class of logicians" – as incomplete symbols. By seeing a range of terms as incomplete, Russell saw that one could explain the meaning of sentences containing them without committing oneself to a corresponding range of entities. So mathematics can be understood without needing to suppose that there is an infinite range of abstract objects – such as classes. He finally thought that he could do away with propositions themselves by thinking of them as having a meaning only within the context of propositional attitudes such as judging. This, however, seems to have been a step too far and Wittgenstein (1979: 122) shot down Russell's (1992) programme in flames.

An important influence of the theory of descriptions (and of the notion of an incomplete symbol) is that the logical form of a sentence may be quite different from its apparent logical form: although sentences involving definite descriptions seem to be about particular objects, in fact they are generalized statements asserting the existence of a certain entity. Thus philosophical analysis is needed to reveal the true logical form of our sentences.

2.5 Kripke's attack on descriptivism about names

Finally we consider Kripke's (1980) defence of our original analysis, namely that the meaning of a name is its reference. A descriptivist is anyone who thinks that the meaning of a name is given by a definite description associated with it. Russell is a descriptivist because he identifies a name with a definite description:

the name is an abbreviation for the description. Frege might be seen as a descriptivist because he thinks that the meaning of a name is, in part, its sense, and sense is a way of determining reference. One way of being able to determine the reference of a name would be to have descriptive knowledge of its bearer. So, for instance, if I understand the name "Barack Obama" by grasping its sense, I might associate a definite description with that name, for example, "The current president of America". But, it seems, that need not be the only way – one might for instance simply have an ability to recognize the bearer of the name when it is appropriately presented to one. In essence, Kripke assumes that such an ability must consist in implicit descriptive knowledge. His attack on descriptivism looks at the way we ordinarily use names successfully to refer and then looks at the use of names in modal contexts, contexts involving talk of necessity or possibility.

2.5.1 Is there a meaning-determining description for each name?

We shall look first and look reasonably quickly at the arguments based on our use of names and then look at the modal argument. One problem in thinking about the sense of names as being given by definite descriptions is that there seems to be a circularity here. We give the sense of "Barack Obama" as "The current president of America" but this description itself uses a name: "America". So what is its sense? Well, maybe "The land of the free and home of the brave". Perhaps, and, if so, this would be fortunate because now we would have come to an end. But what guarantee is there that, in general, we shall come to an end, that we shall not trace out circles among the names in language? It is difficult to know how such an investigation would go but at least it seems plausible that at some point we come up with descriptions that are linked to objects present to sensation, or to uniquely individuating definite descriptions involving no names, or to definite descriptions involving no names but uniquely individuating in context.

Another of Kripke's arguments is that frequently one uses a name and knows a great deal about the bearer. For instance, I know that George W. Bush was the president of the USA in 2007, is the son of ex-President George Bush, was the opponent of Al Gore in the American election of 2000, was the closest international ally of Tony Blair, was Osama Bin Laden's most feared enemy and so on. Which of these pieces of information encapsulates the sense I associate with the name? There does not seem to be an answer to this question. Put another way, any of these beliefs might change without that change being viewed as a change of meaning. Maybe the right response here is to follow Searle (1958) and to say that the sense is not given by any individual description; rather, the referent of the term is that individual who satisfies a majority from a cluster of descriptions. So the cluster in some way gives the sense of the name.

If we move away from names of famous people it seems even less likely that there is a publicly agreed sense for a name. I may know Bertha as the woman who rides a titanium bicycle, won the Cape Argus cycle race twice and had a bicycle accident last year. You may know her as the woman who has fourteen dogs, eight cats and an African grey parrot. Do we mean different things when each of us says "Bertha has just won the lottery"?

I may use a name to refer to someone and yet not know anything that uniquely distinguishes that person. For instance, I may not know much about Brazilian football and so know simply that "Ronaldo" is a Brazilian footballer. So my knowledge will not distinguish Ronaldo from Ronaldinho. Still, if I were asked in a quiz show who was the last Brazilian to score in a World Cup Final I might guess that it was Ronaldo. And if I did so, I would rightly get my points because I would have referred to Ronaldo. However, and here is the trouble for Russell and Frege, my reference would not be courtesy of descriptive knowledge.

A response might run as follows. It might well be claimed that I have an incomplete grasp of the meaning of Ronaldo; I am not, for instance, capable of gleaning all the information carried by the statement "Ronaldo faces a ban in Brazil's next international". However, this does not mean that I cannot refer to Ronaldo by using the term "Ronaldo". I can do so because language is a social institution and this means we can recognize a linguistic division of labour (to use Hilary Putnam's happy phrase – 1975: 228). I successfully refer in my use of "Ronaldo" because I defer in my use of the term to the judgements of football experts in my community. Given that they know the sense of the term "Ronaldo", I can use the term to refer to Ronaldo provided I accept their judgements about how the term is correctly used.[6]

Kripke will not accept this argument since he supposes that, for instance, it may be the case that all that any of us know about Gödel is that Gödel discovered the incompleteness of arithmetic. Nevertheless, he suggests that the following may, in fact, have happened. The now sadly forgotten Schmidt discovered the incompleteness of arithmetic and was then murdered by the nefarious Gödel, who then took the discovery and published it as his own. When we now use the name "Gödel", are we referring to Gödel or to Schmidt? According to Kripke we are referring to Gödel, but Frege and Russell would have to say that we are referring to Schmidt. The point about this example is that no one in our current speech community could act as an appropriate expert. Nonetheless we may suppose that our speech community includes those individuals going back in time who spoke the same language. Those speakers would have grasped an accurate sense for the name "Gödel".

2.5.2 The causal account

What we have been presented with so far is a set of observations about our use of names that certainly taxes the orthodox Fregean and Russellian views. But it does not seem clear that this is a knock-out blow. So, in large measure, our judgement about whether or not to stick with some version of descriptivism will depend on whether there is a better explanation of the observations. So I want now to look at Kripke's positive account before we look at his modal argument against descriptivism.

The phenomena we need to account for are these (see McCulloch 1989: 268):

1. *Reference*: the information a speaker or community associates with a name may not determine its reference since (i) it may be false of the bearer and (ii) it may not individuate the bearer uniquely.
2. *Availability*: the information particular speakers may associate with a public name may be widely disparate and in many cases speakers will be unable to supply a description.
3. *Proliferation*: no information about the bearer of a name can be singled out as distinctively part of the meaning of the name when we focus either on the community or on individuals within it.
4. *Inextricability*: the information about the bearer of a name may not be specifiable in terms that do not involve use of names.

Kripke takes the lesson of the observations to be: (i) that the information associated with a name is not part of its meaning (from all of the above) and (ii) that this information need not be involved in the mechanism by which reference is determined (from 1 and 4). Thus he offers an account of the working of names that makes nothing of the information speakers may or may not have about the bearer of the name.

His account and similar accounts are often subsumed under the title "the causal theory of names", but although it is true that he offers a causal *account* of names, Kripke denies that he is offering anything like a *theory*. His view is that what fixes the reference of a name is not information associated with the name but a chain of causal links that connect one use of the name with previous uses and that ultimately link an original or baptismal use with the object that is the bearer of the name. That is the basic scheme, but it is obvious that the basic scheme is false.

My friend Lord Amberley has a prize pig called "Horatio", after Horatio Nelson. So when Lord Amberley says, "Horatio has just cleaned out his trough of slops", his use of the name "Horatio" is causally linked to other people's use of "Horatio" in such sentences as "Horatio was victorious at Trafalgar", uses, that is, that are causally linked to an original baptism of Nelson as "Horatio". So it would seem that Lord Amberley is referring to Nelson when he says, "Horatio has just cleaned out his trough of slops". This is clearly muddled. Kripke solves the problem by noting that Lord Amberley does not intend his use of "Horatio" in that sentence to preserve the reference of "Horatio" in such sentences uttered by others as the one about the battle of Trafalgar. So what is necessary and sufficient for a use of a name to refer to an object is that that use is causally connected by a chain of uses, *each of which involves an intention to preserve reference* to that object.

2.5.3 The modal argument

Let us consider Kripke's modal argument. We can see Russell as saying that there is a philosophical analysis of each name that reveals it to be synonymous with a definite description. But, as we noted in discussing the business of analysis, we must be able to use the analysis to explain the use of the name in all its occurrences. Kripke's modal argument shows this to be false in relation to sentences involving modal notions. The strength of this argument is that it applies in a case where there is just one uniquely identifying description of the bearer of the name and it is known by the speaker. Indeed, Kripke even concedes that the description might be used to fix the reference of the name. What he contends is that the description does not give the meaning of the name. Since the name and the description are not synonymous, the latter does not give the sense of the former. An example that fits the case – Dummett's – might be that of the name "St Anne" and the description "the mother of Mary".

The argument can be seen as a *reductio ad absurdum* of the descriptive view of names, namely that each name is synonymous with a definite description. If the descriptive view of names holds, then the name "St Anne" is synonymous with a definite description that, for the sake of argument, we shall assume is the description "the mother of Mary", there being, in the circumstances, no plausible alternative. Thus the sentence "St Anne is the mother of Mary" is necessarily true. Why so? Because the sentence "The mother of Mary is the mother of Mary" is necessarily true and the sentences differ just by replacing one term with a synonymous one. Kripke's argument will be that, in a certain sense, our conclusion here – that "St Anne is the mother of Mary" is necessarily true – is wrong. Thus the descriptive view is itself mistaken. But we need to be careful to get clear about the sense in which our conclusion is wrong.

One thought you might have is the following. St Anne, you realize, might not have been interested in parenthood and might instead have pursued a career in merchant banking; so surely it is true to say "St Anne might not have been the mother of Mary" and does not this contradict our claim that "St Anne is the mother of Mary" is necessarily true? Well, no, it does not. We might have exactly the same thoughts about the mother of Mary – she might also have shown little interest in parenting and thus have become a banker instead. So the sentence "The mother of Mary might not have been the mother of Mary" is also true. That sentence does not contradict the claim that "The mother of Mary is the mother of Mary" is necessarily true; so the truth of "St Anne might not have been the mother of Mary" does not contradict the claim that "St Anne is the mother of Mary" is necessarily true.

But let us think for a moment about the possible situation we have envisaged, that is, the situation in which St Anne (or the mother of Mary – *that* woman) becomes a career girl and steers clear of motherhood. Assume too that someone else gives birth to Mary.[7] To say of those circumstances that St Anne is the mother of Mary is to say something false – she is not; she is a successful banker – but to say of them that the mother of Mary is the mother of Mary is to say something true. In other words the sentence "St Anne is the mother of Mary" is false in those circumstances; the sentence "The mother of Mary is the mother of Mary" is true. So there are possible circumstances in which the one sentence is true and the other false. Therefore the sentences are not synonymous. And, since they differ only by replacement of "St Anne" with "the mother of Mary", those terms must fail to be synonymous. And this contradicts the descriptive view, which is therefore shown to be false.

The difference between our two terms is clearly this. When we describe our possible situation, the term "St Anne" picks out the career-girl banker whereas the term "the mother of Mary" picks out the mother of Mary (naturally enough). Because the two terms pick out different individuals in these possible circumstances, our sentences have different truth-values. Contrariwise, this difference in truth-values demonstrates the difference in function between the terms and thus shows up their difference in meaning.

2.5.4 Rigidity

Kripke explains the disanalogy in the behaviour of names and definite descriptions in this way. A name functions as a rigid designator: it designates the same object in each possible world. A definite description can be used as a non-rigid designator, namely to designate the object that is the unique satisfier of the description in each possible world. Thus,

(i)   Necessarily, St Anne is the mother of Mary

and

(ii)   St Anne is necessarily the mother of Mary

express the same proposition, since each claims that the person St Anne has the property of being the mother of Mary in all possible worlds. However, in

(a)   Necessarily, the mother of Mary is the mother of Mary

the first definite description functions non-rigidly, and in

(b)   The mother of Mary is necessarily the mother of Mary

the first definite description functions rigidly. So, given that St Anne is the mother of Mary, (b) makes a claim equivalent to (i) and (ii); but (a) makes a quite different claim.

2.5.5 Necessity

Consider the sentence

(*)   St Anne is the mother of Mary.

We have just argued that this is not necessarily true. However, Kripke allows that the definite description "the mother of Mary" is uniquely associated with the *meaning* of the name "St Anne" since it may be used to *fix the name's reference*. So there is a kind of necessity attaching to (*): one can know (*) to be true on the basis of knowing the meaning of "St Anne", that is (*) is *a priori* knowable or *epistemically necessary*. Kripke thus distinguishes between *metaphysical necessity* and *epistemic necessity*. What we have discovered is that a proposition might be metaphysically contingent – true in some worlds, false in others – yet epistemically necessary. (The opposite combination – metaphysical necessities which are known *a posteriori* – is, importantly, also possible.)

2.6 Analysis and singular terms

Russell and Kripke agree that definite descriptions and logically proper names are distinct logico-syntactic categories; Frege disagrees. Russell distinguishes logically proper names from ordinary proper names; Kripke and Frege do not. Russell and Kripke agree with the analysis of the meaning of a name as its referent when the name is logically proper; Frege resists this *tout court*. Each philosopher's view about the nature of the expressions in need of analysis depends heavily on his views about how that analysis will proceed and on his views about the semantics of the relevant terms. There is no philosophically uninformed place to begin analysis, and the role of analysis is found within a theory about how this region of language functions.

3. Analysing sentence-meaning

3.1 Specifying sentence-meaning

What we wanted as a starting-point for analysis were ordinary sentences involving the ascription of meaning to a kind of linguistic expression. When we come to the case of sentences, it is hard to see how this would work if we focus on specifications of the form:

s means m.

What would we replace "m" by when, for instance, s is "snow is white"? One might just be prepared to contemplate the following:

"snow is white" means the state of affairs that snow is white.

Two things are worth noting: first, the notion of a state of affairs is a term of art invented as a way of conceiving of the meanings of sentences as some type of entity – a controversial proposal; and secondly, in characterizing states of affairs we have to use the "that" locution and this suggests taking a much more straightforward, less controversial set of sentences ascribing meaning to sentences. We might choose to focus on sentences such as

s means that p,

for instance, the true sentence,

"snow is white" means that snow is white

or the false sentence,

"snow is white" means that grass is green

Our aim would be to characterize what makes the first sentence true and what makes the second false. So our analysis attempts to fill out the question mark in

s means that p iff ?

Grice (1957)[1] offers us just such an account. The account is however complex, proceeding in two stages. The first stage characterizes speaker-meaning, that is, what it is for a speaker, A, to mean that p by uttering a sentence, s. Grice then defines sentence-meaning, that is, what it is for s to mean that p, in terms of speaker-meaning. We begin, however, with a much more general distinction in our notions of meaning.

3.2 Natural and non-natural meaning

Grice approaches linguistic meaning by thinking about meaning more generally. We say that smoke means fire, dark clouds mean rain, his slamming of the door means he is in a temper and so on. So here we have one event that indicates another. These are cases of *natural meaning*. Given the relation of indication between these events, it is likely that an observation or belief about the one (the smoke, the clouds or the slammed door) will induce another belief about something else (the fire, the rain or his temper). Grice wants to distinguish such cases from what he calls non-natural meaning. A clear difference between natural and non-natural meaning is that if, for instance, smoke means fire, then there must be a fire. Contrast this with the following: if Joe's statement "There is a fire" non-naturally means that there is a fire, then it does not follow that there is a fire. Grice's thought is that we can arrive at an understanding of non-natural meaning – that is, meaning that results from attempts to communicate – and then base an account of meaning in language on this notion of *non-natural meaning*.

3.3 Speaker-meaning

Consider a case of someone exiting a room, slamming the door behind him. Here it might be appropriate to say that his slamming the door means that he is in a bad temper, but it would be wrong to say that *he* means that he is in a temper by slamming the door. His slamming the door naturally means that he is in a temper. What more might we need to build into the picture of his slamming the door to arrive at a case where it becomes appropriate to say that he means by slamming the door that he is in a temper? Well, first, his slamming the door might be non-intentional, in which case it means that he is in a temper in exactly the same way as his red face, prominent veins and clenched fists might do so. But even if he intends to slam the door that clearly does not get us to what we want since that just makes the slamming a deliberate act – it does not show that there was any attempt to communicate, and that is what we need for the second description to be apt; we would still only have a case of natural meaning. So let us suppose that he intends not simply to slam the door but that he intends *thereby* to get one to believe that he is in a temper.

This too surely is not sufficient. A deliberate act performed with the intention of inducing a certain belief does not give rise to meaning. For instance, I may want to induce in you the belief that there are pink elephants and so I may spike your drink intending *thereby* to produce such a belief in you. Does this imply that spiking the drink means that there are pink elephants? Clearly not. Another example: I may want to induce in you the belief that X is the smartest student in the class and I may figure that a way to achieve this end is to leave X's essay on your desk. Do I mean that X is the smartest student in the class by leaving the essay on the desk? Again, it seems not. We perform many actions with a variety of purposes. On occasion, our purpose is to induce one or another belief in someone but that alone does not make the act communicative and does not confer meaning on it.

What is missing? Well, from the perspective of the audience, one is simply presented with evidence (even though this may have been deftly engineered by the would-be communicator) that induces one to believe something. So from this perspective there is no noteworthy change from natural meaning. What we would need is for there to be a recognition on the part of the audience that the evidence she is presented with is the product of the would-be communicator's intention to induce a certain belief. So from the would-be communicator's perspective, she would need (i) deliberately to perform an action with the intention of inducing a certain belief in her audience, and (ii) intend the audience to recognize this intention. Satisfaction of the second intention ensures that the audience recognizes that the evidence she is presented with is of a "special" sort.

And now, contrast the case of the essay with this one: if I leave photographs of X and of the class medal on your desk with the intention of inducing you to believe that X is the smartest student in the class, it seems more plausible to say that by those photographs I do mean that X is the smartest student in the class. Why? Because, in order for you to form that belief you would (most likely) have had to wonder why someone would leave those precise photographs on your desk. That might well lead you to recognize that someone intended to induce a belief about X's deserving the class medal and, if you trust the likely "someone's" opinion, you might form the belief about X being smart. In contrast, if you thought that the photographs had arrived there accidentally you would be most unlikely to form the belief about X's smartness (contrast with the case of X's essay arriving accidentally on your desk).

Let us suppose that in the essay case you see me place the essay on your desk. So you recognize that I have an intention to induce a certain belief in you (the evidence is "special" since it arises from my intention). So both cases satisfy (i) and (ii). But in the essay case (ii) plays no role in your formation of the belief about X's smartness – it is entirely incidental. Thus, in placing the essay on the desk, I do not mean that X is the smartest student in the class. To achieve that, we need a third condition, which is only satisfied in the case of the photographs: (iii) the would-be communicator must intend that recognition of her intention in (ii) plays a role in the audience's formation of the belief. As Grice says, "'A meant$_{NN}$ something by x' is (roughly) equivalent to 'A intended the utterance of x to produce some effect in an audience by means of the recognition of this intention'; and we may add that to ask what A meant is to ask for a specification of the intended effect" (1957: 385). Notice that meaning is construed here purely in terms of the speaker's communicative intentions. We might then dissect this complex intention as follows (I shall suppose that the intended effect is the production of the belief that p):

S means that p by φing:
1. S φs with the intention of producing the belief that p.
2. S intends her audience to recognize this intention.
3. S intends her audience's recognition of her intention to play a role in her audience's formation of the belief that p.

We shall need to consider whether this analysis provides a non-circular account of the necessary and sufficient conditions for S meaning that p by φing. But let us set that task aside for the moment. What role is the analysis supposed to play? The scenarios we have been considering are one-off cases in which a communicator intends to communicate a belief to an audience. According to Grice, the fulfilment of these communicative intentions is the basis of meaning in language.

The development of that point depends on the following two features of our ordinary use of language. If, when I am asked my opinion of Grice's book, I say, "It has an extremely interesting cover", then, on the one hand, what *the sentence* I uttered means is that the book has an extremely interesting cover. But what *I* mean by the utterance is that the book is tedious and dull. So, whatever one's view about language, it seems that we should distinguish between *sentence-meaning*, on the one hand, and *speaker-meaning* on the other. Grice's account of meaning in terms of communicative intentions is supposed to be an account of speaker-meaning and his thought is that we should explain sentence-meaning ultimately in terms of speaker-meaning.

Let us just apply the Gricean account to this case of speaker-meaning. Obviously I utter "It has an extremely interesting cover" with the intention of producing in you the belief that the book is dull. I intend you to infer that my purpose in choosing to comment only on this aspect of the book is that I intend to induce that belief in you. And I intend that these beliefs about my intentions play a role in your formation of the belief that the book is dull. So:

1. I utter "It has an extremely interesting cover" with the intention of producing the belief that the book is dull.
2. I intend you to recognize this intention.
3. I intend that your recognition of my intentions plays a role in your formation of the belief that the book is dull.

Thus in uttering "It has an extremely interesting cover" I speaker-mean that the book is dull.

This may be confusing, so let me clarify the situation. I have focused on this abnormal case because the case itself highlights the distinction between speaker-meaning and sentence-meaning. What is abnormal about the case is that speaker-meaning and sentence-meaning here come apart, but this need not be the case and, importantly for Grice, is not the case most of the time. We shall expand on this point below but the relation between speaker- and sentence-meaning is complex and, I am afraid, is apt to be confusing. First let us turn to the account of sentence- (and word-) meaning in terms of speaker-meaning.

3.4 Sentence-meaning

Grice's approach is often described as being that of explaining meaning in terms of intention plus convention. We have just seen the role of communicative intentions in fixing speaker-meaning; so it seems natural to think that we then need simply to see sentence-meaning as emerging from grafting conventions on to regularities in communicative practices. In fact this is not Grice's approach. Although he flirts with the notion of convention, his considered view is that conventions are not necessary to linguistic meaning.

> It seems plausible to suppose that to say that a sentence (word, expression) means something ... is to be somehow understood in terms of what users of that sentence (word, expression) mean on particular occasions. The first possible construal of this is rather crude: namely, that usually people do use this sentence, etc., in this way. A construal which seems to me rather better is that it is conventional to use this sentence in this way; and there are many others.

Now I do not think that even the most subtle or sophisticated interpretation of this construal will do, because I do not think that meaning
is essentially connected with convention. What it is essentially connected with is some way of fixing what sentences mean: convention is
indeed one of these ways, but it is not the only one.   (1989: 298)

Grice's first thought is to focus on the idea that a string of signs, *t*, means that
p for a speaker, *S*, if and only if *S* has a "policy (practice, habit)" of using *t* to
speaker-mean that *p*. But the account fails because the analysis provides neither
necessary nor sufficient conditions for *t* to mean that *p* for *S*. The analysis is not
necessary because, although *t* may mean that *p* for *S*, it may also have some other
meaning, in which case it will not be *S*'s policy to use *t* *only* to speaker-mean
that *p*. The analysis is not sufficient because, although *t* may mean that *p* for *S*,
some other expression *r* may have the same meaning, in which case it will not
be *S*'s policy to use *t* whenever *S* speaker-means that *p*. Thus Grice supplements
his account with the notion of having a certain procedure in one's repertoire.
So the meaning of an expression does not dictate a set of uses (it cannot do so
because it may have more than one meaning and may share its meaning with
another expression); rather, its having a certain meaning makes available certain
ways of using it. So we have

t means that p for S iff S has in her repertoire the procedure of using t to
speaker-mean that p.

What the account fails to capture is the sense in which language provides a
speaker with a resource for communicating. To be sure, the speaker has the
procedure as part of her repertoire and thus the procedure is available to her
as a resource in communicating, but on each occasion the procedure is supposed to work afresh. The efficacy of the procedure (as opposed to the speaker's
adoption of the procedure) never owes anything to what has been established.
What we seem to require is not merely that the speaker have the procedure in
her repertoire but that she intends her audience to know her procedure and to
react appropriately on the basis – at least, in part – of this knowledge. We shall
return to this issue below. First let us complete the Gricean picture by tackling
the question of word-meaning.

Here Grice offers only the merest sketch, but it is a sketch whose limitations
are themselves revealing. To proceed, Grice claims, we need to be given an
account of the semantic structure of the various complex expressions included
in the language. Although we have a huge amount of work to do in achieving such an account, this need not overly concern us since this is a problem
for linguists not for philosophers. What we, as philosophers, need to reassure
ourselves about is that it is likely that we shall be able to build an account of
word-meaning on the basis of linguists' dissection of language. And here the

general strategy will be that we can dissect the procedure that a speaker adopts relative to a complex expression into those procedures that she adopts relative to the components. Of course those components will occur in other combinations, so the procedure we are interested in is a general procedure that dictates how that component procedure figures in the construction of those complex procedures related to those other complex expressions. So the idea is that there will be a procedure associated with the expression "Fred" that is a component of the procedure associated with such sentences as "Fred is red", "Fred is tall" and so on; and likewise for the predicate "is red" and so on. Of course this is just to map out a scheme of composition. The important thing for Grice is that we need to see this scheme as built on procedures that relate ultimately to speaker-meaning. Thus we have the following:

(Pred) For "*F*" to mean the same as "*G*" for *S* is for *S* to have in her repertoire the procedure of uttering "*F*"-"*a*" in order to speaker-mean that the R-correlate of "*a*" is *G*.

(N) For "*a*" to mean the same as "*b*" for *S* is for *S* to have in her repertoire the procedure of uttering "*F*"-"*a*" in order to speaker-mean that *b* is the D-correlate of "*F*" (see Grice 1989: 133).

The next step is to explain the notion of correlation (D-correlation for predicates and R-correlation for singular terms). It will not be worth our while following Grice very far down this route because, first, the account already limps and, secondly, Grice does not manage to travel very far himself and manages only to arrive at a position in which there are "as yet unsolved problems". His idea is to tackle the issue in stages, the first of which is to explain what it is explicitly to set up a correlation. This one does by making an utterance (e.g. "I hereby correlate 'shaggy' with all and only those hairy-coated creatures") in which one establishes a relation between the word and the relevant objects and makes the utterance with the intention of establishing such a relation. The account is then extended to non-explicit establishment of a correlation. And here the problems are twofold. First, how do we ensure extensional adequacy if, say, we focus on uses such as ostensions? For instance, how do we know that the correlation is between "shaggy" and all and only hairy-coated creatures and not to those that look hairy-coated to *S*? Secondly, if we try to reduce the non-explicit case to the explicit case by saying that the correlation is that which the speaker *would have* explicitly set up, then the problem is in saying under what conditions the speaker would have explicitly done so and in understanding how such an account is not going to be regressive; we cannot explicitly correlate all our terms because it takes some correlated terms in order explicitly to state the correlation.

Let us set aside these problems with the notion of correlation and return to the above specifications. If *S* means that Fido is shaggy by "Fido is shaggy", then

S has in her repertoire the procedure of uttering "Fido is shaggy" in order to speaker-mean that Fido is shaggy. But what our clause for the meaning of "Fido" will now commit us to is, roughly, if *S* means that Fido is shaggy by "Fido is shaggy" then *S* has in her repertoire the procedure of uttering "Fido is shaggy" to speaker-mean that Jones's dog is shaggy, where "Fido" is R-correlated with Jones's dog. The fault is obvious: *S* may well speaker-mean that Fido is shaggy without speaker-meaning that Jones's dog is shaggy since "speaker-meaning that" is intensional.[2] In effect the approach runs afoul of Frege's problem of substituting co-referential terms into the context of a *that*-clause. We *might* be able to surmount the objection were we able suitably to restrict specifications of correlations. But in order to do so, we would need to justify the claim that in speaker-meaning that *a* is *F*, *S* speaker-means that the R-correlate of "*a*" is *F*. Consequently "*a*" and "the R-correlate of '*a*'" would have to have the same semantic content for *S*. But this simply demonstrates the vicious circularity of the account. The role of clause (N) is in specifying sameness of semantic content, but its adequacy is suspect unless we can ensure that the terms it uses have the same semantic content. Thus it is entirely useless.

3.5 Problems for Grice's account

3.5.1 Problems for the account of speaker-meaning

Is the account circular?
As we noted, the Gricean account focuses simply on speakers' intentions in the construction of meaning. But if we restrict our focus in this way, then it appears that anyone can mean whatever they want to by anything – they just need to have an appropriate, even if daft, set of intentions. The account degenerates into a "Dumpty" theory of meaning. Witness this dialogue between Dumpty and Alice:

> "I don't know what you mean by 'glory'," Alice said.
>
> Humpty Dumpty smiled contemptuously. "Of course you don't – till I tell you. I meant 'there's a nice knock-down argument for you!'"
>
> "But 'glory' doesn't mean 'a nice knock-down argument'," Alice objected.
>
> "When *I* use a word," Humpty Dumpty said, in a rather scornful tone, "it means just what I choose it to mean – neither more nor less."
>
> "The question is," said Alice, "whether you *can* make words mean so many different things."
>
> "The question is," said Humpty Dumpty, "which is to be master – that's all." (Carroll 1982: 184)

Dumpty's position should strike you as utterly implausible – that is the point of Carroll's playing with the absurd – and the major reason for this is that meanings cannot be conjured so easily from the whims of speakers; language could not be a communicative tool were speakers to be complete masters of the meanings of their words.[3] Grice's account of speaker-meaning runs close to Dumpty's theory since it makes meaning dependent on the speaker's intentions. To separate Grice from Dumpty one wants to place some constraints on the meaning-determining communicative intentions. A seemingly minimal constraint is to demand that these intentions be *reasonable*.[4] Patently Dumpty's intentions are unreasonable because when Alice protests "I don't know what you mean by 'glory'" Dumpty betrays his irrationality by agreeing: "Of course you don't – till I tell you". Grice suggests that constraints of reasonableness must function:

> [I]f as an examiner I fail a man, I may well cause him distress or indigna-
> tion or humiliation; and if I am vindictive, I may intend this effect and
> even intend him to recognize my intention. But I should not be inclined
> to say that my failing him meant$_{NN}$ anything. On the other hand, if I cut
> someone in the street I do feel inclined to assimilate this to the cases of
> meaning$_{NN}$, and this inclination seems to me dependent on the fact that
> *I could not reasonably expect* him to be distressed (indignant, humili-
> ated) unless he recognized my intention to affect him in this way.
>
> (1957: 384, emphasis added)

In this example my intention that the effect be brought about through recogni-
tion of my intention to bring it about is reasonable in the latter case but not in the former. Thus the latter is a case of meaning$_{NN}$, the former is not.

So let us restrict the account in some way to intentions that one can rea-
sonably expect to be fulfilled. There are two problems, however, with such an attempt; the first is a problem about the nature of such reasonable intentions when linguistic meaning is the issue, and the second is that the restriction promises to be insufficient: given enough imagination we can engineer situations that, although far-fetched, are such that the expectation of fulfilment of the intentions is not unreasonable (see the discussion of Searle below). I want, however, to focus on the first problem, questioning whether it is so much as legitimate to restrict the intentions to reasonable intentions.

The first point concerns the arbitrariness of a word's relation to its meaning. How could it possibly be reasonable to use the sentence "The avocado is over-
ripe" to mean that the avocado is over-ripe except for what those words mean? More fully, one's utterance of "The avocado is over-ripe" with the reasonable intention of bringing one's audience to believe that the avocado is over-ripe and with the reasonable intention that this intention is recognized and plays a part in one's audience's formation of the belief is an *impossibility* if those words do not have certain meanings. What makes one's intentions reasonable here *is* the

meaning of the relevant words. Contrast the situation with that of drawing an appropriate picture. Here the account stands a chance of working because there is a non-arbitrary relation between the picture and what it is taken to mean that enables one's communicative intentions in producing the picture to be seen as reasonable. But since the relation of a word to its meaning is arbitrary, the only way to come to see the intentions as reasonable is to appeal to the actual meanings of the words. Grice's aim is to account for linguistic meaning in terms of repertoires of procedures that are acts performed with communicative intentions. But the repertoires must take hold on acts performed with *reasonable* communicative intentions, and those intentions cannot be recognized, or even conceived, *as* reasonable without bringing in the meanings of the words spoken. So the account presupposes what it sets out to explain.

But Grice can simply respond as follows. True, there could be no having the reasonable communicative intentions were there no meanings. So the reasonable communicative intentions cannot *precede* the establishment of the repertoire of procedures. And that, to be sure, is a grave fault were Grice in the business of offering a story about the genesis of linguistic meaning. However, that is not his goal; his goal is to offer an analysis of linguistic meaning and this he does in terms of the notions of reasonable communicative intentions and a repertoire of procedures. Although in some cases making sense of the particular reasonable communicative intentions requires linguistic meanings, the general notion of a reasonable communicative intention is independent of the notion of linguistic meaning. Thus we can use the former notion in an analysis of the latter.

I am not sure, however, how impressed we should be with this response. I have two concerns. The first relates to the obscure notion of having a procedure in one's repertoire. One thinks of this as a kind of standing ability to perform an act that is itself independent of that standing ability. For instance, one might have been able on some occasion to tie a knot but one may have no generally reliable capacity so to do; the tying of the knot is not dependent on having that ability as part of one's repertoire. However, on the current account, this would be nonsense in the linguistic context. There *is* no speaker-meaning something by a sentence unless that sentence has a meaning and the sentence has a meaning only if there is a procedure of using it with a certain speaker-meaning. Speaker-meaning and sentence-meaning thus necessarily coexist and the problem now is not that Grice does not give an account of the origin of sentence-meaning – that may not have been his interest – but that it is difficult to see how sentence-meaning *could* arise on his account of what it is.

There is a response to this problem on Schiffer's (1972: §V.3) rather different view of things. On his account we have to think of an initial situation in which, for whatever reason, it *is* reasonable for a speaker to use a "sentence" with a certain speaker-meaning. His example: the speaker utters "Grrr" to speaker-mean that she is angry; the communicative intentions can be seen to be reasonable in the circumstances because the speaker believes that her audience will associate the sound with the sound that dogs make when they are angry and thus she can reasonably intend her audience to respond appropriately. Once that communicative situation has occurred, it itself provides a reason and a different reason for thinking that the audience will be able to respond appropriately – at this point history of use can take over the role of grounding the reasonableness of the relevant communicative intentions. So the relation of an expression to its meaning can be arbitrary, provided that there is an initial situation in which it is not arbitrary but is supported by specific features of the situation. What Schiffer's account possesses and what Grice's lacks is a conception of the kinds of features that render a communicative intention reasonable and, importantly for Schiffer, those features must be seen to evolve – from specifics to history – in the origin of linguistic meaning. So this nod in the direction of genesis affects his analysis.

Schiffer attempts to explain sentence-meaning not in terms of having procedure in one's repertoire but in terms of convention. Roughly – we shall be more careful below – a sentence has a certain meaning just in case it is conventional for speakers to use it with that speaker-meaning. Although Schiffer is somewhat sympathetic to Lewis's account of convention, his tentative account does not take the resolution of coordination problems[5] as central but instead focuses on the role of precedence and of explicit agreement in stipulation. Since linguistic meaning cannot be entirely a matter of explicit stipulation, precedence is thus seen to have an essential role not merely in the genesis of language but in understanding what language is. We thus need some account of the emergence of the precedent and, since Schiffer thinks the basis of the precedent is a communicative situation, we shall have the account just rehearsed – at some point the relevant communicative intentions are made reasonable by some relevant but incidental fact (such as that "grrr" sounds like the noise dogs make).

Now, as an account of the origin of language among some small group of people, this is believable, because we may suppose that speakers' intentions are reasonable given the shared history based on some original use; but nonetheless it is mere speculation. However, as an account of almost all speakers' linguistic experience it is a gross distortion. Most of us meet language fully formed; there is no relevant connection of the word with its meaning, nor need one be created in the learning situation. And the precedent that may have played a role in establishing that meaning is not available to us. In fact, the precedent that we are concerned with appears not to be a precedent that is a Gricean communicative exchange; rather, what may well set up the precedent is precisely repetitive situations whose role is *not* communicative, that is, drill and training in the use of linguistic terms. Now, although this does not show that a Gricean account is mistaken, it does throw into question the point of such an account. If it needs to be based on a speaker's reasonable communicative intentions, and if those intentions are rendered reasonable by a history of training in the use of terms which one intends to employ, then it appears that Grice's account presupposes an account of the effects of training and thus of the meanings of speakers' terms. It would thus be redundant. A virtue of Grice's approach, as I have mentioned, is that from the first it weds meaning in language to speakers' rational use of language. But in adopting this as its exclusive focus it seems to ignore the role of training and thus to over-intellectualize the origin of linguistic understanding.

A second point relating to our original concern is this. Our puzzlement concerns linguistic meaning and, if Grice is to be any help to us, he must be able to explain the notion of linguistic meaning. And so it seems he does: he explains linguistic meaning in terms of the general notion of a reasonable communicative intention. However – and this is the crux – if that general notion is to be any use in my grasp of linguistic meaning, I must have an understanding of reasonable communicative intentions *in the relevant circumstances*. And the objection is that making sense of reasonable communicative intentions in the circumstances of the use of language will, because of the arbitrariness of a word's meaning, require an understanding of the notion of linguistic meaning. The notion of a reasonable communicative intention is, to be sure, independent of linguistic meaning in the sense that such intentions can be had and can be made sense of independently of language. But some concepts seem to have a quality of extensibility,[6] that is, as circumstances and contexts change, the concept acquires uses that arise out of its previous uses but also involve some enriching of the concept. The point here is that once we enlarge the space of reasons that are available in rationalizing a communicative act, we extend the notion of a reasonable communicative intention; in particular, the addition of reasons involving the meaning of expressions in a language precisely has this affect. So the question is whether the notion of a reasonable communicative intention is extensible in this way or whether, in contrast, it is definite. I am not sure what my intuitions tell me, but the absence of a clear verdict one way or the other should raise suspicions about the programme of analysis here.

Counter-examples to the necessity of the analysis
Consider the following case. Triumphantly concluding his proof, Pythagoras asserts, "The square of the hypotenuse equals the sum of the squares on the other two sides". Clearly Pythagoras intends his audience to believe that the square of the hypotenuse equals the sum of the squares on the other two sides and intends his audience to recognize his intention to get them to form such a belief, but does he intend them to form the belief on the basis of recognizing this intention? Certainly not! He intends them to form this belief on the basis of the foregoing proof – his intentions should be entirely irrelevant in his audience's formation of the belief and should be rendered so by the proof he has rehearsed. However, surely we want to say that Pythagoras means that square of the hypotenuse equals the sum of the squares on the other two sides by his assertion.

Now consider this case. Pythagoras has no audience as he works through the proof in his study, "uttering" sentences either orally or in writing. He has no communicative intentions – not even with respect to his later self – but simply aims to do some mathematics. His "utterances" certainly appear to be meaningful – to fulfil their function they must be meaningful to Pythagoras and would be meaningful also to some suitably qualified eavesdropper – but they do not owe their meaning to any communicative intention of Pythagoras.

Finally, consider a case in which I know that you know that the justified true belief analysis of knowledge is false. Nonetheless, realizing that an epistemological claim you have just made commits you to the justified true belief account of knowledge, I now assert "The justified true belief account of knowledge is false". Since I know that you have this belief, I am not intending you to form this belief. However, what my assertion means is surely that the justified true belief account of knowledge is false.[7]

Counter-examples to the sufficiency of the analysis

There is a variety of counter-examples in the literature that attempt to show that the analysis is insufficient because there can be situations in which a communicator has all the Gricean intentions but because of some other deceptive intention we would not want to say that the meaning ascribed by the Gricean account is correct. Consider the following:

> S intends by a certain action to induce in A the belief that p; so he satisfies condition [(1)]. He arranges convincing-looking 'evidence' that p, in a place where A is bound to see it. He does this, knowing that A is watching him at work, but *knowing also that* A *does not know that* S *knows that* A *is watching him at work*. He realizes that A will not take the *arranged* "evidence" as genuine or natural evidence that p, but realizes, and indeed intends, that A will take his arranging of it as grounds for thinking that he, S, intends to induce in A the belief that p. That is, he intends A to recognize his [(1)] intention. So S satisfies condition [(2)]. He knows that A has general grounds for thinking that S would not wish to make him, A, think that p unless it were known to S to be the case that p; and hence that A's recognition of his (S's) intention to induce in A the belief that p will in fact seem to A a sufficient reason for believing that p. And he intends that A's recognition of his intention [(1)] should function in just this way. So he satisfies condition [(3)].
>
> (Strawson 1971: 156)

Strawson's claim here is that although S satisfies all of the Gricean conditions for communicating, this is clearly not a case of communication. Clearly the example hinges on the emphasized qualification. S's intentions are reasonable only on the condition that S knows (or believes) that A fails to know (or believe) something about the situation. So it is tempting to respond to the case by adding a Gricean intention:

(4) S intends that A should recognize S's intention (3).

Although this provides an immediate fix, counter-examples along the same lines can be constructed involving S knowing that A lacks some higher-order piece of knowledge about her intentions. Again we could remedy the situation by adding yet more intentions on S's part that A recognize her lower-order intentions. But since examples can continually be reproduced, we develop an infinite regress.

Let us turn now to our second worry, that is, to the question of whether the restriction to reasonable communicative intentions is sufficient. Consider the following example:

> Suppose that I am an American soldier in WW2 and that I have been captured by Italian troops. And suppose also that I wish to get these troops to believe that I am a German officer in order to get them to release me. What I would like to do is to tell them in German or Italian that I am a German officer. But let us suppose that I don't know enough German or Italian to do that. So I attempt to put on a show of telling them that I am a German officer by reciting those few bits of German that I know, trusting that they don't know enough German to see through my plan. Let us suppose that I know only one line of German, which I remember from a poem I had to memorize in a high school German course. Therefore I, a captured American address my Italian captors with the following sentence: "Kennst du das Land, wo die Zitronen blühen?" (Searle 1969: 229–30)

Here the American intends to induce the belief that he is a German officer and intends to do so by virtue of his captors' recognizing that intention. So according to Grice the American's utterance of "Kennst du das Land, wo die Zitronen blühen?" means that he is a German officer. But again this is radically implausible. The utterance means: "Knowst thou the land where the lemon trees bloom?"

One way of reading Searle's example is simply that, even if we build the requirement of reasonableness into the relevant communicative intentions, we can counter-exemplify Grice's account of speaker-meaning. So we might be tempted to react simply by amending the account of speaker-meaning. And this is, in fact, one lesson Searle intends us to learn. His thought is that we need to consider the different sorts of effect that a communicative act may set out to achieve and we need to restrict the legitimate effects that figure in communicative, meaning-determining, intentions. He borrows Austin's distinction between the illocutionary and perlocutionary. On Austin's account we need to consider (at least) three sorts of acts that may be associated with a doing-by-saying. There is the saying, that is, the use of a certain set of words (with a given meaning) – this is the act *of* saying something or, as Austin says, the locutionary act. However, one may and usually one does *do* something *in* saying something – and this Austin ([1962] 1975: ch. 8) calls the illocutionary act. Thus I may utter the words "The cat is on the mat" and perform the locutionary act of uttering a sentence that means that the cat is on the mat and, in doing that, I may perform the illocutionary act of asserting that the cat is on the mat. But, further, I may thereby intend to inform you that the cat is on the mat and this further act is perlocutionary. The point is this: an illocutionary act succeeds just when the communicative intentions with which it is performed are recognized: the aim of communication is just to lay bare these intentions to one's audience. "If I am trying to tell someone something, then … as soon as he recognizes that I am trying to tell him something and exactly what it is I am trying to tell him, I have succeeded in telling it to him" (*ibid.*: 47).

In contrast, the perlocutionary act is not purely communicative; rather, one performs the illocutionary act with the aim of achieving a certain perlocution-ary effect. But, whether or not one does so will depend on whether one's audi-ence reacts as one wishes, and this cannot be guaranteed purely on the basis that they recognize one's intentions. Thus I may intend to inform you that the cat is on the mat but you may resist receiving the information even if my illocutionary act succeeds. You may appreciate just what I want to do but treat the information as suspicious because, say, you know that I am bad at identifying cats (perhaps bad at identifying mats too). Correspondingly we have the following sorts of intention. An illocutionary *intention* is one that is fulfilled simply on the basis of the audience's recognition of the intention. A perlocutionary *intention* is not so fulfilled. If you recognize my intention to promise that … in uttering "I promise …", then I have promised that …; if you recognize my intention to ask a question in uttering "Is …?", then I have asked a question. These are all illocutionary intentions. Contrariwise, if you recognize my intention to induce the belief that … in uttering "XYZ", then it does not follow that my intention is fulfilled – you may remain incredulous; if you recognize my intention to offend you in uttering "Ugh blugh blug", then it does not follow that my intention is fulfilled – you may be thoroughly thick-skinned (see Searle 1969: 47).

So Searle's thought is that we need to restrict the intentions we consider in the account of speaker-meaning to illocutionary intentions. And this enables us to deal with the particular example of his American soldier since his intention here is to bring about a certain belief in his audience and this is a perlocutionary, not an illocutionary, intention. To be sure, this amendment seems necessary: perlocutionary intentions should not be taken as meaning-determining. And it seems well suited to solve some of our other problems. In presenting his proof, Pythagoras has a perlocutionary intention to produce a belief in his audience that the square of the hypotenuse equals the sum of the squares on the other two sides, but this intention is not communicative. Rather, the communicative intention might be that he intends his audience actively to entertain the thought that *p*. Similar remarks would apply to cases of reminding.

But, as Searle readily concedes, the emendation is insufficient to counter the *sort* of example he raises. For the example would lose none of its absurdity were we to think of the soldier as having the intention to *assert* that he is a German officer by uttering "Kennst du das Land, wo die Zitronen blühen?"

In the foregoing we have been treating Searle's case as a counter-example to the Gricean account of speaker-meaning. That account winds up being amended, but counter-examples can still be manufactured easily enough. I think that approaching the problem in this way fails to acknowledge the full force of the worry, which is much more an internal worry about the structure of the view. As we have mentioned repeatedly, Grice's account consists of two components – an account of speaker-meaning and an account of sentence-meaning based on it – but, as stated, there is no guarantee that the two components will not war with one another. This is just what Searle's example reveals: the established meaning of a sentence may conflict with that attributed to it on an occasion of use by the account of speaker-meaning. There is no reason that one should not use a sentence in defiance of one's procedures for using it;[8] this is just what the American officer does. Searle's focus is linguistic conventions, since he views the American officer as knowingly flouting the conventions governing the German sentence. I shall frame the discussion in terms of conventions*, which I shall treat as being neutral between Searle's notion and Grice's conception of procedures in one's repertoire. If we are to move forward by placing a restriction on the relevant communicative intentions, we need to find restrictions that ensure that there can be no conflict of this sort between the two components of the account.

Imagine a case where Jack wants to promise Jill that he will love her forever but is too embarrassed to say this in English. He may utter some romantic French doggerel verse (which means something completely other) with the intention of thereby effecting the promise (thinking that Jill is bound to pick up on the romantic intentions).[9] Now his intention is illocutionary but he does not mean "I'll love you forever" by the French sentence because, according to Searle, he has not uttered it with the intention of respecting the conventions* of French. And this is the second emendation that he insists on: "If he is using words literally, he intends this recognition to be achieved in virtue of the fact that the rules for using the expressions he utters associate the expression with the production of that effect" (1969: 45).[10] Note that this intention seems to be well suited to play the role of filling the gap we have diagnosed. The gap allowed for there to be play between the two components of the account and, by insisting that the intentions constitutive of speaker-meaning explicitly involve the conventional* aspect, we seem to have closed that gap. Although, of course, it is true that some of the gap has been closed, it is not clear that the gap has been closed either sufficiently or in quite the right way. First, note again that the intention to conform to the conventions* of the language needs to be reasonable. Jack may have a completely baseless intention to conform to the conventions* of French – and indeed may miraculously do so – but there would still be something troubling in supposing that, in these conditions, he might mean that he will love Jill forever in uttering "Je t'aimerai toujours". It is not even clear that making the intention reasonable would be enough – say Jack recalls being told by his friend Jacques, whom he takes to be a fluent French speaker, that "Je t'aimerai toujours" means "I'll love you forever". Jack's intention is reasonable if his belief in Jacques' French competence is reasonable. But suppose that the belief is both reasonable – because he saw Jacques reading *L'Etranger* by Camus – and true but that Jacques was not reading the book but simply attempting to cut a dash in the eyes of an existentialist inamorata. Here Jack has a reasonable intention and in fact succeeds in following French convention*, but does his remark mean that he will love Jill forever? It is hard to think that it does because, in the circumstances, the thing that makes his intention reasonable might just as easily have resulted in him using some other string of words. Alter the case to one in which his linguistic adviser is not Jacques but José, who knows no French but gives apparently good evidence of being a French speaker and misadvises Jack that "Avez vous une bicyclette?" means that I shall love you forever in French. This is an interesting case: clearly Jack fails the test of intending to conform to the conventions* governing the sentence he utters, yet he does intend to conform to the conventions* governing the language of the sentence uttered.

Intuitions will vary here just as they do with analogous cases in epistemology. However, what the examples suggest is that it is not merely enough to intend to conform to the conventions* governing the sentence one utters or of the language of that sentence, but that that intention must be informed by an *awareness* of those conventions*. Using a sentence to mean something is thus based on an understanding of the relevant sentence. Of course this is, in a sense, thoroughly unsurprising. It does, however, entail that the modified Gricean account explains the use of language in communication on the basis of what it is to understand language. It does not illuminate the nature of that understanding and thus only builds on and does not address a central (perhaps the central) question in the philosophy of language. The next section will pursue this issue by looking at Schiffer's work. In attempting to remodel the Gricean account of speaker-meaning so as to deal with what seems to be an endless series of counter-examples, Schiffer constructs a notion that seemingly has the ability to explain speakers' awareness of linguistic conventions*. If so, then the modified Gricean account may have some mileage in it.

Notice too that we would have to build further layers of Gricean intentions into the Searlean intentions. For suppose now that it is Jacques (having given up on his erstwhile existentialist beloved) convincing Jill of his love in similar circumstances. In this case Jacques might choose to utter "Je t'aimerai toujours" with all the appropriate reasonable communicative intentions and reasonable intentions about adhering to conventions governing French usage. Would he mean that he will love her forever by his remark when it is clear that he knows that a whole slew of other remarks – with quite different meanings – would have done as well? If not, we might then be tempted to insist that Jacques have the reasonable intention that Jill recognize his intention to conform to the conventions* of the language and he reasonably intends that her interpretation of his utterance proceeds by means of this recognition. And now the other Gricean intentions appear to drop out of the picture: if the conventions* determine meaning, then Jacques' intentions in relation to the conventions seem sufficient to confer a meaning on his utterance.

The problem is that we were supposed to be offered an account of linguistic meaning in terms of speaker-meaning plus conventions*. But, if Searle is right, speaker-meaning must involve intentions that relate to conventions*. The problem is one of circularity. Sentence-meaning is explained in terms of convention* and speaker-meaning. Speaker-meaning is then explained in terms of (reasonable) communicative intentions, some of which relate to conventions*. But the convention* is that of making an utterance with certain communicative intentions. So we do not know what the convention is until we know what the intentions are. But, at least in part, the intentions concern the conventions*. So we do not know what the intentions are until we know what the convention* is. We have no way of breaking into this circle and so no way of knowing what either sentence- or speaker-meaning is.

3.5.2 Speaker-meaning, mutual knowledge and conventions

Let us return to Strawson's problem with the account of speaker-meaning. As we noted, the possibility of such counter-examples depends on the speaker having an intention that is hidden from her audience. So a seemingly neat response is that of Blackburn (1984: 115), who amends the Gricean account to include the fact that the communicating speaker intends all her intentions in performing the relevant act to be recognized. The problem with the clause is that it seems to rule out deception, which often depends on successful communication. I cannot lie successfully if *all* my intentions in so acting are recognized, and thus I cannot both lie and rationally intend that all my intentions in so acting are recognized. Thus there needs to be some restriction on the sorts of intentions that are to be recognized. I am not clear what the relevant restriction should be but I think that any restriction will be problematic. Consider, for instance, the suggestion that we restrict attention to illocutionary intentions. Thus the communicator has the intention *that all her illocutionary intentions are recognized*. The problem here is that we necessarily include the restriction in the content of the catch-all intention. And this is radically implausible; most of us communicate well enough without any conception of what an illocutionary intention is. Indeed, most of us communicate well enough without any conception of what the appropriate restriction is, which would be impossible were the restriction required. Thus the proposal requires a restriction but none can be provided. The proposal should thus be rejected.

Schiffer offers a rather different conception of openness in communication that hinges on the notion of mutual knowledge. By definition, S and A mutually know that p iff each of S and A knows that p; each knows that the other knows that p; each knows that the other knows that she knows that p; each knows that the other knows that she knows that the other knows that p ... Thus in cases of mutual knowledge each knower knows an infinite sequence of pieces of knowledge but the sequence in each case is fully determined. So the notion appears well suited to our problem, provided, of course, that we can make sense of the idea of possessing an infinitude of pieces of knowledge. Obviously our mutual knowers need not be able to avow all their pieces of knowledge; rather, each simply needs to be able to avow each of these infinite pieces of knowledge and this she can do by recognizing easily appraisable aspects of the situation of mutual knowledge: the fact that one's access to a piece of knowledge is available to one's mutual knower and that her access to that same knowledge is available to oneself. Under these circumstances the notion of mutual knowledge is not mysterious. Schiffer's revision of Grice's account of speaker-meaning then proceeds as follows:

> S means that p by doing φ iff S φed with the intention of bringing about a situation, E, in which (or in which it is intended by S that) S and A have mutual knowledge that E obtains and that E provides good evidence that S φed intending:
> (1) to produce a response r_p in A,
> (2) A's recognition of S's intention in (1) is part of A's reason for responding r_p,
> (3) to bring about E.   (cf. Schiffer 1972: 39)

Typically, E is the situation of S having φed. So what becomes mutually known is that S φed *and* that S's φing is good evidence that S φed with the relevant Gricean intentions. On the version of the proposal that includes the bracketed alternative it is not clear that we do not run into similar problems as we found in Blackburn's account. What Schiffer needs to ensure is that, in some sense, our mundane practice is informed by an implicit conception of mutual knowledge. It is one thing to point to occasions in which knowers have mutual knowledge, but quite another to point out situations in which they conceive themselves to be mutual knowers.

How does the notion of mutual knowledge enable us to deal with Searle's counter-example? Our American officer intends the following:

(i)   that his audience believes that he is a German officer[11]
(ii) that his audience forms this belief on the basis of recognizing intention (i).

Schiffer fills in the detail of the example as follows. The American believes (a) that his captors will take his utterance to be German, (b) that they will take him to believe that his audience speaks German (and that he does too), and (c) that, in the circumstances, they will infer that his utterance means that he is a German officer. That is the basis they are intended to have for forming the relevant beliefs about the American's intentions (i) and (ii). However, this is clearly not the basis they are intended to think they are intended to have. Why? Well, since they are intended to believe that the American believes that they speak German – something he clearly hopes is false – they are intended to think that the basis they are intended to have for their belief about the American's intentions is simply their understanding of the sentence "Kennst du ...".

The question is: how does the requirement of mutual knowledge help? We had better not focus on the knowledge component of this requirement since the audience's beliefs will not amount to knowledge since they are largely built on the false belief that the American believes that they speak German. Schiffer is anyway content to frame the requirement in terms of mutual belief. Now though there are elements of the situation that clearly fail any mutual belief requirement; what we need to focus on is mutual belief about the communicative intentions (i) and (ii). Let us call these (I). Obviously the American believes (I); these are *his* intentions. The reasoning just rehearsed in the previous paragraph both explains how the audience might form a belief in (I) and, since it is the American's reasoning, explains how he would form the belief that his audience believes (I). And, having formed the belief about the American's intentions, the audience can rehearse our reasoning (these are *his* intentions) to form the belief that the American believes (I). And the American can do this too. Thus we have the following steps in the sequence:[12]

$$B_S I \qquad\qquad B_A I$$
$$B_S B_A I \qquad\quad B_A B_S I$$
$$B_S B_A B_S I$$

It is the next step – getting to $B_A B_S B_A I$ – that promises to be difficult because we do not want to ascribe awareness of the beliefs that sponsor the American's belief $B_S B_A I$. From that point on, however, there should be no problem; since the American is apprised of the relevant fact, if we manage to construct a rationale for the formation of the belief $B_A B_S B_A I$, then this will be a rationale he can mimic and so form the relevant higher-order belief about his audience's beliefs (and so on at each stage). Thus there will not be a bar to extending the sequence on the left-hand side provided we can extend the right-hand side. So let us get back to our problem. How do the captors form the belief that the American believes that the captors believe I? They obviously do not suppose that he believes that they have rehearsed the complicated reasoning that, in fact, they did rehearse. However, they also believe that the American believes that they are in a pretty normal communicative situation – namely, one in which both parties understand the language spoken (German). And given this (false) belief, it would be *surprising* if they *failed* to form the belief given by $B_A B_S B_A I$. So the sequence extends. As long as we focus on belief rather than knowledge, the situation should appear by Schiffer's lights to be one of communication since the reciprocal beliefs are vouched safe on the one side by a false belief and on the other by an awareness of the false belief. To be sure, there is the discrepancy that Schiffer highlights, but this fails to affect the formation of the higher-order beliefs required for mutual belief. The counter-example stands.

Let us consider sentence-meaning. Take the following very simple account:

> *s* means that *p*, for *S* iff there is a convention that *S* speaker-means that *p* by uttering *s*.

Then take the following simplified Lewisian[13] account of convention (cf. Lewis 1969: 42):

> A regularity, *R*, is a convention amongst a population *P* when they are in a recurrent situation *T* iff it is mutually known[14] between members of *P* that in any instance of *T*:
> (i)   everyone conforms to *R*;
> (ii) everyone expects everyone else to conform to *R*;
> (iii) everyone prefers to conform to *R* on condition that the others do

The result is:

> *s* means that *p*, for *P* iff it is mutually known between members of *P* that in any instance of *T*:
> (i)   everyone utters *s* to speaker-mean that *p*;
> (ii) everyone expects everyone else to utter *s* to speaker-mean that *p*;
> (iii) everyone prefers to utter *s* to speaker-mean that *p* on condition that the others do.

Let us now encapsulate the set of Gricean intentions in the phrase "M-intention" (see Grice 1989: 105). Then the account of sentence-meaning in terms of speakers' intentions runs as follows:

> *s* means that *p*, for *P* iff it is mutually known between members of *P* that in any instance of *T*:

(i) everyone's utterance of s is mutually known to provide evidence that she M-intends that p;

(ii) everyone expects everyone else's utterance of s to be mutually known to provide evidence that she M-intends that p;

(iii) everyone prefers that her utterance of s is mutually known to provide evidence that she M-intends that p on condition that the others prefer likewise.

Note the iteration of mutual knowledge; it is supposed that members of P have mutual knowledge of mutual knowledge. How are we to construe this? One approach would be to take mutual knowledge of mutual knowledge that p to consist in mutual knowledge of each piece of knowledge involved in mutual knowledge that p. If so, then I think the idea is unproblematic. If S and A mutually know p then we shall have pieces of knowledge of the form $K_S K_A \ldots p$ and $K_A K_S \ldots p$. What we then need for mutual knowledge of mutual knowledge is that each of these pieces of knowledge is mutually known. Consider the situation from S's perspective. We then need to consider whether we have $K_S K_S K_A \ldots p$ and $K_S K_A K_S \ldots p$. The latter is a piece of knowledge included in the original sequence of mutual knowledge and the former is a species of self-knowledge, which, though not guaranteed, we can take to be given unless there are countervailing considerations. Similar remarks clearly apply to A; but now we need to show that each piece of knowledge just demonstrated is available to A. For the first A needs to ascribe a piece of self-knowledge to S, which he can do by mimicking our argument and the second once again simply generates another piece of knowledge from the original sequence of mutual knowledge. Thus, if we can help ourselves to a degree of self-knowledge and an awareness of this self-knowledge, mutual knowledge of mutual knowledge is, on this construal, given with mutual knowledge. However, I think this is not what is meant by mutual knowledge of mutual knowledge that p. Clearly the opening clauses here will be of the form $K_S K^*_{SA} p$,[15] which is not a piece of knowledge that would be generated in the account just rehearsed. It is quite different from all those pieces of knowledge since it involves an ability to reflect on the generation of a whole infinite series of pieces of knowledge, an ability that is notably absent in the description just given. On this construal mutual knowledge of mutual knowledge (indeed knowledge of mutual knowledge) is a comparatively rare and sophisticated piece of knowledge. Certainly it is nothing one would wish to ascribe as fundamental to speakers' understanding of their language.

Let us move on to Schiffer's account of word- and sentence-meaning, which proceeds by assigning wordly to linguistic items and, on the basis of this, distinguishing those sentences that have the property we shall call T. A (simple) sentence is T just when the object assigned to its name has the property assigned to its predicate. Thus intuitively T is truth under the given assignment, but this is not assumed. Rather, we consider the characterization of T-conditions; we have just said, in general, when a sentence is T and we can give a particular characterization in each case. So we shall have clauses of the form "s is T iff p". We then can think of the meaning of the sentence in these terms:

> s means that p iff there is a convention to utter s only if speakers mean that p by uttering s and s is T iff p.[16]

The nature of the proposal is obscure. What we seem to have been given is two characterizations of the meaning of the sentence: one in terms of a convention governing speakers' individual acts of meaning and another in terms of the truth-conditions of the sentence. Each clause seems to be sufficient, especially since Schiffer adds refinements to ensure that the specification of truth-conditions is not merely extensionally correct but plausibly captures those truth-conditions that specify meanings. However, one might suppose that the second clause is insufficient since, as it stands, T has not been assumed to be truth. Thus T cannot be assumed to capture truth-conditions, and, without that assumption, it cannot be taken as a specification of meaning. I think that something like this reading is right. We can thus begin with this clause:

> s means that p iff there is a convention that speakers utter s only if they mean that p.

We also have:

> s means that p iff s is T iff p.

The point then is that if we read the second clause in the light of the first we can take T to be truth and, perhaps more importantly, we have seen how to generate clauses of the second form from clauses governing words. Thus we learn that the convention governing the use of the sentence first secures a truth-condition for the sentence and, secondly, through this, secures semantic properties for words. In a sense, we learn how the convention operating at the level of sentences develops conventions operating at the level of words. Once we have this we can see how the semantic properties of words might combine in novel ways to issue in the meanings of novel sentences.

Importantly, the programme helps itself to the findings of an investigation to which it cannot contribute, namely, a dissection of language into its primitives and an assignment of wordly items to linguistic items. Thus the programme depends on far more than mere analysis of problematic concepts such as speaker- and sentence-meaning. Secondly, the aspect of the programme focusing on communicative intentions will make itself redundant if the truth-conditional account were to be constrained by something *other* than conventions governing speaker-meaning. This, we shall see, is a good way to view Davidson's programme, where the truth-conditional account is constrained by the needs of an interpreter. And indeed something like Davidson's view may well prove to be an attractive option, especially given the difficulties that beset these attempts to give an analysis of speaker-meaning and sentence-meaning that can be success-fully combined without circularity, without implausibility and without falling prey to counter-examples. We should also note that the terms of the analysis – conventions and communicative intentions and their like – are by no means uncontentious. Certainly they will be contended by Quine's examination of the analytic approach, which we look at in Chapter 4. Finally, what recommends the current approach is that it insists that the semantic account we offer of language must be measured against the facts of speakers' use of language. Here we con-ceive of those facts in terms of conventions governing (communicative) acts of meaning; but there are other ways of securing this connection. To mention but two: we might focus on the role that the semantic account of language plays in understanding speakers' general behaviour (Davidson) or we might focus on the norms that operate in linguistic practices.

4. Analysing synonymy

Our attempt to elucidate the notion of meaning via analysis seems to depend solely on how one rates Grice's attempt to analyse sentence-meaning. It is worth noting that even if that account does not face internal difficulties, it still does not resolve the question of meaning itself but reduces linguistic meaning to mental meaning plus convention. But there is another potential starting-point for analysis. Rather than analysing an assignment of meaning to an expression, one might instead try to analyse *sameness of meaning* or *synonymy*. Our aim in analysis will accordingly be to arrive at true sentences of the form:

e_1 means the same as e_2 iff ?

or,

the meaning of e_1 is the same as the meaning of e_2 iff ?

where we are attempting to fill in the question mark.

The appeal of this is manifold. First, sentences of the form "e_1 means the same as e_2" are ordinary sentences of English. Secondly, they remain grammatical no matter what expressions take the place of "e_1" and "e_2". Third we resist any presuppositions about meanings being entities or about what sort of entities they are.[1]

However, it might seem that we are only analysing sameness of meaning rather than meaning itself. So it might seem that we are falling short of our goal. When Frege (1953: §§62–9) was interested in analysing the concept of number, he began by analysing sentences of the form "the number of Fs is the same as the number of Gs". In other words, his starting-point was the notion of sameness of number or equinumerosity. His reason was that he felt it important, when introducing a new range of objects – here numbers – to have a criterion of identity applicable to those objects; the notions of identity and of objecthood go together. Now Frege himself thought that this was only the first stage of the analysis, the second stage would say what numbers are in a manner that shows that they do indeed satisfy the analysis of equinumerosity. But it can easily strike one that Frege's demands here are excessive.[2] It is easy to say when the number belonging to one concept is the same as that belonging to another, or to say when the direction of a line is the same as the direction of another line, but very hard to say what a number is or what a direction is. For we have:

> The number of Fs is the same as the number of Gs iff there is a one-one matching of the Fs and the Gs.[3]
> The direction of a is the same as the direction of b iff a is parallel to b.

And the question is: why is our understanding of the new range of objects not captured in these statements about when objects in that range are identical? Frege claims that the lack here gives rise to the so-called "Julius Caesar" problem, namely that the account of numerical identity fails to give us a means for deciding whether or not Julius Caesar is the same as the number of Fs. He had his particular reasons for this insistence, but many others have felt that asking our analysis of *number* to decide this question is itself asking it to decide too much. So perhaps we can make progress with an analysis of sameness of meaning.

For historical reasons Quine's focus of attention is not, at the outset, the notion of synonymy but the notion of analyticity. We soon discover that they are, however, interlinked. His argument will be that an (informative) analysis of synonymy is impossible. And, if so, then an (informative) analysis of meaning is impossible too, since the latter would yield the former. Thus from the perspective of this negative argument there is every reason to focus on synonymy rather than on meaning itself.

4.1 The analytic–synthetic distinction

In "Two Dogmas of Empiricism", Quine (1961: ch. 2) sets himself against empiricist adherence to (i) the analytic–synthetic distinction; and (ii) reductionism – the two dogmas. The first is a view that sentences divide into two: those whose truth is grounded in fact and those whose truth is independent of fact, of the way things happen to be. The second insists that each meaningful sentence can be analysed as a logical construct of terms whose meanings refer to immediate experience. A reductionist will always adhere to the analytic–synthetic distinction, although one might adhere to the latter for reasons distinct from reductionism. In analysing sentences to reveal their empirical content, we show how the truth-value of a sentence depends on two components: its meaning, a contribution made by us; and empirical fact, a contribution determined by the world. Some sentences are probably thereby shown to be true in virtue of the first component alone and, indeed, those sentences expressing the results of analysis will fall into this camp. These sentences are therefore true no matter what: these are the analytic sentences.

The form of Quine's argument is to ask for a basis for the distinction, or for a definition of analyticity. He considers a number of alternatives, pointing out that none is satisfactory since it defines the target notion in terms that are equally problematic. He concludes that there is here a circle of *putative* concepts into which we cannot gain entry. He goes on to describe a picture of how he sees language as functioning and, in terms of this, he then seems to offer a replacement for the traditional notion of analyticity and notes that no sentence counts as analytic on this scheme. So, although there is an acceptable notion of analyticity, it has no application.

If we give up the view that meanings are entities (what Quine calls the museum myth of meaning – each word is a museum-type label for a meaning), then we may content ourselves with identifying sameness of meaning – synonymy – among terms and analyticity of statements. We then might define an analytic statement as one that can be transformed into a logical statement (true purely in virtue of form) by substituting synonyms for synonyms. But this will not do as it stands since the notion of synonymy is as much at issue as is that of analyticity.

So the question becomes: what makes one phrase synonymous with another? One thought might be that synonymy is a consequence of definition: "spinster" means "unmarried woman" as a matter of definition. But although this account might be acceptable for an artificial language, in which we are permitted to introduce new terms only by strict or stipulative definitions, it distorts the case of natural language where these supposedly definitional connections are set up by the nature of our linguistic use. So the resulting definition is an encapsulation of use; indeed, it is no more than a report of synonymy. So the notion of definition presupposes that of synonymy and thus cannot ground it.

Can we define synonymy in terms of the interchangeability of expressions without change of truth-value, *salva veritate*? If two terms are synonymous, then there is a sense in which they each perform the same linguistic function. So, can we be more precise about characterizing this sameness of function? One, seemingly promising, thought is that two expressions are synonymous if one can always be used in place of the other without thereby affecting a change in truth-value between the original and resulting sentences. We need, however, to be clear about the richness of the language in which we suppose this process to be occurring. The two expressions "featherless biped" and "human" can be intersubstituted *salva veritate* in a number of sentences simply because all and only featherless bipeds are human. The expressions, however, are obviously not synonymous. So we need, at least, to suppose that we have *modal* notions, notions of necessity and possibility or the like. For example, "bachelor" is synonymous with "unmarried man" because we can substitute "bachelors" for "unmarried men" in "Necessarily all unmarried men are unmarried" to get "Necessarily all bachelors are unmarried"; "featherless biped" and "human" are not synonymous since "Necessarily all featherless bipeds are featherless bipeds" is true but "Necessarily all featherless bipeds are human" is false. However, once again, the notion of necessity is as problematic as that of analyticity. The point is that only in an *intensional* language rather than an *extensional* language is interchangeability a plausible criterion for synonymy. But an intensional language incorporates, and thus presupposes, the very terms and concepts we are trying to explain.

It is worth noting that the definition in terms of interchangeability *salva veritate* is fine in rich-enough languages. There is nothing circular or uninformative about the stated definition. But Quine's more general concern might be seen as asking how the richer intensional language is grafted on to its merely extensional base. The definition obviously is now clearly impotent since its adequacy depends on having an intensional language and so Quine's question remains: how is the intensional language to be introduced?

This point reveals something of an ambiguity in Quine's account. At first it seems he is raising a philosophical concern about the legitimacy of certain putative concepts. In order to answer that concern we need a philosophical account of those putative concepts and, here, a philosophical account is seen as providing a (reductive) definition. This, in itself, is a large and perhaps revealing philosophical assumption: why would one restrict the nature of a philosophically illuminating account to the provision of definitions unless one were oneself in the grip of a conception of philosophy as purely analytic? Certainly an adherent of the analytic–synthetic distinction need not suppose that analyticity can itself be defined, nor even that any interesting concept can be analytically defined; perhaps analytic statements simply spell out necessary conditions for the application of a concept without ever achieving sufficiency. But although it might take a hefty philosophical argument to get one to share Quine's assumption, it is not even sufficient to fund his argument. Why not? Well, what we have just discovered is that the definition of synonymy in terms of intersubstitutability *salva veritate* is perfectly adequate if the language we are concerned with is intensional. So, to resurrect Quine's worry, we have to ask how the intensional locutions entered the language. And now we have to insist not merely that the *philosophical legitimation* of those concepts requires a (reductive) definition, but that the *introduction* of those concepts requires such a definition. And this, as Grice and Strawson (1956) point out, is far-fetched indeed. There are innumerable concepts that we grasp successfully without need of a (reductive) definition. My sense is that there is a better reconstruction of this phase of the argument; it will help, though, to have the next phase in front of us before we turn to it.

Let us return to Quine's exploration of possible definitions of analyticity. Another thought is that we should retreat from natural language, whose rules are inexplicit and imprecise, and consider the notion of analyticity in artificial languages, whose semantic rules are explicitly given. The thought would then be that in a given artificial language L we can stipulate, by means of these rules, the sentences that are analytic in L. But Quine points out that this fails to capture a notion of analyticity since all we have is a class of sentences that are categorized as analytic-in-L. We do not have the general concept of what it is for an arbitrary sentence to be analytic in an arbitrary language L. The only help provided by the move to artificial languages is that we now have neat technical ways of delineating the class of sentences that are analytic but we understand the character of sentences in this class only if we have a prior notion of analyticity. The technical apparatus gives us no insight into the *point* of classifying a sentence of L as analytic-in-L. (Ease of picking out the items that the term "analytic" should apply to is no help in clarifying the meaning of the term. For example, you may be very good at picking out stressed people by measuring their blood pressures but also have no idea what "stress" means, and what the point is of so classifying them.)

Now let us return to the attempt to define synonymy in terms of interchangeability *salva veritate*. What we discovered is that this definition is adequate only for an intensional language. Thus we face a similar problem to the retreat to formal languages: we do not yet have an account of synonymy for an *arbitrary* language. Moreover, although we can easily enough pick out languages that are *not* purely extensional, not every non-extensional language is "sufficiently intensional" to legitimate the definition. Say the language includes one non-intensional context: "Linnaeus believes that …". Assume also that, good taxonomist as he is, whatever Linnaeus believes of creatures with a heart he believes of creatures with a kidney. Thus in this non-extensional language, "creature with a heart" is intersubstitutable *salva veritate* with "creature with a kidney" and would be decreed to be synonymous according to our definition. Hence, in order to have a partial definition that is extensionally adequate, we would need a conception of a sufficiently intensional language, and the difficulty is going to be in trying to form that conception without helping ourselves to a conception of meaning-properties, or of synonymy and so on. After all, a "sufficiently intensional" language just seems to be one in which only *synonymous* terms are intersubstitutable *salva veritate*.

Quine's final thought is to consider the verification theory of meaning. Let us suppose that the meaning of a statement is given by its method of verification and/or refutation. Then statements are synonymous if and only if they are confirmed and infirmed in the same circumstances. This view impinges directly on the second dogma of empiricism: *reductionism*. A statement is meaningful only in so far as it has determinate conditions of confirmation and infirmation. So every meaningful statement must be translatable into a logical construction of statements about immediate experience. Thus for each statement there is a set of experiences that will confirm it and a set of experiences that will infirm it. In other words, statements are tested singly against the deliverances of experience. Quine finds this suggestion implausible. He famously insists that "our statements about the external world face the tribunal of experience not individually but only as a corporate body" (1961: 41). No matter how loosely one treats the doctrine of reductionism, it insists that certain courses of experience should lead us to a view about the truth-value of a given sentence (either because such-and-such course of experience renders it true; or because such-and-such experiences render it likely; or because such-and-such experiences render the statement false etc.). Quine rejects this notion on two grounds: (i) no one has been able to achieve any such reduction for significant regions of science or even for talk about physical objects; and (ii) certain experiences may call for us to modify our system of beliefs – our theory of the world – but the experience cannot, in any circumstances, dictate what modification is called for (and this is just what reductionism denies). This last view is the basis of Quine's semantic holism.

We shall turn to that soon, but we need now to draw a moral from this phase of the discussion. Quine takes his attack on analyticity to constitute an attack on the respectability of the notions of meaning, synonymy, analyticity and syntheticity. And many, notably Grice and Strawson (1956), have attacked him on this score. I am sympathetic to these worries. As I mentioned, it is far from clear that we need to restrict genuine understanding of a concept to that which accrues through a reductive definition. Accepting that restriction is indeed to endorse a large assumption; but at this stage of our argument it is an assumption we are endorsing relative to the philosophical understanding of the concepts that Quine is concerned to examine. We are currently in the business of trying to decide whether we should seek philosophical illumination of the concept of meaning or of synonymy through the construction of a reductive definition. And the resounding reply returned by Quine is that we should not. It is a reply I think we have to endorse. Quine goes on, however, to use this result to cast doubt on the bona fides of these concepts. And that is a step it would be premature to take; we can give up Quine's excessive restriction and investigate other approaches. So the suggested conclusion of this part of the book is that the programme of analysis seems to grind to a halt: its most favourable starting-point cannot make any interesting progress.

4.2 Holism

In focusing on the verification view of meaning, Quine suggests that there *appears* to be an acceptable notion of analyticity: that of a statement that can be held true come what may, or of a statement whose truth-value cannot be revised.[4] The reductionist dogma encouraged the idea that there are two distinct components – one of fact and one of meaning – determining the truth-value of any statement. This makes it seem that the factual component can, on occasion, vanish, leaving us with an analytic statement. Quine now denies that there is any such category: *any* statement can be held true come what may if we make drastic enough adjustments elsewhere in the system (1961: 43). If, for instance, certain observations seem to refute our theory, we are not bound to modify the theory. We might claim that the observations were mistaken, that the instruments on which those observations depended were at fault. And, even if we decide to modify the theory, it is not determined which modification we shall adopt. Suppose for instance that a certain heavenly body fails to appear in the night skies at a time and place predicted by our theory. We might decide that something in our theory needs to be changed. But a number of things might be changed: we might change our view about the constitution of the heavenly body; or we might change our view about its trajectory; or we might modify the law of gravity; or we might modify the laws of motion; or we might even modify the logic by means of which the prediction was inferred! Thus there are not two distinguishable components – a meaning component and a worldly component – determining the truth-value of a sentence.[5] Instead, our theory as a whole has to meet the test of experience. When we encounter a recalcitrant experience, no particular revision in our system is imposed on us. So how do we go about making revisions in our theory in the face of recalcitrant experience? Quine's suggestion is that we make changes in line with the pragmatic maxim of minimizing further changes in the system – Quine's pragmatic maxim of minimum mutilation. So we revise the system so as to cause least possible fuss. There is no injunction against revising a basic scientific principle or a logical law in response to experience (and indeed some recommend revising the distributive law of classical logic in response to quantum-mechanical phenomena), but we would be unlikely to do so since it would impose further and radical disturbances elsewhere on our system.

The upshot is that it makes no sense to think of a sentence as having empirical content; the only thing that has empirical content is one's theory about the world. Certain courses of experience cohere with the theory; others are recalcitrant. The theory can thus be tested empirically. We seem to be able to test a part of the theory but when we do so we *choose* to hold the other parts fixed.

If one were persuaded by Quine's description of how language functions, then certainly one would question the validity of the analytic–synthetic distinction and, possibly, Quine's attack on the distinction is motivated by his independent inclination to endorse the holistic picture. Be that as it may, we should note here a threat to the project of philosophical analysis. If Quine's holism is right, then there are no analytic sentences and, since it is the goal of philosophical analysis to produce analytic sentences, there can be no viable project of philosophical analysis. Conversely a philosophical analyst will have to reject holism. Thus far the jury is out on this conflict: we have not been given an argument in favour of the holistic view.

It is, however, far from evident that the phenomena cited by Quine, even if accepted as genuine, sponsor his holistic view. What the phenomena force on us (as Grice and Strawson [1956] point out) is an acceptance, first, that no sentence has confirmation/infirmation conditions in isolation and, secondly, that any sentence may have the assignment of truth-value to it revised. The first point simply entails that the confirmation/infirmation conditions of a sentence have to be taken against a background of assignments of truth-value to other sentences. Two sentences then can be said to be synonymous just when they have the same confirmation/infirmation conditions relative to each assignment of truth-value to other sentences. The second point is, in a sense, banal: any sentence may have its truth-value revised if its meaning changes. So Quine's claim is that there is no distinction between revisions in truth-value sponsored by a change in belief and those sponsored by a change in meaning. In consequence, the argument needs to shift to the question of whether or not this distinction has any substance.[6] However, even then one might accept Quine's claim here but still reject the negative conclusion about meaning and synonymy. How might one do so? One might well think that certain revisions of meaning are a response to change in belief. Thus there would be no dichotomy between those revisions that result from change in meaning and those that result from change in belief; one might say that rejecting the dichotomy here is not to reject the distinction. We shall return to this question towards the close of the book.

5. Radical translation

One reading of Quine's argument in "Two Dogmas" is that it advocates a sceptical view about notions such as analyticity, synonymy and meaning. However, Grice and Strawson (1956) rightly point out that if we are to view the argument in this way, then the argument makes a huge assumption. It assumes that if a concept is legitimate, then we should be able to define it. Quine gives no justification for such an assumption and consequently scepticism about meaning and cognate notions is not warranted. However, Grice and Strawson's objection makes a significant concession to Quine; it concedes that there is no informative definition of these notions. This might not discredit them but it does entail that (analytic) definition is not the way to shed philosophical light on them.

We might, though, proceed somewhat obliquely. Rather than take the very direct road of analysing synonymy, we might instead try to reflect on the nature of synonymous relations by imagining an enterprise that would precisely be sensitive to those relations. In this way we might be able to show how those relations are part of the fabric of the world, despite our inability to offer an appropriate definition. Although one might not be able informatively to say what facts constitute relations of synonymy, it would be significant and would be a rebuttal of scepticism to be told how sensitivity to a certain range of facts enabled one to be sensitive to relations of synonymy. In a sense, we could think of this as a version of a genealogical approach. In genealogy one attempts to understand a phenomenon by understanding aspects of its genesis or of its possible genesis. The current approach, although it does not attempt to provide the genealogy of meaning and/or synonymy – we do not try to tell a story about how *meaning* comes to be – is a genealogical approach to the *concepts* of meaning and synonymy – we tell a story about how we might come to employ such concepts.

What enterprise advertises itself as revealing relations of synonymy? Well, restrict your attention (initially) to relations of synonymy between languages, and the answer is of course: translation.

5.1 The indeterminacy of translation (the argument from below)

In the second chapter of *Word and Object* (1960) Quine sets out with great thoroughness a thought experiment. The thought experiment is that of radical translation. We are asked to imagine the business of a field linguist whose task it is to write a translation manual for a foreign language. The target language, though, shares no kinship with the home language, either in terms of some commonality in cultural setting or in terms of having had a common source – or, at any rate, must not be assumed so to do. So the linguist's own experience of her language is to provide no help in her translation project. This is what makes the enterprise *radical*. It is also what makes the enterprise something of an idealization and, supposedly, philosophically informative. Quine is interested in the scientific respectability of the notion of meaning. Essentially he is asking, from the perspective of his naturalism (the belief that all truth is amenable to scientific investigation), whether there is any fact of the matter about linguistic meaning. His way of asking that question is to turn to radical translation. If there is a fact of the matter about what a native means by her utterances, then that fact should be one that determines the translation scheme that the radical linguist adopts (provided only that she carries out her method properly). Quine's conclusion is that translation is indeterminate. We shall need to clarify: first, the linguist's approach to her problem; secondly, the reasons for the indeterminacy; and, finally, the consequences of Quine's argument.

5.2 Methodological considerations

5.2.1 The context principle

How should translation begin? What data can we, plausibly, suppose are available to the linguist? A first point to note is that the data a linguist observes will relate to utterances in response to specific environing stimuli, and Quine takes it that the minimum unit of linguistic utterance is a sentence, so our evidence base will consist of speakers' use of whole sentences. Our task will then be to work back from conclusions based on this evidence to facts about the meanings of words. Many philosophers have been keen to assert some version of this priority of the sentential. In Quine the priority is a consequence of the evidence available through speakers' use of language, which consists, at base, of utterances of whole sentences, even when the sentence is a one-word sentence. Frege too offers a version of the priority in his famous context principle – the injunction never to ask for the meaning of a word except in the context of a sentence, that is, except in terms of its contribution to the meanings of sentences in which it occurs. For Frege this principle has a more metaphysical air about it. The point is that we need to think of the meanings of words as being combinable to form the meanings of sentences. So the meaning of the word must be explicable in terms of its ability to combine with that of other words to form the meanings of sentences. So the principle is at once an insistence that we explain word-meaning in terms that allow for a appreciation of language as compositional in structure and a methodological piece of advice to condition our investigation with this end in view: simply correlating a word with an extra-linguistic entity will fail on its own to explain the how the meanings of words combine to form the meanings of sentences.

There is a certain obvious truth in the idea that the minimum meaningful move in language involves use of a whole sentence: merely uttering a word is not meaningful. And this is the basis for Quine's focusing the data on speakers' uses of sentences. But some may claim that this concession does not go far enough: a speaker's meaningful use of a sentence cannot be disentangled from her propensities to use the rest of her language. Indeed we could see Quine as precisely making this point in "Two Dogmas of Empiricism", where the minimum unit of empirical content is not the sentence but the whole theory. Here in his discussion of translation Quine will be making a similar point; the meaning of a speaker's sentence will depend on her dispositions in relation to a whole range of other sentences and these dispositions are the joint product of belief and meaning. But he does not help himself to any of these conclusions at the outset. To begin, we have speakers' uses of whole sentences and observations about the stimuli that cause those uses.

5.2.2 Stimulus-meaning

Quine's approach is behaviouristic. The linguist can observe the stimuli (in the form of surface irradiations of the speaker's sensory apparatus) and can then elicit assent to or dissent from a sentence, given the stimulus. This presupposes that the linguist has succeeded in identifying typical assent and dissent behaviour and, in itself, this is not trivial. It requires, first, an identification of certain behaviours as being those of assent or dissent and then a categorization of one set as being assent and the remaining set as being dissent. However, this step is necessary for the possibility of translation and we can suppose that, perhaps after having rejected a number of inoperable hypotheses, the linguist lights on a workable assignment.

The next phase in the programme can begin. We need a set of concepts for describing language consistent with this austere approach. The linguist distinguishes dispositions to assent to or dissent from a sentence given certain stimuli. We can thus begin with a notion of the stimulus-meaning of a sentence. We can think of stimulations as coming in two sorts: those that would prompt a speaker's assent – the affirmative stimulus-meaning – and those that would prompt dissent – the negative stimulus-meaning. The stimulus-meaning of a sentence is given by *both* of these since the one set does not determine the other: there may be stimuli that are neutral. Note also that we are talking about what *would* prompt a speaker's assent or dissent. So we are trying to fix on a speaker's dispositions to assent and dissent, these dispositions being captured in subjunctive conditionals; for example, "if speaker S were to be stimulated thus-and-so then she would assent to *t*".

Two points about stimuli are worth noting. First, the stimulus will last some time. So we need to specify what time period we are considering in identifying stimuli. (Quine calls this the modulus.) Also, stimulus-meanings will be specific to speakers at certain times: we cannot presume community-wide agreement and we must allow that a speaker's use of language may change. Secondly, stimuli are *types* of events. That is, in talking of a stimulus, *s*, we are talking of all events of a particular form. So the very same stimulus can be repeated.

Stimulus-meaning is a notion that describes an aspect of a speaker's use of a sentence. Depending on the sort of sentence considered, it can provide a more-or-less accurate indication of what we would normally call the meaning of an expression. So Quine's next task is to classify sentences and to discuss the way in which they relate to their stimulus meanings. Note that although Quine proceeds here by considering how stimulus-meaning relates to different sorts of sentences in the *home* language, this is not to compromise the radical nature of the translation project. Such assumptions will be made in translating *any* language; they are not legitimated by any specific assumptions about the relation between the foreign and the domestic languages.

Standing and occasion sentences: An occasion sentence is one whose truth-value varies from time to time so that no response of assent or dissent is appropriate if it is not a response to a relevant stimulus. Examples are: "This is wet"; "There's a priory"; "Rabbit!" Standing sentences, intuitively, are sentences whose truth-value should be settled once and for all but are better seen as sentences whose truth can be discussed without there having to be an appropriate prompting stimulus. So, for instance, I can simply ask whether or not you assent to or dissent from "The moon is made of green cheese". Quine does not suppose that there is a sharp divide between the two sorts of sentence. (Rather, the time gap between requisite re-promptings can progressively decrease until we reach typical occasion sentences where the time gap is less than the modulus. This technical nicety will not concern us here.)

A problem now concerns the way in which collateral information can effect what prompts a speaker to assent to a sentence. Take Quine's famous native utterance "Gavagai.",[1] which, intuitively, we want to translate as "Rabbit." Now it may be that the natives know that a certain distinctive fly hovers around nothing but rabbits. So if she sees these flies, a native will assent to "Gavagai." Should this stimulus count as part of the stimulus meaning of "Gavagai." or should it be regarded as the employment of collateral information? The general question here is whether there is a principled way to decide whether a change in the use of an expression corresponds to a change in meaning or to a change in belief.[2] Quine is suspicious of this supposed distinction so the lack of a clear way of deciding the question in the case of stimulus-meaning is no form of threat to him; it will however have important consequences.

Observationality: The possible intrusion of collateral information marks a sentence off as being less observational, since what prompts assent and dissent will often be a matter of background belief. For instance, the use of "He is a bachelor." in contrast to, say, "That's green." is massively dependent on background information. So there is a distinction to be marked out here between cases where a sentence has a certain meaning but the use is guided by collateral information and cases where such facts are simply part of the stimulus-meaning of the sentence. Quine resurrects a version of this distinction simply by widening his gaze from an individual speaker to community-wide use. As a community we agree about the meaning of "Jake is a bachelor." but differ widely in our use because that use is heavily guided by collateral information. Conversely, if a sentence is observational, then its use will vary little as we move across the community, considering as we do so speakers in possession of different collateral information.

Stimulus synonymy: Stimulus-meaning is a very bad guide to the meaning of non-observational sentences: although the stimulus-meaning of "Lo, a bachelor." may differ hugely for you and for me, the meaning of the sentence is the same. So it would seem that the linguist's notion of meaning is vastly inadequate as soon as we move away from observation sentences. This has to be admitted. However, a workable notion of *synonymy* can be rescued. If we concentrate on an individual speaker, then the two sentences "Lo, a bachelor." and "Lo, an unmarried man." have the same stimulus-meaning. If this sameness is preserved as we move across different speakers, then we can say that the two terms are stimulus synonymous. This is despite the fact that, in communal terms, it makes no sense to talk of the stimulus-meaning of either sentence.

5.3 The indeterminacy of translation

The crucial thesis of the indeterminacy of translation emerges in two movements: first, when we move from translating the stimulus-meanings of observational *sentences* to translating the meanings of *words*; and, secondly, when we then move back to the translations of sentences as determined by the translation of words: if the translation of the words is indeterminate, then there will probably be non-observational sentences that have incompatible translations according to the different schemes. The thesis of the indeterminacy of translation is itself a thesis purely about the sentential level: it is the claim that there are indefinitely many empirically adequate translation schemes that are incompatible with one another in the sense that they provide translations of sentences that are not (even stimulus) synonymous.

Let us grant that the field linguist has determined that "Gavagai." has the same stimulus meaning as "Rabbit." Even so, we cannot infer that the terms "gavagai" and "rabbit" have the same meanings since we cannot even infer that they are true of the same things. It may be that "gavagai" means the same as any of the following: "temporal stage of a rabbit"; "undetached rabbit part"; "rabbithood"; "rabbitting" and so on. Any of these translations will ensure that "Gavagai." has the same stimulus meaning as "Rabbit.". This phenomenon is *the inscrutability of terms*.

Of course if we had a way of talking about sameness we might distinguish between some of these translations: the stimuli of the head and then the hindquarters of the same rabbit will prompt an assent to "Same rabbit." but not to "Same undetached rabbit part." The obvious problem with this is that it presupposes that we have succeeded in translating the natives' term for "same". It may however be that the assent is to the statement (to the effect) that this gavagai belongs with that gavagai. The repercussions for the notion of stimulus synonymy are immediate. Even though the *sentences* "Bachelor." and "Unmarried man." are stimulus-synonymous, we cannot say that the *terms* have the same meaning, otherwise we could similarly deduce the sameness of meaning of "gavagai" and "rabbit" from the stimulus synonymy of "Gavagai." and "Rabbit." We shall look in more detail at examples of this sort soon but, for now, let us pursue that translator's project further.

However, Quine supposes that one set of terms *can* be translated: those terms (terms of logic) whose definitions are truth-functional. These can be translated because the truth-functional definitions have direct correlates in terms of assent and dissent. So, for example, a term will translate as "and" if whenever a speaker assents to two sentences concatenated by this term she will assent to each sentence individually and vice versa. We can define stimulus-analytic sentences as those sentences that are stimulus-synonymous with a denial of a contradiction (not-(p & not-p)). So the linguist can: (1) translate observation sentences; (2) translate truth functions; (3) recognize stimulus-analytic sentences; and (4) recognize stimulus-synonymous sentences (for given speakers).

To proceed, the linguist needs to impose analytic hypotheses on her scheme of translation. That is, she will need to catalogue the foreign vocabulary and set up a correlation between that and her domestic vocabulary so as to accord with her discoveries, of the sort just listed.

Adoption of a set of analytical hypotheses imposes the structure of the home language on to the target language. Provided it agrees with the finite store of linguistic data, the resulting translation manual enables us to form indefinitely many supposedly grammatical foreign utterances and to provide each such utterance with a translation. The indeterminacy of translation is then a consequence of the supposed fact that there are indefinitely many ways of imposing a set of analytical hypotheses, which, though confirmed by the available data (of (1)–(4)), issue in divergent, that is, stimulus non-synonymous, translations for sentences not included in (1)–(4). Given a choice of how we correlate certain foreign words with our own words, for example, "gavagai" with "undetached rabbit part", we can then preserve consistency with (actual and possible) data by making accommodations elsewhere in the system, for example translating some other phrase not as "same" but as "belongs with".

There is no fact of the matter about which translation scheme is correct since to suppose otherwise is to suppose that the facts of the matter transcend verification. One might suppose, though, that there is nothing wrong with the idea of facts that we cannot access and that the argument simply shows that meaning-facts are of this sort. But, as Quine points out at the beginning of the chapter, since meaning is a public phenomenon, to suppose "a distinction of meaning unreflected in the totality of dispositions to verbal behaviour is a distinction without a difference" (1960: 26). How, for instance, could someone learn a language if she was required to pick up on a difference in meaning that is not available in speakers' dispositions to use language, which, after all, is the only evidence a learner of language has to go on? How could such a language be deployed in communicating with one another?

It is true that linguists, in practice, would not encounter the radical indeterminacy that Quine suggests. But this is because many of the rival schemes would appear clumsy or contrived. However, we should not read into the fact that we *can* project our own forms of speech onto the native utterances anything other than a lack of constraint in how we are *forced* to translate their utterances.

Let us summarize how these different elements of the picture combine. As Quine explicitly acknowledges in "On the Reasons for the Indeterminacy of Translation" (1970: 182), the gavagai example shows that the *word* "gavagai" can be translated in many ways given the stimulus-meaning of observation sentences in which it occurs. As we have noted, he calls this the *inscrutability of terms* and points out that this is not the same as the *indeterminacy of translation*, which is the thesis that some *sentences* of the foreign language can be translated by distinct sentences of the domestic language, which are not synonymous (in any sense). The route to that conclusion from the inscrutability of terms is to note that, given our choice of analytical hypotheses and our consequent choice of different translations for terms, it will be highly likely that certain non-observational sentences will admit of a variety of non-equivalent translations. Now you might think that if we face a choice of translating a sentence by two sentences that are not stimulus synonymous (for us), then we could test either choice against the use that the native makes of her sentence. But this is false. It is false because we are using facts about natives' use to solve simultaneously both for meaning and for belief. We can thus account for the fact that a native's use of her sentence might vary from the use we would make of the corresponding translation of that sentence by attributing to her beliefs that diverge from our own. We may, says Quine, charitably assume that the native's beliefs are right (by our own lights) and that charitable assumption may help us choose between translation schemes. But on Quine's view the charitable assumption is a pragmatically useful device for constructing workable translation schemes; it is not a response to the linguistic facts of the matter.

5.4 Quine's conclusions on meaning

Radical translation can be brought home. If there is no fact of the matter determining how to translate the natives' utterances, there is no fact of the matter about how I should translate my fellows' utterances, and, indeed, I cannot suppose that my own utterances are in any way different. If the only thing that could determine meaning – speakers' dispositions to use language – fails to do so, then meaning must be indeterminate. In Quine's view, the facts available to a field linguist are precisely the same facts as those available to a first-language learner. The latter has the task of learning the meanings of terms in the language and the former carries out the same task by means of translating into her home language. Since the linguist's task can be accomplished in too many ways, reflection on that task shows that it fails to discriminate determinate meanings. Since the first-language learner does not have a home medium in which to mark the possibility of alternatives, indeterminacy is not a live problem for her. But this fails to alter the essentials. The evidence available in either case is the same, and the evidence underdetermines meaning. For Quine the facts are the scientifically respectable facts and if these fail to determine meanings, then meaning is not a scientifically respectable notion. But, even if Quine is wrong about the general identification of facts with those available in science, it might, at first sight anyway, be plausible to suppose that in the case of language the demands on language learning require such an identification. As we saw previously, the lesson that Quine urges fits in with his physicalism. There are no intentional facts, so talk of meaning and ascriptions of belief must be given an instrumental account.

5.5 Evans's response

Gareth Evans argues that, although we might concede Quine's thesis of the indeterminacy of translation, we need not also concede his radical conclusions about meaning: indeterminacy of translation does not entail scepticism about meaning. Evans's paper "Identity and Predication" (1985: ch. 2) is a subtle piece of work but his basic point is not too difficult to grasp.

Quine's thought is that if there are facts about meaning, then these facts will constrain the business of translation. Since translation is indeterminate, there are no facts about meaning – at least none other than those that are captured by the ersatz notions of stimulus-meaning and its cognates: stimulus analyticity and stimulus synonymy. This thought of Quine's assumes that the project of translation will be sensitive to all relevant facts about meaning. But why should that be so? If we focus on observational sentences – our "basis" for translation – all that translation aims at is to arrive at translations of the relevant words that give rise to translations of sentences in the foreign language into stimulus-synonymous sentences in the domestic language. But that is a very weak constraint indeed and so it is not surprising that the resulting project of translation is indeterminate.

To appreciate this point, it helps to distinguish between the project of translation and the project of constructing a theory of meaning. The latter project aims to present a theory that systematically portrays the facts about meaning for some given language.[3] It will do this by explaining the meanings of certain primitive expressions in the language and then the meanings of complex expressions in terms of the meanings of their components and the significance of the way they are combined in the complex expression. If the project of constructing a theory of meaning were indeterminate, then Quine's conclusion would follow. But, as yet, we have no reason for thinking that indeterminacy in the translation project carries over into indeterminacy in the project of constructing a theory of meaning. What Evans tries to show is that there is no reason to think that the sort of indeterminacy that arises in translation will show itself in the project of the theory of meaning, because here additional constraints come into play.

We shall get to that point in just a moment. But, before we do so, I want to make a couple of remarks about the notion of compositionality. Language is apparently a highly structured entity: it consists of a finite set of primitive expressions and modes of combining those primitives grammatically, but allows the formation of an indefinite (perhaps infinite) range of complex expressions (and of sentences, in particular). Given that we are interested in a finite scheme of translation – since, as field linguists, we can only use such a scheme – we shall need to have a scheme that translates the primitive expressions and then delivers translations of the complex expressions on the basis of these (e.g. "regnig" means the same as "ginger"; "gavagai" means the same as "rabbit"; so "regnig gavagai" means the same as "ginger rabbit"). But the only constraint on this project is that we arrive at stimulus-synonymous sentences (at least if we restrict our attention to observation sentences). According to Quine, this means that we must adopt a set of analytical hypotheses – hypotheses about how to break down the language into its constituent words – but doing so is not a straightforward matter since it may be difficult to tell when something is a complex and when it is simple: also, given that some words are ambiguous, it is not obvious when a sign should count as one word or more than one. Now the indeterminacy of translation is really a product of the fact that our choice of analytical hypotheses is not determined by speakers' assent and dissent behaviour; that is, we can reconcile more than one choice of analytical hypotheses with this behaviour of speakers. So much for translation; what about the theory of meaning?

Like a translation scheme, a theory of meaning will aim to be compositional: it will characterize the meanings of primitive expressions and then character-ize the meanings of complex expressions in terms of the meanings of these primitives. But the point of so doing differs from that of compositionality in a translation scheme – at least, it is arguable that it differs. Whereas in the case of translation we want a compositional account because this is the only sort of theory a *linguist* can use, in the case of a theory of meaning we want a compo-sitional account because we think that this is the only way of making sense of, of explaining, *speakers'* semantic capacities, that is, the capacities that constitute the ability to speak a language. So the difference is this: a translation scheme is simply a theory that the linguist can use to arrive at adequate translations; a theory of meaning is a theory that explains speakers' semantic capacities. And this means that a theory of meaning is responsible to facts that a translation scheme can safely ignore.

What facts are these? Well they are facts about speakers' semantic capaci-ties and specifically they are facts about speakers' abilities to understand new sentences on the basis of understanding a range of others. At its simplest, the thought runs roughly as follows. If a speaker understands the sentences "Fred is green" and "Mary is red", she is able to understand the "new" sentence "Fred is red". The way we explain this is to say that the speaker has a capacity in rela-tion to the word "Fred" that enables her to understand sentences in which it occurs with other terms she understands, similarly, she has a capacity in rela-tion to the predicate "is red" that enables her to understand sentences in which it occurs with other terms that she understands. When these two capacities are exercised together, she is able to understand the sentence "Fred is red". These capacities constitute her understanding of the relevant words. So the point is that we are forced by our need to explain speakers' abilities to understand new sentences to pick out distinct capacities associated with "Fred" and with "is red" and so we are forced to break language down or to analyse it in a particu-lar way.

How does this work in the "gavagai" case? Recall that the one, plausible, suggestion called for us to widen our gaze to sentences containing "gavagai" other than "Gavagai." In particular we looked at sentences about sameness. So take the sentence "Hit gavagai emas hat gavagai",[4] which is stimulus synony-mous with "This rabbit is the same as that rabbit". We noted that this does not help us determine whether "gavagai" means the same as "rabbit" or the same as "undetached rabbit part" since we do not know that "emas" means the same as "same" or means the same as "is an undetached part of the same rabbit as" (i.e. the sentence is also stimulus synonymous with "This undetached rabbit part is an undetached part of the same rabbit as that undetached rabbit part").

But now let us consider things from the point of view of the theory of meaning. Here we shall not have clauses that specify translations; rather, we shall have meaning-specifying clauses.[5] For example:

THEORY I:

"gavagai" means *rabbit*
  (or: "gavagai" applies to rabbits)
"emas" means *the same*
  (or: x ^ "emas" ^ y is true iff the referent of x is the same as the referent of y)

THEORY II:

"gavagai" means *undetached rabbit part*
  (or: "gavagai" applies to undetached rabbit parts)
"emas" means *undetached part of the same rabbit as*
  (or: x ^ "emas" ^ y iff the referent of x is an undetached part of the same rabbit as the referent of y)

Note that here we do not simply quote a synonymous expression on the right-hand side; rather, we explain the meaning in one way or another.

Both theories explain speakers' abilities to arrive at an understanding of "Hit gavagai emas hat gavagai". So, thus far, there is no distinguishing one from the other: translation and the theory of meaning are in the same boat.

But now note that Theory I enables us to explain speakers' abilities to understand sentences involving "emas" that do not involve gavagais. So *if* speakers can go on to understand novel sentences of this sort, then that is evidence in favour of Theory I and against Theory II; if not, then vice versa.

If we stick with translation there is no need for us to take this sort of evidence into account: we could treat "emas" as ambiguous or we could add an ad hoc clause (the strategy is suggested by Hookway [1988: 154–5]). For example,

"emas" means the same as (i) "an undetached part of the same rabbit", in the context of terms for gavagais or as (ii) "same" in all other contexts.

You might think that we could rehabilitate Theory II by a similar manoeuvre:

x ^ "emas" ^ y is true iff (i) the referents of x and y are undetached rabbit parts and the referent of x is an undetached part of the same rabbit as the referent of y or (ii) the referents of both x and y are not undetached rabbit parts and the referent of x is the same as the referent of y.

But here it would be mysterious as to how a capacity that correlates with the first part of the clause goes together with a capacity correlated with the second part of the clause. These seem to be distinct capacities and thus there is no explanation for why they would come and go together.[6] The Quinean reply, however, is obvious: we have begged the question by supposing that these capacities are distinct. What objective criterion do we have for sameness and difference of capacities?

Let us leave things inconclusively here. Our journey to the cul de sac fails to notice a branch in Evans's argument, a branch, indeed, that he claims is more important than that on which we have hitherto focused. Consider the following clauses, first from a translation scheme and then from a theory of meaning.

(T) "Dummy" $^\wedge$ x means the same as (i) Trans(x) $^\wedge$ "is a part of a muddy rabbit", when x is a term for gavagais, or (ii) Trans(x) $^\wedge$ "is muddy", otherwise.

(M) "Dummy" $^\wedge$ x is true iff (i) the referent of x is a part of a muddy rabbit, when x is a term for gavagais, or (ii) the referent of x is muddy, otherwise.

The problem is that, when all our predicates are so construed, if x and y are both parts of the same rabbit, they are indistinguishable in the language: whatever predicate applies to x will apply to y. Moreover, since, as long as we stick, as the proposal insists, to clauses taking this form, no extension of the language will enable such a distinction; so this phenomenon cannot be dismissed as a mere contingent expressive weakness in the language. Our translation scheme thus forces us to conceive of the natives as operating with a range of terms with diverse reference but as being unable to discern these differences in reference. Or, to put the point differently, if we distinguish the relation of identity as relating x and y just when $(\forall F)(Fx \equiv Fy)$, then "emas" will be identified as the relation of identity and not as the relation "is a part of the same rabbit as". And now the crucial point comes in: while this is a crushing objection to the clause of the theory of meaning, it is not an objection to that in the translation scheme. The reason for this is that taking our native's terms to be terms for rabbit parts violates the following constraint: "[I]t is unacceptable to discern predication of As in sentences of a given kind unless those sentences are such that their systematic mastery requires mastery of the identity conditions of As" (Evans 1985: 39). The constraint is a constraint on the semantics of predicates drawn from consideration about the nature of understanding. It is thus a constraint on an adequate account of meaning; it is not a constraint on the mere business of finding a translation scheme. So we have a reason for rejecting a meaning-theory that adopts the above clause, (M), but none for a translation scheme adopting its respective clause, (T). And this, Evans claims, is the deeper worry he thought he had revealed.

His point relies on the fact that the semantic theorist will restrict her attribution of semantic properties to those for which there is evidence. She has evidence that speakers are sensitive to the identity conditions of rabbits because we either systematically describe their use of language explicitly as involving reference to or predications over rabbits, or we think of them as referring to and as predicating over rabbit parts but explain the satisfaction conditions of those predicates by reference to rabbits. Another way of making this point is simply to note that the sentence x ^ "emas" ^ y of the native's language is stimulus synonymous with Trans(x) ^ "is the same rabbit as" ^ Trans(y),[7] so in this sense the natives are sensitive to the identity conditions of rabbits. So we are justified in thinking of their apparatus of predication as involving predication over rabbits; we are not similarly justified, given the description of the case, in discerning an apparatus of predication that involves predication over rabbit parts. Were we to do so, we would allow that apparatus of predication to float free of the apparatus of identity; we would be attributing semantic properties for which there is no evidence.[8] As it happens, that principle is one Quine would accept;[9] the basis of the thought experiment of radical translation depends on it. We suppose that if there are to be facts of the semantic matter, then there must be evidence for such facts. Quine's *additional* assumption is that the evidence should be available to the radical translator. His argument then attempts to show that when the translator fails to find the requisite evidence she is forced to deny the existence of the relevant semantic facts. Evans's riposte is to point out, somewhat ironically, that the relevant evidence escapes the translator's notice because *translation* bases itself only loosely on the evidence – *any* translation scheme is acceptable provided it preserves testable stimulus synonymy. The irony is thus that, given Quine's insistence on constraining our discernment of semantic facts by the evidence, the project of translation was a singularly inapt project for him to have focused on.

The worry we have been concerned to emphasize clearly applies to meaning-theoretic clauses that follow the pattern suggested above in (M), because the first element in the clause is made conditional on our *terms* referring to gavagais. As long as all predicates follow this model, we shall be unable to distinguish between terms that ostensibly stand for different parts of the same rabbit. But there is a slightly different form the account might take,[10] which we ought to consider as part of a mopping-up operation; rather than think of the relevant linguistic context by reference to the *terms* that are used, we might think of it by reference to the *predicates*. For example:

"Dummy" ^ x is true iff (i) the referent of x is part of a muddy rabbit, when "Dummy" occurs with the predicate "Gavagai" or (ii) the referent of x is muddy, otherwise.

If the referent of x is a muddy part of a muddy rabbit and the referent of y is a non-muddy part of the same rabbit, then "Dummy" ^ x will be true, and "Dummy" ^ y

false. So, on this account, the referents of x and y *are* distinguishable. But now consider the sentence "Dummy" ^ "gavagai" ^ y. According to our scheme, it will be interpreted as "the referent of y is a part of a muddy rabbit", which is true. But this conflicts with the obvious fact that "Dummy" ^ "gavagai" ^ y formally entails "Dummy" ^ y (or, put differently, it conflicts with the facts that "Fi" ^ "dummy" ^ "gavagai" ^ y ^ "neht" ^ "dummy" ^ y^{11} is (stimulus) analytic). So this scheme runs aground because it distorts the formation of complex predicates; the manner in which the complex predicate applies to a term is not explained in terms of the application of its components. Or, perhaps better, we could base our choice about how to translate "gavagai" on whether "Fi" ^ "dummy" ^ "gavagai" ^ y ^ "neht" ^ "dummy" ^ y is stimulus analytic for our natives.

If this argument is right, it has not shown that indeterminacy *is not* a problem. It suggests that there may be a way to resolve some of the indeterminacy Quine highlights but does not demonstrate that all such indeterminacy can be expunged. But, if Evans is right, then Quine's case *is unproved*. Moreover, it suggests an alternative approach to the attempt philosophically to understand language; rather than pursue our aim through the modestly ambitious project of radical translation we should instead consider the project of constructing a theory of meaning.

The immediate focus of Evans's attack is not the thesis of the indeterminacy of translation but rather that of the inscrutability of terms. Of course, if that thesis is dethroned and if Quine's assumption that our adoption of analytical hypotheses will be dictated purely by pragmatic considerations is similarly jeopardized, the thesis of the indeterminacy of translation will indeed be left hanging by a thread. What thread will that be? Well, Quine recognizes that for many sentences of a speaker's language the stimulus-meaning will be a very poor guide to the sentence's actual meaning because the use of the sentence will be heavily dictated by collateral information (we have already noted this point). So we might construe a speaker equally coherently as having one combination of meanings and beliefs or as having a quite different combination. What dictates our choice here will be whether we find it plausible to attribute the one set of beliefs or the other. As Quine says,

> The maxim of translation underlying all this is that assertions startlingly false on the face of them are likely to turn on hidden differences of language … The common sense behind the maxim is that one's interlocutor's silliness, beyond a certain point, is less likely than bad translation.
> (1960: 59)

He links the maxim with Wilson's (1959) Principle of Charity, which label has now stuck. For Quine the maxim can only ever aspire to pragmatic virtues; it is not a deep truth about speakers or translation but a feature of constructing workable translation schemes.

We shall move now from the project of translation to the project of interpretation, from Quine's writings to those of his student Davidson. We can read
Davidson as having learned some of the lessons I have been concerned to present
in this chapter. First, interpretation (by construction of a theory of meaning) is
a rather more ambitious project than is mere translation and thus promises to
be more tightly constrained by the nature of speakers' understanding. Secondly,
Davidson is exercised by the status of the Principle of Charity, which he argues
is no mere pragmatic maxim but an essential guide to the enterprise of interpretation. However, before we are in a position to concentrate on Davidson we
need to think more generally about the theory of meaning.

6. The structure of a theory of meaning

Two recent chapters (3 and 5) have closed with suggestions about theories of meaning: in Chapter 3 we left Schiffer speculating on how a Gricean approach might be developed to give a systematic explanation of the meanings of words and compounds thereof – the upshot of this project would be a theory of meaning; and Chapter 5 suggested that the indeterminacy of translation reveals no deep truth about the nature of meanings but an inadequacy in the project of translation, which should therefore be replaced by that of constructing a theory of meaning. The preliminaries to that project are sketched in this chapter.

6.1 What is a theory of meaning?

A terminological nicety for openers: there is an ambiguity here that, on occasion, it will be important to guard against. "Theory of meaning" is often taken to signify a view about the nature of meaning or, quite distinctly, a theory that specifies or delivers specifications of the meanings of all expressions in some given language. Michael Dummett suggests the following disambiguating terminology. Let "meaning-theory" stand for the second use and let "theory of meaning" stand for the first use. Then we can talk about the philosophical discipline that is the theory of meaning and about a meaning-theory for Xhosa, or for Spanish or for Hebrew. The current proposal is thus that the best way of pursuing the theory of meaning is to consider how one would construct, and what form would be taken by a meaning-theory.

So, again our approach to questions about linguistic meaning is oblique. Rather than attempt to say what meaning is, we aim to throw light on the notion by thinking of an enterprise that will be sensitive to or constrained by the facts of linguistic meaning. Our focus is not however synonymy – a relation that is a consequence of meaning-facts – but the central notions of meaning and understanding themselves. As in the thought experiment of radical translation we do not envisage the actual construction of a meaning-theory; instead we are concerned with how such an edifice would be constructed, what form it would take as a whole, and what form specific, philosophically puzzling bits of it will take. In this chapter we shall secure some basic thoughts about the general enterprise. But then, in the following chapters, we return to Davidson's work and to his central claim that we ought to consider the construction of a meaning-theory as part of the enterprise of radical interpretation. Philosophical insight into the nature and function of language accrues *both* through an understanding of the nature of the meaning-theory that will be constructed and through an appreciation of *how* it would be constructed. But this is all work for much later; let us return to some general points about meaning-theories.

An important, if somewhat subtle, point needs to be registered at the outset. When we say that the meaning-theory must enable one to specify the meaning of every term of the language, this does not mean that the theory will deliver clauses of the form: expression *e* means such-and-such; or, sentence *s* means that so-and-so. Rather, the theory might only deliver clauses of a quite different form. For instance, on Davidson's proposal the theorems of the theory take the following form:

s is true iff *p*

What we shall then need to ensure is that we can treat this clause as giving the meaning of *s*, possibly because we can be sure that *if the theory states* that *s* is true iff *p*, then we can be sure that *s* means that *p*. Alternatively we might find reasons for thinking that the theory will not directly specify meanings at all. Perhaps what the theory will do is to state what it is that a speaker knows when she understands a term (cf. Dummett 1993: essays 1–3) or what practices or abilities suffice to enable one to deploy a vocabulary (cf. Brandom 2008). Since when one understands a term one knows its meaning, the theory will be stating that knowledge that comprises knowledge of meaning; that is, meanings are characterized in terms of what it is to know them. The theory thus characterizes meanings indirectly by characterizing knowledge of meanings. So decisions about the overall shape of the theory will be called for. Can we be more specific about the form of the theory independently of those decisions?

6.2 Systematicity

Since the set of expressions that belong to a language is at least potentially infinite, we cannot expect a tractable meaning-theory to contain more than a mechanism that enables the meaning-theorist to generate a specification of the meaning of every expression in the language. Such a mechanism will presumably involve truths about the meanings of basic expressions in the language plus a set of principles detailing how the meanings of complex expressions depend on those of their components. In just this sense the meaning-theory (in effect just because it is a *theory*) will be systematic. In other words, the theory is systematic not on account of the nature of its subject matter – linguistic competence – but on account of the theorist's requirements (as a being with finite capacities).

In this sense of systematicity a meaning-theory differs in no interesting way from a translation manual and thus, in all probability, a meaning-theory so conceived will not enable us to escape the bind of indeterminacy that infected the project of translation. Thus we ought to demand more of systematicity in a meaning-theory and, as a matter of fact, for this or for other reasons, most writers do make such demands. What we want is for the meaning-theory to reflect, in some sense yet to be made precise, what is involved in linguistic competence. At its weakest we might require reflection of linguistic competence to amount only to this: a theorist apprised of a meaning-theory for the language *L* will be able to speak *L*. Thus the meaning-theory does not attempt to mirror the capacities of competent speakers in any way more refined than in issuing in an overall competence that matches speakers' competence. We might however strengthen the requirement of reflection in a whole array of ways by insisting that portions of the theory correspond with certain competencies possessed by competent speakers. The array would then be generated by how one carves up the portions of the theory. One might, for instance, demand that certain sub-theories corresponding perhaps to particular subject matters – say, colour talk or use of the tenses – relate to capacities of speakers. Or, at its most extreme, one might require that each clause of the theory be related to a particular linguistic capacity. And one might also have reasons for adopting something of a mongrel position, varying the focus from individual clauses to sets of related clauses.

How does the requirement that the meaning-theory reflect speakers' capacities relate to systematicity? This is a good question and an important one too. Speakers, we mentioned, are able to understand an indefinite number of sentences; their limited experience of language somehow results in knowledge enough for them to arrive at an understanding of indefinitely many hitherto unencountered sentences. Similarly it is unthinkable[1] that speakers' linguistic competence comes into being fully formed. Rather, one's access to linguistic expertise is a stage-by-stage process. One might explain both features of language by supposing that linguistic competence is itself systematic: more basic competencies combine in novel ways to produce new linguistic abilities and understandings of novel sentences. The supposition thus is that complex abilities are complex because they can be dissected into the composition of more basic competencies. Thus complex capacities arise systematically from more basic capacities. Now, if we insist that the meaning-theory to some degree reflects speakers' capacities, then, depending on the extent of that reflection, we enforce a degree of systematicity in the meaning-theory.

For now the question of what degree of reflection we ought to enforce will have to remain hanging. What one needs to keep in mind is that the meaning-theory derives its systematicity from two sources: (i) the demands of theory-construction; and (ii) the need to reflect speakers' capacities.

6.3 The distinction between sense and force

Consider the following speech acts:

> Amanda asks, "Are the truffles grated?"
> Renée says to Paul, "Grate the truffles."
> Jessica asserts, "The truffles are grated."
> David says in conjecture, "The truffles are grated."
> Ethan declaims, "Would that the truffles were grated."

A natural thought is that here a variety of speech acts has been performed but that the same content – which we might designate as "that the truffles are grated" – has been deployed on each occasion: Amanda has used that content interrogatively; Renée has (depending on context) issued Paul with an order with that same content; Jessica has claimed that the content is true; David simply entertains a thought with that content; and Ethan expresses a wish that the content were true. Different speech acts thus might share a content, and differ-ent contents can be the subject of the same sort of speech act. It is thus tempting to suppose that every speech act can be dissected into a component comprising its content and a component that accounts for what is done with that content. In Frege's terms each speech act consists of a *sense* that is used with a certain *force*. The sense of a sentence – a thought – thus can be used with, at least, interroga-tive, imperative, optative or indicative force.

An interesting question is: what are the marks of the different forces? Another is whether the distinction, natural though it might seem, is robust. The distinc-tion is clearly congenial to the systematic approach because the dissection of a speech act into a sense and a force means that a systematic theory will aim first for a systematic characterization of senses and then go on to explain how a sense is at the disposal of a number of forces; the account of sense would be apportioned to the semantic theory and the account of force to the pragmatic theory for the language.[2]

So far we have left it unclear what modes of force there are. All we have done is to suggest that there is something in common between utterances of "Grate the truffles" and "Move your bike" and a different thing in common between "Grate the truffles" and "The truffles are grated". But we can acknowledge this without having to suppose that there is a determinate set of modes of force (say the four standardly mentioned and listed at the end of the last paragraph but one). If there is not such a determinate set, then there is no way of *systematically* decomposing the meaning of an utterance into its sense and its force. For the systematic theory cannot encompass an indefinite range of possible forces. In other words, if the distinction is to be capable of doing any work for us, we have to be able to wed a *theory* of sense to a *theory* of force. But we cannot have a theory of force if the range of possible forces is indeterminate.

Another challenge to a theory of force would arise if each type of force marked out only a superficial feature of a speech act. For instance, Renée's utterance to Paul may seem like an order in one context – Paul is her underling in the cuisine and his role is to help Renée make the soufflé – but alter the context and the utterance might seem like a piece of advice – Paul, making a soufflé for the first time, is wondering what next to do and Renée is vastly more experienced. So perhaps there is no real unity to these similar speech acts; rather, there is a range of acts that superficially resemble one another.

Let us not pursue these questions any further here. Rather, we should record these possible reasons for doubt and note that it is a widespread, though not uniform, assumption that we can build on the sense–force distinction. We shall return to examine the validity of the distinction but it will be rather easier to do so once we have seen what weight meaning-theorists place on it.

6.4 The centrality of assertion

To adhere to the validity of distinguishing between sense and force is to suppose that we can divide the task of constructing a theory of meaning in two: that of constructing a theory of content or sense; and that of constructing a theory of force. At first sight there seem to be two equally plausible ways of proceeding. What we want is a theory of content and a theory of how the content can be deployed in different speech acts with different forces. We might thus construct the theory of content by focusing on a property of sentences that is independent of their use with one or another force. On the other hand we might take one type of force as fundamental and use the sentence's role in utterances with that force as explanatory of the sentence's content. The latter sort of account attempts to explain the overall use of a sentence in terms of a restricted class of its uses. We might thus call accounts of this sort "use-based". The first sort of account tries to explain the content of a sentence in terms of its relations to non-linguistic items. We might thus call accounts of this sort "semantic".

As a matter of philosophical tradition it is clear that assertion is taken as central. There are a number of possible reasons for this. On the one hand there is the evident fact that assertions are the sorts of things that can provide and can be provided with *reasons*. So an account of assertions links very directly with an account of rationality. Now, given that philosophers are interested in rationality, it is clear that that interest will develop an interest in assertion; but there is a more intrinsic motive for focusing on assertion given assertion's link with rationality. Many have thought that what marks us off from the purely natural world is the fact that we are reason-giving creatures and that what enables our giving of reasons is our use of language. Now this speaks in favour of the idea that an account of rationality will depend on an account of language use but it does not in itself speak in favour of the proposal that the account of language will take reason-giving or asserting as central. Why should language not serve some more basic function that explains its ability to function in the business of giving reasons? We can, it appears, imagine practices that resemble those of language use but that do not have a role for assertion. Consider Wittgenstein's builders:

> A is building with building-stones: there are blocks, pillars, slabs and beams. B has to pass the stones, and that in the order in which A needs them. For this purpose they use a language consisting of the words "block", "pillar", "slab", "beam". A calls them out; – B brings the stone which he has learnt to bring at such-and-such a call. – Conceive this as a complete primitive language. (1958: §2)

Here the appearance is that we have a language consisting only of imperatives[3] – there is no practice of assertion. Now if such a language is genuinely conceivable as a complete language, then it would seem that assertion cannot be the explanatorily central function of language: if it were, then there would be no explaining our builders' language.

Well, perhaps. But one might one wonder, first, whether the builders' language is indeed conceivable; secondly, whether it could be explained without appeal at least to the notion of judgement; and thirdly, whether one could concede the possibility of such a language yet still claim that in an account of a language resembling ours there would still inevitably be a central explanatory role for the notion of assertion. Let us take each of these points in turn.

Wittgenstein's use of the various language games he describes in the opening sections of *Philosophical Investigations* is a source of contention. Witness this remark: "It is easy to imagine a language consisting only of orders and reports in battle. – Or a language consisting only of questions and expressions for answering yes and no. And innumerable others. – And to imagine a language means to imagine a form of life" (1958: §19). Undoubtedly one point that Wittgenstein is trying to make here is that the limits placed on the conceivability of a language game are set, not by abstract requirements of logic or of the nature of representation, but by the conceivability of different forms of life. So the question about conceivability of the builders' language is a question about whether one can conceive of such a complete language in a form of life.

Let us consider the second point. Take Wittgenstein's example of a language consisting of questions. Importantly, such a language could not consist only of questions; there has to be a means of answering the questions – expressions for answering yes and no. And now it is clear that such answers will amount to assertions. Answering yes in response to the question "Are the truffles grated?" is to assert that the truffles are grated; answering no to the question "Are your toes poking through your socks?" is to assert that your toes are not poking through your socks. So we could not account for such a language without, in effect, also giving an account of assertion. Say, for instance, that we wanted to explain the content of a question. A promising strategy would be to explain the question's content by explaining when it was right to answer yes and/or when right to answer no. But as we have just noticed, these answers are making claims about the world and are thus closely akin to assertions.

And what of a language consisting purely of orders? Well, here it is impossible to imagine such a language without also incorporating the idea that the language somehow includes a mechanism for signalling when an order has been complied with and when it has not. Does A repeat the order to B, if B fails to respond? What does A do if B brings a slab when she had called for a block? Without answers to such questions it is hard to see this as a genuine practice of issuing orders; orders require a system of enforcing compliance and thus there needs to be a way of signalling both successful compliance and failure to comply. Thus the language will have to include ways of expressing judgements about success and failure to comply, judgements that make claims about the world and thus are akin to assertions.

This survey is of course far from exhaustive – could there be a language consisting only of greetings? – but it indicates that even very simple languages and languages that differ vastly from our own will need to be understood in terms of notions very similar to assertion, that is, they will need to be seen as incorporating an ability to make claims about the world.

Consider now the third point: just how similar is the builders' language to our own? Let us suppose that the description of the builders' language substantiates the possibility of a language consisting purely of orders. Our meaning-theorist will thus infer that it is equally likely that her account of content will be based on assertions as imperatives. Presumably if the latter tactic is adopted the account of content will focus on what constitutes compliance with an order. Two points should then be noted: one concerns the nature of compliance and the other concerns the possible range of orders. The stunning simplicity of the builders' language might beguile one into thinking that one might understand what it is to comply with an order in terms of performing simple bodily movements – this is just what I believe about compliance with parade-ground orders. But if the orders in the builders' language are indeed anything like orders in our language, then compliance might be accomplished in any number of ways. Say, B is in the habit of hauling a slab on to her back and moving it over to where A is every time A calls "Slab". Now she has the following idea. She places the beam so that it pivots over a pillar, places a slab on the lower end of the pivot thus created and drops a calculated block on the other end every time A calls "Slab", so projecting the slab to A's desired location. Has she complied with A's order? Quite probably she has. The point is that what constitutes compliance with the order is bringing about a certain state of affairs. How one brings about those states of affairs is irrelevant to whether or not one has complied with the order. Indeed, it is possible to issue and understand an order without having the slightest idea of how it is to be fulfilled. I can instruct my lawyer to sue the pants off someone who has slandered me; neither I nor my lawyer need know quite how she will do this, yet both of us understand the order because both of us understand just when my slanderer will have had his pants sued off.

A second point reveals a sharp difference between our language and that of the builders. Our language includes the means of both making assertions and issuing orders; it includes the ability to make not a limited range of commands but an indefinite range of utterances. Now the easy grammatical transition between an apparent command and an assertion may make it seem as if orders and assertions stand on all fours. But this is deceptive. I can indeed move back and forth between "The truffles are grated" and "Grate the truffles" or between "The book is on the cat" and "Put the book on the cat", but can I genuinely move from the assertion "Absolute zero is $-270\,°C$" to "Make absolute zero $-270\,°C$"? The latter merely has the grammatical form of a sentence apt to be used in an order but in no sense can it be used to make an order – except doubtfully to God. The institution of orders requires that an order only make sense if there is a reasonable expectation that the fulfilment of the order lies within the power of one's commandee and that the commander has an appropriate authority to issue an order with that content. It is impossible to imagine what would give one the power to bring it about that absolute zero has a value different form that which it actually has, nor what authority would give one the right to issue such an order. So the order is merely sham. The lesson the meaning-theorist should draw from this is that if she wants a theory that will encompass all the contents we are able to express in a language such as ours, then she should focus on assertions; assertions are central because whatever content we are able to express is a content we are able to assert.[4]

6.5 Use-conditions versus truth-conditions

The clash between a use-conditional approach to meaning and a semantic approach will be a major preoccupation of this book. The use-conditional account is both easier and harder to get a grip on. It is easier since, if the account of meaning proceeds via use and if assertions are taken as central, then meaning will be characterized in terms of the conditions governing the making of assertions. It is harder to get a grip on since it is harder to focus on just what the relevant conditions are and harder to see just how achieving the right focus will deliver an account of meaning. We shall return to these questions in due course. For the moment we shall concentrate on the semantic approach, which is the dominant paradigm in contemporary philosophy of language.

Our question is: what property of sentences can be taken as central in accounting for their use in assertions? The answer we are given is: the sentence's truth-condition. One way of elaborating this answer is Davidson's. Accordingly a meaning-theory for a language will be a theory of truth applicable to it. We shall need to be just a little clearer about what a theory of truth is, but we can then quickly see why a theory of truth might function as a meaning-theory. A theory of truth will deliver clauses specifying necessary and sufficient conditions for each (declarative) sentence in the language to be true. So we shall have clauses of the form:

(T) s is true iff p

where s names a sentence of the language in question and p gives the necessary and sufficient conditions for its truth. So we might have, for example, "Schnee ist weiss" is true iff snow is white. What is important, though, is that the theory of truth will provide us with a means of systematically generating clauses of this form – the theorems of the truth-theory – for each sentence of the language. Tarski taught us how to achieve this for formal languages and Davidson's idea is that we can deploy the Tarskian machinery in the setting of natural language and use it, not to define truth, but to elucidate meaning.[5]

Tarski's problem was both technical and philosophical. On the technical front he had to construct a systematic means generating clauses of the form (T). His aim was to provide an explicit definition of truth and thus the major technical innovation was the introduction of machinery that converts the recursive characterization of truth into an explicit definition. Davidson chooses to make nothing of this innovation and thus his conception of a truth-theory is merely a recursive characterization of the application of the truth-predicate. On the philosophical front, Tarski (1944)[6] had to ensure that the clauses so generated were correct. His thought was that we could ensure the correctness of (T) just in case the sentence replacing p is a translation of – a synonym of – the sentence s in the language of the theory (a translation from German into English in our example); this is Tarski's Convention-T. Another way of capturing this is to say that (T) is correct if the following is true:

(M) s means that p

Davidson's insight is that we can, in a sense, reverse this process. If we can replace Tarski's criterion of correctness by something else – crucially something whose application does not rely on access to meanings in the language – then we can treat the truth-definition as a theory of meaning. Why? Because then we shall be able to treat clauses of the form (T) as clauses of the form (M).

Another way of seeing this point is to note that at least one theory of truth will be a theory that pairs each sentence, s, in the target language with its meaning-specifying correlate, p. So at least one theory of truth is a meaning-theory. If we can set out criteria – whose application crucially does not depend on access to meanings in the language – for when such a theory of truth issues in the right correlations, then we can treat that theory of truth as a meaning-theory. Thus a meaning-theory is an adequate theory of truth. In other words, if one knows that what one has is an adequate theory of truth, which involves both knowing that the theory is a theory of *truth* and that it is adequate, then one knows that one has a meaning-theory. Thus if we assume grasp of the concept of truth we can access meaning.

The important question is obviously: what are the criteria for an adequate theory of truth? The detailed answer to that question will have to await Chapter 7, but the brief answer is itself interesting. Tarski gives us a criterion for the correctness of each clause of the theory (strictly: definition): the *theory* is correct if it issues in *correct* clauses. Once again Davidson upturns the thinking here. The clauses of the theory can be taken to be meaning specifying if the theory is itself correct and the theory is itself correct if it is interpretational; that is, if it successfully enables interpretation of speakers of the target language. So the correctness of the theory will be determined by what it is successfully to interpret speakers. That enterprise Davidson entitles radical interpretation – "radical" because, in line with our insistence that the criteria for an adequate theory of truth must beg no questions about meaning, the interpreter must begin from a position of assuming nothing about meanings in the speakers' language. Davidson and Quine are as one here.

6.5.1 The bearing of Frege's distinction between sense and reference

A Davidsonian truth-theory will systematically generate specifications of truth-conditions for the sentences in the language based on specifications of the references of terms and satisfaction-conditions of predicates in the language. One might be tempted to think that this is in conflict with Frege's argument for distinguishing sense from reference. But this would be a mistake. The point is this. Were a Davidsonian theory to include clauses of the form: the meaning of "Fred" is the referent of "Fred" (namely, Fred), then the theory would conflict with Frege's advocacy of senses. But this is not Davidson's intention. First, he is not interested in constructing a theory of meaning by specifying the meanings of expressions. Indeed he claims that meanings are, in fact, irrelevant in a theory of meaning. Quine is suspicious of intentional entities such as meanings because he thinks that such entities have no clear identity-conditions, but

Davidson thinks that even if we set this reservation aside, meanings should be eschewed in the theory of meaning because they have no explanatory power. If we take Davidson's example (1984: 17–18) of the sentence "Theaetetus flies" and apply a Fregean scheme of assigning senses to expressions as their meanings, we learn that the sense of this sentence is that thought that results when the sense of "Theaetetus" is the argument to the function that is the sense of "*x* flies". But this putative explanation is vacuous, says Davidson: we knew before we started that the meaning of "Theaetetus flies" is a product of the meanings of its components – that was given by our adherence to compositionality – and Frege's supposed account simply dresses up this piece of knowledge; it does not unpack it. As he says, Frege's account labels rather than solves our difficulty. Thus he recommends that, strange as this may sound, the theory of meaning should have no truck with meanings. And this because *they are explanatorily redundant*: they do not do any useful work. Davidson's conclusion is perhaps a little overstated – there is clearly a sense in which meanings as entities fail to allow a fully explanatory role. This is because there is no explanation of how these entities combine to form the meanings of complex expressions. However, if the assignment of meanings is correct, such a reification of meaning will explain the decomposition of the complex meaning. In other words, we shall not have an inkling about how the meanings combine but at least we shall know which meanings need to combine. True, this latter piece of information is of relatively little value if it cannot be supplemented by an account of the mechanism of combination – so the information about the composition of complex meanings might be better encapsulated in another form. Thus the moral of this parable is that meanings are no help in constructing a theory of meaning. That is, we should not be aiming to provide clauses of the form "*S* means *m*".

So the basic clauses of a Davidsonian theory will not have the form: the meaning of "Fred" is Fred; rather they will have the form of specifications of reference: the referent of "Fred" is Fred. But note that when we say that a competent speaker knows (among other things) that "Fred" refers to Fred, we are not saying that the speaker knows the referent of "Fred". So, rather than saying that the speaker has a bare knowledge of the referent of a term, we are saying that she knows the referent as the referent of "Fred", because we use the term "Fred" to specify the reference. Now this may not be exciting news, but is undoubtedly correct. Note also that if Frege is right that only terms with the same sense can be intersubstituted in the context of propositional attitudes, then saying that *S* knows that "Fred" refers to Fred is characterizing *S*'s knowledge in a manner that is sensitive to the sense of the term "Fred". Were it the case that Fred is identical with Mary's goldfish, then, *S* knows that "Fred" is Mary's goldfish would not be a correct characterization of *S*'s knowledge *qua* competent speaker. The proposition expressed by "'Fred' refers to Fred" differs from that expressed by "'Fred' refers to May's goldfish"; the former correctly characterizes what *S* knows the latter fails to do so.

Note an important consequence of this. Our aim is not to specify the meanings of expressions in the language, but to characterize, informatively, what knowledge is possessed by competent speakers. So conceived, a meaning-theory is, as Dummett is fond of reminding us, a theory of understanding. A question that we shall come to in due course is thus whether and how a Davidsonian manages to give an informative account of what competent speakers know. Before we turn to that question we shall need to examine much more carefully what Davidson means by an interpretative truth-theory – that will be business for Chapter 7. Before we turn to that task we should map out use-based conceptions of theories of understanding.

6.6 Use-conditional theories of understanding

An alternative approach to giving an account of meaning would be to focus on the use-conditions governing the making of assertions. Here, as opposed to the truth-conditional case, we still face a number of important choices. What we want to do is to explain the use of assertions and then use this in a characterization of content that can be fed into an account of the use of that content in utterances with the other modes of force. But there is a number of facets of the use of an assertion that might, *prima facie*, be taken as meaning-determining. One might, for instance, focus on conditions warranting the making of assertions, conditions in which an assertion is justified, conditions of verification of an assertion, conditions in which an assertion is deniable, conditions in which it is falsified or conditions in which it should be withdrawn, or indeed some combination of such conditions. We shall need to press those questions but now is not the right moment to do so – we shall return to this in Chapter 14.

What we need to register immediately is a point that should be quite obvious but is apt to be missed. Let us suppose that we aim to characterize the meaning of a sentence in terms of its conditions of warranted assertion.[7] Thus, to focus on an example we might have clauses that detail that a meaning-determining warrant for assertion of "Jones is in pain" is that Jones is exhibiting pain behaviour.[8] Now a facile objection to assertibility-conditional accounts of meaning is that this misconstrues things: if one asserts that Jones is in pain, one does not assert that Jones is exhibiting pain behaviour. Indeed the two claims "Jones is in pain" and "Jones is exhibiting pain behaviour" are from any perspective distinct in meaning since either might be true and the other false. But this is not the assertibilist's claim. Rather, she is aiming to characterize what a speaker knows how to do, so her claim is that the speaker knows (in some sense that wants considerably more probing) that "Jones is in pain" is warrantedly assertible when Jones exhibits pain behaviour. Of course there still remains the question of how one distinguishes between "Jones is in pain" and "Jones is exhibiting pain behaviour", since both are warrantedly assertible when Jones is exhibiting pain behaviour, but that is a further question to come under our lens later.

Mathematics is the only field for which we have a well-worked-out assertibility-conditions account of meaning. There the aim is to characterize a sentence's proof-conditions in terms of those of its components. The aim is thus to be able to formulate the condition a construction must fulfil if it is to be a proof of our target sentence. How does this deliver an account of meaning? Well, we then deploy this in saying just what a speaker who understands the sentence is able to do: she is able to discriminate between those constructions that are proofs of our sentence and those that are not. In effect, we characterize a proof-*relation* – construction c is a proof of sentence s – and claim that, in understanding s, a speaker internalizes this proof-relation.

The point is this. The use-conditional theorist aims to construct a theory of meaning that is a theory of understanding, so she aims to characterize what it is a speaker knows when she knows how to use a sentence to make assertions. The characterization of the sentence's content is thus ineradicably indirect: we never construct clauses of the form s means that p.

A question that may have been troubling the reader is this. Why this sharp division between use-conditional and truth-conditional accounts of meaning? Could not we regard the truth-conditions of a sentence as conditions governing its assertion? After all, in one sense it is objectively right to assert a sentence just when it is true and incorrect to do so just when it is false. The relation between use- and truth-conditions is important because, whichever one takes as primary, one will want to have some account of the other. However, there is one good reason – a reason much emphasized by Dummett – for not identifying use-conditions directly with truth-conditions. The reason is this. For many sentences of our language we are incapable of putting ourselves in position of determining whether or not the truth-conditions hold. Take a sentence about the distant past – "Ivan the Terrible was partial to figs" – or a sentence about distant regions of space – "There is a carbon-based life form in a galaxy over a hundred light years from the earth" – or Goldbach's conjecture – "Every even number can be expressed as the sum of two primes"; although we can, on occasion, know whether a sentence of this sort is true or false, we cannot, in general, guarantee to be able to do so. The world might just be stubbornly unrevealing despite all our best efforts to determine whether or not such a sentence is true. So in these cases, *if you suppose that the world determinately either fulfils or fails to fulfil the sentence's truth-condition*; that is, if you suppose, as we are wont to do, that the sentence is either true or false, then the truth-condition of the sentence does not directly relate to its use-conditions. For there is nothing that the speaker can do that demonstrates that her use is guided by grasp of these truth-conditions.[9] Contrast this with a sentence such as "There is no coffee cup on the desk at the moment". Here a good survey of the surface of the desk is guaranteed to determine whether or not the sentence is true. So here one might say that truth-conditions do relate directly to use-conditions: grasp of the truth-conditions dictates one's preparedness to assert or to deny the sentence. It will be an important question for us much later (Chapter 14) and has been an important question in contemporary philosophy for the past fifty years whether speakers do indeed grasp truth-conditions construed in the way we have just described. What we have just done is to raise a worry about the account because it is unclear how grasp of such truth-conditions dictates a speaker's use of a sentence. But, in itself, that is not a conclusive objection to the truth-conditional account of meaning; it still needs to be argued that a speaker's grasp of meaning must be capable of being fully displayed or manifested in her use and, even if that can be established, we need to see what response the truth-conditionalist can muster.

As I said, these are issues that it will take us a good deal of work to find our way back to with a sufficiently sophisticated tool-kit. What we need to do next is to spend some time thinking about what makes a truth-theory interpretational and so fit to be treated as a theory of meaning. That will be the topic of Chapter 7.

7. Radical interpretation

7.1 Constraints on an adequate theory of truth

The claim we had isolated as central to Davidson's view of the theory of meaning is that an adequate theory of truth is a theory of meaning. A theory of truth, we noted, will be a systematic specification of truth-conditions for each sentence in the language. Many theories of truth cannot be treated as theories of meaning. So what qualifies a theory of truth as adequate and therefore as a theory of meaning?

7.1.1 Compositionality

Davidson wants a theory of meaning that will make sense of the idea that the meaning of a sentence is determined by the meanings of its parts and the way they are composed in the sentence. Without such an account, he claims, we would be bereft of an explanation of speakers' ability to learn language and their ability to understand novel utterances. These accomplishments are explained by supposing that what underlies or constitutes speakers' linguistic capacities are competencies that relate to a finite vocabulary and to ways in which these elements may be combined grammatically with one another. A speaker's ability to understand novel utterances is an ability to deploy these components of linguistic understanding in hitherto unencountered ways. The *theory* of meaning reflects this aspect of speakers' understanding by providing the resources for deriving a meaning-specification for every sentence of the language from a finite set of axioms. The axioms will be specifications of the meanings of the expressions in the basic vocabulary and recursive clauses specifying the meanings of allowable combinations of expressions in terms of the meanings of the expressions being combined. A theory of meaning of this form will be called compositional.

Davidson is, as remarked, concerned to make some sense of this line of thought. But he recognizes that the thought is crude and somewhat vague. It is not precisely clear just what epistemological principle is being invoked in insisting that the complex linguistic ability *must* be seen as a complex of simple abilities: what is meant by "simple" and "complex" here? And as long as this is unclear, it is not clear when we shall have provided an adequate compositional theory of meaning. Secondly, it is plausible to suppose that the meaning of a word just *is* its contribution to the meaning of a sentence in which it occurs.[1] So the meanings of words are derived from the meanings of sentences. In this case it is hard to see how we could *explain* the meaning of a sentence in terms of the meaning of the words it contains. For, to do so, we would need to think of the meaning of the sentence as based on the meaning of the words, and that would make the whole account circular.

7.1.2 Interpretationality

Interpretation versus translation

It is important to be clear that Davidson's programme is one of *interpretation*, not one of *translation*. That is, he is not concerned to pair off synonymous expressions in two languages; rather, he wants to be able to interpret the utterances of native speakers. A translation yields an interpretation only if we assume an understanding of the language into which the translation is made, and this language need not be the language of the theory: we could present a translation manual between French and German in English. In contrast, a theory of interpretation will be framed in a home language – since all theories are framed in some language – but will interpret utterances of the native speakers. One way in which this difference is made clear is in an adaptation of Tarski's procedure from formal to natural language. Natural language involves many indexical devices that give rise to sentences whose truth-values may vary from one occasion of utterance to another. But a theory is a body of standing sentences: sentences whose truth-value is stable. So while one might *translate* the sentence "J'ai faim" as "I am hungry" (i.e. "J'ai faim" means the same as "I am hungry"), one could not have a truth-*theory* that includes the following:

"J'ai faim" is true iff I am hungry.

Since the sentence on the right-hand side is a sentence in the theory, we would then have a theory that includes indexical elements: the sentence "I am hungry" will alter its truth-value from one occasion to another. Or, put differently, the biconditional sentence will be true on any occasion of utterance but the truth-condition we ascribe to the French sentence will depend on who utters the English sentence. So we shall not be able to think of ourselves as having a truth-theory for French since the *content* of the theory varies from one context of utterance to another. The clause winds up being false if it is applied to numerous utterances of the French sentence by French speakers – whether or not Jacques' utterance of "J'ai faim" is true does not depend on whether or not *I* am hungry – and thus can be used to interpret only my current utterances of the French sentence. The source of the problem is that it is muddled to think that the French *sentence* has a truth-condition; what has a truth-condition is the *utterance* of the sentence on a specific occasion. So we shall have to change the goal of our theory; instead of giving a theory of truth of *sentences*, we shall give a theory of the truth of a sentence *as uttered by a certain speaker at a certain time*. So we shall get:

"J'ai faim" as uttered by x at t is true iff x is hungry at t.

Here the indexical element has (supposedly) been removed: the sentence "x is hungry at t" is either true or false once x and t have been determined. In essence, the indexicality of "J'ai faim" is eliminated by explicitly stating the relevant context, which Davidson supposes is given by a speaker and a time. So the sentence on the right does not *translate* the indexical sentence named on the left; it *interprets* an utterance of that sentence.

Now it is an essential feature of Davidson's programme that we should be able to eliminate indexicality in this way. What is clear is that indexical expressions cause sentences in which they occur to have unstable truth-values because the indexical expression has a different reference (or semantic value) on different occasions of use. And this is because the reference of an indexical expression is determined by the context of use. Davidson's assumption is that we can give a complete account of these contextual features (essentially he thinks that all the work can be done by filling in the context of the speaker and time of utterance). And one might well doubt this: is it clear that the reference of a demonstrative (e.g. "this" or "that") is determined by the speaker and time of utterance rather than intentional aspects of the situation, for example, the speaker's perceptions (and what is salient among those perceptions), interests and purposes?

We had advertised the truth-conditional account by claiming that we can replace the "filling"-in clauses such as "*s* means that *p*" by "is true iff", provided that the specification of truth-conditions has been managed in the "right" way. Consequently, the question, which we need to go on to address, is: what might we mean by "right"? However, we should notice the effect that the treatment of indexicals has. It is implausible to suppose that we might replace "is true iff" in the above clause by "means that":

"J'ai faim" as uttered by x at t means that x is hungry at t.

The clause on the right clearly is not synonymous with the sentence on the left, nor is it clear that it *gives the meaning* of x's utterance. My utterance of "x is hungry at *t*" surely does not have the same meaning as *x*'s utterance; *x* may be unaware of the time or even that he is *x*. Rather, there is a much looser sense in which my utterance is interpretative of *x*'s: it is how I would report what *x* had said; it gives my "best" specification of the truth-conditions of *x*'s utterance. Thus there is a sense in which the notion of meaning retreats into the shadows. What we are concerned with is the construction of a theory of truth that is *interpretative*; that notion now occupies centre stage.

Interpretation and the evidence for interpretation
For a theory of truth to do service as a theory of meaning it must be interpretational; it must, that is, enable one to interpret speakers' utterances. But what is it for a theory to enable interpretation? And, how does the theorist or interpreter (as we have learned she is) plausibly arrive at an interpretative theory?

One thing one might be tempted to say is that a theory is interpretative just in case it issues in clauses of the form:

S is true iff *p*,

where *p* is a sentence that translates the sentence named by S. That is, we might just insist on satisfaction of Tarski's Convention-T. But of course, appealing to a notion of translation, of synonymy, of sameness of meaning is illegitimate when we are in the process of setting out constraints on a theory of meaning and thus are searching for constraints that can be applied independently of knowledge of meanings. So our problem is this: how do we guarantee that *p* translates S without assuming that we have a handle on meanings at all? Davidson's imagined scenario is that of the *radical interpreter*, a character who has the task of interpreting speakers but who is disallowed any assumptions about the meanings of their utterances and so of similarities between the community's meanings and her own (see Davidson 1984: essay 9).[2]

An attempt to interpret an utterance will involve seeing that utterance in the context of a speaker's non-linguistic environment and activities. So we need to light on evidence provided by these that is plausibly available to an interpreter in advance of any insight into the speaker's meanings. But now we seem to face an impenetrable barrier. We could surely make progress in interpreting a speaker's utterances if we knew her beliefs, since we could then take a speaker's sincere assertions to be expressions of her beliefs. However, to gain access to a speaker's beliefs we would need to know what her words mean, since many of her beliefs are identifiable only on the basis of what she says and her other beliefs are not accessible on the basis of behaviour alone: how a person behaves depends on the conjunction of her beliefs *and her desires*. There is no action distinctive of possessing the belief that that is a glass of wine. I might reach out for it if I want a drink of wine and believe, in addition, that the glass is meant for me, but I might not do so because I might want to stay clear headed for the afternoon's lecture. So the interpreter seems barred from using behaviour to break into this holistic circle of interdependence of beliefs, desires and meanings.

Davidson appreciates this circle very well but thinks that we can break into it. He admits that, in general, we cannot access a speaker's beliefs without having access to her meanings. However, there is one class of beliefs that he thinks is plausibly accessible to the interpreter. These are a speaker's beliefs about whether or not a sentence is true. That is, he supposes that the attitude of holding a sentence true is plausibly available to an interpreter. How does he justify this view? First, he claims that this is "a simple attitude applicable to all sentences". So although one's holding a sentence true is to have a contentful belief, it is an attitude that might be taken up with respect to any sentence and thus might be identified in advance of making any discriminations between contents expressed by sentences. It is thus plausibly an attitude that the interpreter might be able to discern in advance of interpretation. So Davidson supposes that there are characteristic ways of behaving towards a sentence that demonstrate that the speaker holds the sentence true *and* that these ways of behaving can be discerned by the interpreter in advance of interpretation. The sorts of things he has in mind are the interpreter's ability to pick out a speaker's assent to a sentence or her sincere assertion of it, and so on. What he cannot allow is behaviour that is sensitive to the content of the sentence, for instance one's willingness to act in a way that is appropriate to the truth of the sentence: how one acts on the basis of the truth of "There's a crocodile behind you" varies drastically (one hopes) from how one acts on the basis of the truth of "There's a cheese sandwich behind you" and this is due in no small part to what those sentences mean (and to one's desires). Consequently this sort of behaviour is not available to the interpreter. Thus, on the one hand, the sort of evidence available is fairly meagre. On the other hand, it is clear that under ideal conditions a speaker's sincere assertions would do to fix the sentences she holds true – provided the interpreter could distinguish these from cases of lying, questioning, ruminating, assuming (all of which might be performed by uttering a declarative sentence)[2] – without presupposing that the interpreter has a grasp of meaning.

Although Davidson does not discuss the question, it is clear that the behaviours indicative of holding a sentence true are likely themselves to be the joint product of belief and desire. For instance, one might well exhibit the appropriate behaviours while not holding the sentence true because one wishes to deceive one's audience into thinking that one holds the sentence true. So Davidson must be supposing that in general speakers use language with a set of desires that is consistent with a motivation to be sincere about what sentences one holds to be true. Lying and other forms of deception are thus subversions of the institution of language, whose prevalence would be self-undermining; we could not be aiming to deceive one another most of the time without depriving ourselves of the ability to speak meaningfully and so to lie.

Right, so we are to assume that we have identified a range of sentences that speakers hold true in certain circumstances and at certain times. The question is: how are we to use this evidence in constructing an interpretative truth-theory? The evidence, as Davidson notes (1984: 135), comes in this form:

(E)   Kurt belongs to the German speech community and Kurt holds true "Es regnet" at t_0 and it is raining near Kurt at t_0.

We gather pieces of evidence of this sort from which we inductively infer certain generalizations, for example,

(GE) $(\forall x)(\forall t)$(If x belongs to the German speech community then x holds true "Es regnet" at t iff it is raining near x at t)

This piece of evidence is now supposed to support a theory containing the following (T)-sentence:

(T)   "Es regnet" is true-in-German when spoken by x at t iff it is raining near x at t.

In arriving at this position we make two problematic inferences. The first is the inductive inference from pieces of data of the form (E) to (GE); the second is the inference from (GE) to (T). The first inference is problematic since our data of sentences held true and the circumstances in which they are held true will include cases in which the speaker is mistaken. So along with (E) we might have:

(E′)   Klaus belongs to the German speech community and Klaus does not hold true "Es regnet" at t_1 and at it is raining near Klaus at t_1.

Given (E′) and its like we can no longer infer (GE). The second inference is problematic because we cannot help ourselves to the inference from the fact that speakers hold a certain sentence true in certain circumstances to the fact that it *is* true in those circumstances: what precludes the possibility of mass error? Clearly what renders each inference problematic is the occurrence of error. As Davidson often reminds us, the source of the problem lies in the nature of our basic pieces of evidence; (E) and (E′) are the products of *two* factors: what our speaker believes and what she means by the relevant sentence. The radical interpreter is trying to access the meaning of the sentence but is frustrated in treating pieces of information like (E) as information relating to meaning because both meaning and belief are complicit in their origin.

As it turns out, our way forward with each inference is forged in the same way. But let us focus first on the second inference. Were our generalization to take the following form, the inference would be unimpeachable:

(GEC) $(\forall x)(\forall t)$(If x belongs to the German speech community then x *correctly* holds true "Es regnet" at t iff it is raining near x at t).

(GEC) is a statement of those conditions in which speakers correctly hold the sentence true and, since the sentence is true when it is correctly held to be true, these are conditions in which the sentence is true. So we can take those conditions specified in (GEC) to be specifications of truth-conditions. That is, we can infer (T) from (GEC). Our problem then becomes one of how we infer (GEC) from evidence that comes in the form (E) and (E′). What we need, of course, is evidence in the form:

(EC)   Kurt belongs to the German speech community and Kurt *correctly* holds true "Es regnet" at t_0 and it is raining near Kurt at t_0.

But how do we sift through evidence of the form (E) and (E′) to determine which of those pieces of evidence is a correct holding true and which is mistaken? Because each is the joint product of both belief and meaning, we cannot check a piece of evidence taken on its own to determine whether or not it is the product of a mistake.

7.2 The Principle of Charity

We need some principled method of assigning "correct" and "incorrect" to our original pieces of evidence, and Davidson's suggestion is that we attempt to assign "correct" as often as possible consistent with forming generalizations of the form (GEC) for the relevant sentences of the language, which in turn give rise to T-sentences that can be seen to be theorems of a systematic theory of truth. Any principle taking roughly this form is a version of Davidson's Principle of Charity. Although, without doubt, this is *a* principled way of going on, the question is whether it is a *justified* principle.

Note how both of our problems are solved. In making assignments of "correct" and "incorrect" we form a data set that allows us to infer generalizations; problematic pieces of evidence such as (E′) can be ignored because they now take the form:

(E′C)   Klaus belongs to the German speech community and Klaus *incorrectly* does not hold true "Es regnet" at t_1 and at it is raining near Klaus at t_1.

Secondly, our generalization now takes the form (GEC), which facilitates the inference to (T). One of the virtues of this approach is that it makes maximum use of the evidence available to the interpreter.[3] In moving from (E′) to (E′C) we effectively discount this piece of evidence and make no use of it in constructing our interpretative scheme. There is very little we can infer about the meaning of "Es regnet" from (E'C), other than, perhaps, that "Es regnet" does not have the truth-conditions of "It is not raining". But obviously there is no point in constraining our interpretation by a claim such as (EC) unless we know that (EC) is true. And how do we know that if all we have is (E)? Put another way, trying to squeeze the maximum content from our data set makes sense only if we think that that content is indeed there to be squeezed out of it. If speakers tend to be mistaken, either in general or about one or another subject matter, then that content is not there to constrain our interpretation and, although this makes the interpretative exercise that much more difficult, that may be an unfortunate fact of life.

As we have pointed out, the *construction* of a scheme of interpretation requires some principled means of sifting through our evidence of holdings true (see Ramberg 1989). And this alone has important consequences for whatever principle we light on. We cannot think of the principle as a way of selecting between interpretative schemes, for there is no interpretative scheme to be had but for the operation of some such principle. Thus the only conception we have of a bad interpretative scheme is that of a scheme produced by a bad interpretative principle. Therein lies a challenge: can we conceive of interpretative principles (other than Charity and its close relatives) that can be deployed in the construction of an interpretative scheme? Quine seems to suppose that Charity pragmatically narrows down the choice of scheme to those that are workable; but to take that view we have to suppose that we can meet this challenge. He does nothing to show that we can.

We shall need to proceed in stages. First we shall look at the content – or possible contents – of the Principle of Charity. Secondly, we shall consider some alternatives. We shall then be in a position to think about just how the principle is essentially involved in the business of radical interpretation. Finally we shall turn to the question of whether the principle is justified.

Above we framed the principle as a plank of the interpretative methodology and, as such, it has reasonably sharp content. Faced with a large but finite set of data of sentences held true in one or another circumstance, our task is to divide that set in two: one set qualified by "correct" the other by "incorrect". And we do this so as to make the set qualified by "correct" as large as possible, consistent with still being able to infer generalizations of the form (GEC). The effect of this is to construe speakers as being as correct as often as possible, consistent with constructing a systematic interpretative scheme.[4] So the fundamental principle from which our piece of methodology emerges is a view according to which speakers must be seen as making the minimum of mistakes or as being correct as often as possible, when judged from our own point of view. Or, slightly differently, speakers' beliefs must agree with our own as often as possible. So the methodological injunction is to interpret so as to maximize or to optimize agreement or to minimize inexplicable error.

We want a theory that satisfies the formal constraints on a theory of truth, and that maximises agreement, in the sense of making Kurt (and others) right, as far as we can tell, as often as possible.   (1984: 136)

We get a first approximation to a finished theory by assigning to sentences of a speaker conditions of truth that actually obtain (in our opinion) just when the speaker holds those sentences true. The guiding policy is to do this as far as possible, subject to the consideration of simplicity, hunches about the effects of social conditioning, and of course our common-sense, or scientific, knowledge of explicable error.

(*Ibid.*: 196)

It is worth noting that, from the outset, the nature of agreement that is envisaged here is not radically implausible. Why, one might wonder, should I construe my interpretee as agreeing with me about the history of jazz in the 1950s and 1960s when she has had no contact with Dizzy Gillespie and his oeuvre or with discussion of either? Well, why indeed? But the good point made by this question – that it is plausible to ascribe a belief only when a believer has had a certain exposure – is not one that the Principle of Charity applied in the business of radical interpretation is ever going to tempt us to flout. Our data come in the form of sentences held true in particular circumstances – circumstances that Davidson often construes as *causes* of one's holding a sentence true. What Charity enforces is an interpretation of those sentences as reflecting those circumstances, or better, it enforces a maximizing of such interpretations. So it will not have any bite in enforcing agreement between interpreter and interpretee in maters that transcend the circumstances or causes – judged by the interpreter – of the interpretee's holdings true. If you have had no contact with "Night in Tunisia", it will not figure in any of the circumstances relevant to your holdings true and thus none of your beliefs charitably ascribed will be about that masterpiece of the bebop era.

In later writings Davidson dissects the Principle of Charity into two subordinate principles: the Principle of Coherence and the Principle of Correspondence.

The Principle of Coherence prompts the interpreter to discover a degree of logical consistency in the thought of a speaker; the Principle of Correspondence prompts the interpreter to be responding to the same features of the world that he (the interpreter) would be responding to in similar circumstances. Both principles can be (and have been) called principles of charity: one principle endows the speaker with a modicum of logic, the other endows him with a degree of what the interpreter takes to be true belief about the world. Successful interpretation necessarily invests the person interpreted with basic rationality. It follows

103

> from the nature of correct interpretation that an interpersonal stand-
> ard of consistency and correspondence to the facts applies to both the
> speaker and the speaker's interpreter, to their utterances and to their
> beliefs.   (2001b: 211)

This suggests a rather more nuanced view than the simple mantra of maximizing agreement. The added nuance calls for a degree of self-consciousness
on the part of the interpreter. For the Principle of Correspondence calls for the
interpreter to have a sense of those of her beliefs – presumably those based on
perception – that are more responsive to features of her environment and, more,
to how those beliefs would change from one perspective to another. In addition,
Davidson takes the operation of the two principles to be much more circum-
spect than that of the original Principle of Charity; we require our interpretee
to have a *modicum* of logic and a *degree* of true belief.

Of course we need to consider the question of whether the Principle of
Charity is justified. But there is another question we should turn to first, and
that this whether the principle is a necessary feature of the radical interpreter's
methodology. No doubt the radical interpreter needs some (plausible) method
of sorting evidence into that which records error and that which does not; but it
is far from obvious that the Principle of Charity is the only such method. Here
is an alternative – one among many in the literature, but one of the earliest to
enter it – from Grandy: the Principle of Humanity:

> If a translation tells us that the other person's beliefs and desires are
> connected in a way that is too bizarre for us to make sense of, then
> the translation is useless for our purposes. So we have, as a pragmatic
> constraint on translation, the condition that the imputed pattern of
> relations among beliefs, desires, and the world be as similar to our own
> as possible. This principle I shall call the *principle of* humanity.
>   (1973: 443)

Grandy's thought is that the purpose of a scheme of interpretation[5] is to make a
speaker intelligible to *us*. So it is a pragmatic failure of such a scheme if it imputes
a pattern among beliefs and their relations to the world that renders them opaque
to us. One might well wonder whether this should be held to be a weakness in
the scheme of interpretation – perhaps the speaker is genuinely opaque to us.
However, our interest at the moment is simply in comparing such a Principle of
Humanity with one of Charity. The relevant contrasts are these: (i) the content
of the Principle of Humanity requires agreement only as a consequence of intelligibility and thus agreement should be sacrificed if doing so conduces to greater
intelligibility; and (ii) the principle is simply a pragmatic maxim (as is Quine's
use of Charity). Grandy's procedure is to offer examples where the Principle of
Humanity seems a better guide to interpretation than the Principle of Charity:

"cases where the natural translation leads us to attribute to the person who is being translated a false belief that is in disagreement with our own views" (1973: 444). The examples are drawn from: the use of definite descriptions to refer; the use of plural descriptions; and the use of theoretical terms. The details of the examples do not matter very much now – we shall look at possible counter-examples to the Principle of Charity when we think about whether or not it is justified. Our present concern is with whether the Principle of Humanity could be a replacement for the Principle of Charity in radical interpretation. What, in effect, the Principle of Humanity calls on the interpreter to do is to impose something much more powerful on her target interpretee than a sharing of her beliefs. Although we might allow those to diverge, we think of them as diverging because we can justify the divergence in terms of the character of the beliefs concerned – the content of the beliefs, the relation of such beliefs to others and the semantic structure of the beliefs or sentences used to express them. This is quite sophisticated knowledge that presupposes fairly extensive epistemological and semantic insight into our own language and system of belief-formation. Set aside the question of whether we are justified in projecting this on to our target; rather, the concern is that the *philosophical interest* of the process of interpretation is undermined by its being informed by this sort of self-consciousness. At what point does a more nuanced replacement for Charity render the project uninteresting? It is not easy or, perhaps, possible to provide a blanket answer to this question, but from Davidson's perspective it would seem that the point has to be arrived at quite soon. For Davidson the project of radical interpretation has to be conceived of in extensional terms – it is a project that, in a sense, legitimates intensional properties by describing how one might become sensitive to them through a project characterized extensionally. So from a Davidsonian perspective there appears to be little attraction in departing from Charity.[6]

There is, however, another doubt one might have about the Principle of Humanity, this time with the coherence of humanity with Davidson's conception of the *role* of radical interpretation. Now, as many commentators have noticed and as Davidson points out, the thought experiment of radical interpretation is his way of conceiving of meanings as public. Meanings are public items because they are guaranteed to be exposed by the radical interpreter's enterprise. So, where that enterprise fails to discover a fact of meaning, meanings become indeterminate: there is no fact of the semantic matter. We shall discuss indeterminacy below and publicity will become a major preoccupation. The present point is just that the fable of the radical interpreter gives a (fairly) clear embodiment of what the thesis might amount to. What the publicity of meaning aims to make sense of is the idea that a speaker's use of language must be fully determinative of meaning – there can be no facts about meanings which are not linked to speakers' use or speakers' capacity to use language.[7] On this view, agreement in use must go along with agreement in meaning; there can be no case where two speakers agree in their use of language but where they diverge in the meanings of their terms. Moreover, it cannot be a mere empirical or *a posteriori* hypothesis – even one that is necessarily or nomologically true – that such speakers agree in their meanings. Of course, in these circumstances radical interpretation informed by the Principle of Charity *will* discern agreement in meanings. However, were Charity (or any such principle satisfying this constraint) a mere hypothesis, then our claim to share meanings, based on the process of interpretation, would itself be a hypothesis. So, whatever principle is taken to inform interpretation, it must satisfy two desiderata: (i) it must guide interpretation in a manner that ensures that agreement in use is agreement in meaning; and (ii) it must have a status of being true *a priori*. So we should note that this would suffice to rule out the status of the principle as simply that of being required for pragmatic reasons. Thus the Principle of Humanity is doubtfully acceptable both in terms of its content and in terms of its status.

Davidson writes:

> The methodological advice to interpret in a way that optimises agreement should not be conceived as resting on a charitable assumption about human intelligence that might turn out to be false. If we cannot find a way to interpret the utterances and other behaviour of a creature as revealing a set of beliefs largely consistent and true by our own standards, we have no reason to count that creature as rational, as having beliefs, or as saying anything.   ("Radical Interpretation", 1984: 137)

So it is a conceptual truth of sorts that if a creature is a believer, is capable of using a language, then it is charitably interpretable. Why so? Davidson thinks this emerges from the nature of belief, specifically the way in which the intentionality of belief depends on truth:

> Beliefs are identified and described only within a dense pattern of beliefs. I can believe a cloud is passing before the sun, but only because I believe there is a sun, that clouds are made of water vapour, that water can exist in liquid or gaseous form; and so on, without end. No particular list of further beliefs is required to give substance to my belief that a cloud is passing before the sun; but some appropriate set of related beliefs must be there. If I suppose that you believe a cloud is passing before the sun, I suppose you have the right sort of pattern of beliefs to support that one belief, and these beliefs I assume you to have must, to do their supporting work, be enough like my beliefs to justify the description of your belief as a belief that a cloud is passing before the sun. If I am right in attributing the belief to you, then you must have a pattern of beliefs much like mine. No wonder, then, I can interpret your words correctly only by interpreting so as to put us largely in agreement.   (*Ibid.*: 200)

A belief (whether true or false) thus fails to be about anything unless it is part of a family of beliefs, many of which are true.[8] Like Frege, Davidson thus thinks that it makes no sense to suppose that a speaker's terms possess an unmediated reference. In Frege's case the reference is mediated by a sense, which the speaker grasps; in Davidson's it is mediated by a set of largely true beliefs. Thus it seems that a position such as Kripke's view of names is in tension with Davidson's view here.[9] Let us focus on this question by looking at proper names.

First let us consider Kripke's attack on descriptivism about names. Take, first, Kripke's modal argument because this is quite straightforward. Nothing in Davidson suggests that a name has its meaning determined (or even its reference fixed) by means of a description. And nothing in his positive proposal should cause him to jib at Kripke's account of the difference in behaviour between names and definite descriptions. Following McCulloch, we had identified four other objections to descriptivism: *reference*; *availability*; *proliferation*; and *inextricability* (see Chapter 2). The holistic character of Davidson's account enables him to deal with the phenomenon of *inextricability*; we do not unpack the name in terms of a description or set of descriptions that then need to be unpacked independently of it until we reach bedrock. No: we assign a referential scheme to the singular terms en masse subject to the requirements of Charity and the other formal constraints. *Proliferation* is no objection since we shall simply have a set of background beliefs; there is no sense in which any should be distinguished as especially related to a name's meaning. Davidson's aim is to think about interpreting one or another speaker; that is, his focus is on idiolects. Thus *availability* is not an issue for him either. The only real concern is raised by Kripke's view that there are some names that have reference in the absence of any true beliefs: the *reference* problem. Let us note this difference: it emerges once again in comparing Kripke's positive view with Davidson's. Here, since Davidson is not giving an account of the mechanism of reference (the interpretative stance relieves him of this burden) nor is he mentioning more than a necessary condition of reference, he is free and likely to admit that there is a causal constraint on reference. If sentences in general represent the circumstances that cause them to be held true, then they are going to be about items causally related to speakers. So the only element of his picture that Davidson will object to is the claim that reference can be *purely* a matter of causal relations, which is, unsurprisingly, the claim that enables Kripke to conceive of reference as functioning, on occasion, quite independently of belief. Evans's view (1985: essay 1) – that the referent of one's name is the dominant (causal) source of one's information – sounds close to Davidson's. However, Evans allows that the information may, in fact, be false of the bearer of the name. And, more than this, the bearer of the name might well be an object other than that about which most of the information is, in fact, true. So here we seem to have a clear violation of Charity. Let us simply note then that the tension between Kripke's and Davidson's accounts (of names) is not as blatant as might be thought. In fact the only real source of tension depends on a controversial plank in Kripke's argument.[10]

Let us grant the dependence of intentionality on truth that the argument requires and ask quite how successful Davidson's thought is here as a justification of Charity. To be sure, if we are to interpret a speaker, in these circumstances, we must attempt to interpret in such a way that there is a preponderance of true beliefs. For, if not, then the likelihood is that we shall not be able to conceive of our speaker as having beliefs about anything. But this fails to show that an intelligible interpretation needs to *maximize* true beliefs. And now there seems to be an uncomfortable dilemma in the offing. Either we accept any principle justified by Davidson's unrefined thought that intentionality depends on truth or we supplement this principle. If the former, then the principle will be so vague that it will not deliver an effective methodology of interpretation. And this is what we need; it will not suffice for Davidson to have given us a vague necessary condition for an adequate interpretation. There are obvious enough reasons for this need: quite simply, how is the interpreter to proceed? But there are less obvious worries too. For, as long as her methodology is allowed to be indeterminate, there are worries about how radical interpretation secures the publicity of meaning. Now, perhaps one can find a way to hang on to publicity without achieving uniqueness in interpretative scheme by claiming that here there is a genuine indeterminacy in meaning; but to make such a claim appears respectable only when we have a clear methodology, in which we can invest our confidence that it will uncover the semantic facts. If we exhaust that methodology without achieving determinacy, then we may have a good claim that the semantic facts themselves are indeterminate. (See the discussion of the indeterminacy of reference below.) However, when we have conflicting possible methodologies, each of which is as acceptable as the other, then we seem not to have a methodology that reveals the semantic facts. So those facts transcend the data supplied by speakers' use. Conversely, if the principle is to be tightened up, we need an argument motivating the more definite principle. Thus far this is entirely lacking. Moreover, we need such an argument that is not based on a reflective understanding of what beliefs need to be in place to secure certain intentional properties: what sort of beliefs are required in order to have a belief about a natural kind, or about one or another sort of object? For then the worry will be that radical interpretation presupposes an impressive reflective understanding of the workings of one's own language: a version of the same worry about more nuanced versions of Charity emerges.[11]

We wanted to be able to conceive of Charity as given *a priori* and as necessarily (conceptually) true. What we have so far, were the argument to be successful, is a justification of the principle as a necessary condition for the possibility of interpretation. This ensures that it is required; it does not secure its truth. In order to achieve that, we need an argument to show that interpretation is possible. And this we find in Davidson, in an argument that is fascinating in its own right, quite independently of the role of Charity.

Davidson claims that any practice we can justifiably think of as linguistic is one we can interpret. So, in a sense, there are no external marks of rationality or of a communicative practice. That is, there is no telling from the outside that a practice is one of speaking a language, of formulating and conveying beliefs, intentions, desires and so on. The only way of determining this is "from the inside", by interpreting it, and to do so requires that you construe it as largely resembling your own practice.

However, compare this with Wittgenstein's famous remark in *Philosophical Investigations* that "[i]f a lion could talk, we could not understand him" (1958: 223), hinting that a lion's form of life would differ so radically from our own that, were lions to talk, we could not interpret their utterances. Thus it seems that he envisages a possibility of uninterpretable speech: we can think of something as a use of language without being able to interpret it. In *Remarks on the Foundations of Mathematics* he makes the supposition more explicit:

> Suppose ... there were a tribe whose people apparently had an under-standing of a kind which I do not grasp. That is they would have learn-ing and instruction, quite analogous to that in [which we teach simple rules]. If one watches them one would say that they follow rules, learn to follow rules. The instruction effects, e.g., agreement in actions on the part of the pupil and teacher. But if we look at one of their series of figures we can see no regularity of any kind. (1978: 348)

Here it seems that he is suggesting that we might be able to ascribe rule-following on the basis of the sort of behaviour that surrounds the practice *even if* we cannot understand the rule itself, and thus that we might be able to ascribe rule-following from an external point of view. But he immediately equivocates: "What should we say now? We *might* say: 'They appear to be following a rule which escapes us,' but also 'Here we have a phenomenon of behaviour on the part of human beings, which we don't understand'" (*ibid.*). Davidson would have us say the second thing here, not the first. However, it marks a significant difference between Wittgenstein and Davidson that Wittgenstein allows that we *might* say the first[12] – allowing that possibility is denying Davidson's position. So more needs to be said about why we should accept it.

Why should we believe that interpretation is always possible? Here is a presentation of Davidson's argument (culled from his paper "On the Very Idea of a Conceptual Scheme", 1984: 183–98) that there are no alternative concep-tual schemes. The relation between the two questions is made clear in the first premise.

1. An alternative conceptual scheme would be one which is expressed in a language which is not translatable into our own.

2. A conceptual scheme is a way of carving up reality: alternative conceptual schemes are different schemes which fit reality.
3. The only sense to be made of a scheme fitting reality is that it is a theory which is (largely) *true*.
4. The only sense to be made of truth as it applies to another language is via translation into one's own language since the truth predicate satisfies Tarski's Convention-T, which is stated in terms of translation.
5. So we cannot make sense of the notion of a conceptual scheme which is expressed in a language not translatable into one's own.
6. Thus translation (or interpretation) is always possible.
7. The notion of an alternative conceptual scheme and thus the notion of a conceptual scheme itself makes no sense.

Step (3) might well give one pause for thought. Why should we think of a theory relating to reality in terms of being *true*? Could we not instead think of the theory as being *about* reality because its terms succeed in *referring* to items in the world? Surely we could. But Davidson will now recycle the argument we have recently been given that intentionality depends on truth; for our terms to refer to things in the world, for our statements to be about things in the world, there must be a range of supporting statements that we would be prepared to endorse which are largely true. So, if we are to make sense of the idea of a theory as being in a relation to the world, then it has to be that the theory is largely true.

Step (4) is also a crucial step in the argument. Davidson has to say that for us to conceive of a language as expressing a truth, we have, because of Tarski, to conceive of a translation of that truth into our own language. Is this right? Surely all I need to conceive is a truth-definition for that language in some suitable meta-language. To assume that the meta-language must be my own language (or, equivalently, that it is one that is inter-translatable with mine) might well be held to beg the question since it is to assume that I cannot make sense of a language which is not inter-translatable with my own.

Davidson's thought seems to be roughly this. In order to make sense of the notion of truth as it applies to the foreign set of beliefs or sentences, I need to be able specify truth-conditions; that is, I need to fill in the question marks in the following schemes:

s is true iff ?
S's belief at t is true iff ?

However, to fill in the question marks in these schemes would be to interpret the belief or sentence. As he says, our notion of truth is linked to Tarskian T-sentences in which the filling in is defined in terms of translation (or interpretation). Let us grant all of this. Tarski's point, though, is that a predicate defined in such a way as to deliver T-sentences will be a truth-predicate. So this condition forms part of a *sufficient* condition for a predicate to qualify as truth. We are not here in the position of having to form a concept of truth, just in that of trying to see how our understanding of the concept of truth enables it to be applied to the foreign sentences or beliefs. For that we do not need to think of the fillings-in of the question marks as delivering T-sentences. All we need to be able to think of is fillings-in that would be true. The point is that we can state truth-conditions in a manner that is not interpretational. That general point is in fact conceded by Davidson in setting out how a truth-theory can function as a theory of interpretation. Not just any theory of truth will be an interpretational truth-theory; rather, only a theory of truth that emerges from the process of radical interpretation. So it is at least possible for us to conceive of specifying truth-conditions in ways that are not interpretational. Can we flesh out this mere abstract possibility? Plausibly we can. Suppose we witness a dog waiting expectantly by the front door. At the sound of a bicycle approaching she grows more attentive, and then becomes very excited as steps approach the door. When the door is opened by her owner she reacts with unbounded glee. Next day at about the same time we find her again sitting expectantly by the front door. One might well then say that the following holds:

The dog's belief is true iff its owner will be home soon.

Does the dog believe that its owner will be home soon? Although it seems natural enough to make the attribution, it may well be hard to sustain. Can she have such a belief without having the concepts of an *owner*, of *home* and of *soonness* – temporal immanence? It is certainly hard to think of the dog as having these concepts, hard to think of her therefore as having that particular belief and hard to think of what other belief she might have. Indeed, it is apt to seem that here we might well have a belief that we *cannot* interpret, although we can think of it as being true and can indeed state its truth-conditions quite adequately. We do not understand the dog in the sense that we are unable to share her belief; but we do understand the dog in the sense that there is much we can say *about* her belief and can explain much of her behaviour on the basis of attributing a belief with a certain truth-condition to her.

Let us sum up our findings about the Principle of Charity. I have argued that there are reasons for thinking that some version of Charity must be a part of the radical interpreter's methodology, since more nuanced alternatives threaten to rob the programme of its philosophical interest. Charity must be guaranteed to hold *a priori*, if radical interpretation is to ground the notion that meanings are public. Davidson motivates Charity as a necessary condition for interpretation because he thinks intentionality presupposes truth. It is not at all clear, though, that this simple thought suffices to motivate any clear methodological principle, and it is a controversial view; Davidson needs an *a priori* argument in its favour. We have left the matter undecided. If we accept that the principle is a necessary condition for the possibility of interpretation, then the universal possibility of interpretation will issue in a justification of the principle as true. However, Davidson's argument here limps; it appears to be both question-begging and, since it neglects a point he concedes, namely, that many truth-theories are not interpretative, it seems invalid. A lesson worth taking away from this discussion is that there is nonetheless a close connection between Davidson's use of the radical interpreter and the Principle of Charity: if we have suspicions about the latter, we should suspect the former too.

7.3 An application: saying that

Davidson wants to apply his method to natural language, and this means that he needs to show how to deal with various natural-language locutions from within a truth-theory taking a Tarskian form. We have looked at how the truth-theory is modified by indexical expressions. What we shall do now very briefly (in part because of its intrinsic interest and connection with Frege and in part because it crops up in Davidson's debate with Foster – our next topic) is to look at his analysis of sentences involving the locution "saying that". So we want an account of the logical form of a sentence such as "Galileo said that the earth moves".

In his paper Davidson (1984: essay 7) critically examines two sorts of approach. The first is a Fregean approach that introduces meanings: anathema to Davidson. The second is the attempt to explain such cases by quoting the sentence that appears in indirect discourse. As I said, some of this discussion is a touch technical and is not what we want to focus on, so what follows is a very brief résumé of Davidson's findings.

Frege and meanings: Recall that Frege's solution to this problem is to say that in indirect discourse an expression changes its reference from its usual reference to what is usually its sense. One problem with such an approach is that we might then be forced into associating an infinite hierarchy of senses with expressions in order to account for their appearance in doubly indirect, triply indirect contexts and so on. Dummett attempts to help Frege by suggesting that we need only the first stage here. We need only (primary) senses since the reference of a term in multiply indirect contexts remains constant: it refers to its sense. Davidson's major worry here is that this means that we can intersubstitute expressions in indirect contexts without changing the truth-value of the containing sentence, provided that they have the *same* sense. But that means that there have to be clear identity conditions for senses. And this Davidson doubts. For him, similarities or differences of meaning are made clear through the business of interpretation. And the correctness of an interpretational scheme is subject to the holistic constraint of maximizing agreement. So there is no suggestion that there is a uniquely correct interpretational scheme: there are no well-defined meanings to be discovered. Since Frege's proposal hinges on seeing such well-defined meanings as the referents of expressions in indirect discourse, it should be rejected.

Quotation: We cannot simply quote the sentence and thus explain "Galileo said that the earth moves" as "Galileo said 'the earth moves'" since:

- Galileo uttered an Italian sentence, "La terra si muove", so our report is simply false.
- The sentence "The earth moves" may have different meanings in different languages. To capture what the original sentence means we would have to specify that the sentence is to have, say, its English meaning.

We cannot build in a reference to the language by explaining our sentence as, say, "Galileo uttered a sentence which meant in his language what 'The earth moves' now means in mine" since:

- When we translate "said that" into French the indexical reference to English will shift, as we desire, to French, but we shall still have a name for an *English* sentence.
- The reference to languages is suspicious since meanings and languages have just as ill-defined identity-conditions as one another. Imagine, for instance, that my language changes slightly from Monday to Tuesday. Then my report, made on Monday, might be true but the corresponding report, made on Tuesday, false. How can we say when a report should be accepted and when an analogous report should be rejected without having a criterion for sameness of language or for the sameness of meaning of two utterances?

The paratactic analysis: The proposal nearly gets it right since it aims to capture the idea that an utterance of Galileo's has the same meaning as an utterance of mine. The problem is that as soon as we move over to quotation, I am not making an utterance; I am simply naming a sentence. So what we want is a situation in which I make an utterance (with the same meaning as one of Galileo's) and assert that Galileo and I are therefore "samesayers". So I shall have to utter the sentence "The earth moves". What we have then is:

The earth moves.
There is an utterance of Galileo's which means the same as my last
    utterance.

(Davidson puts it in terms of "samesaying": There is an utterance of Galileo's which together with my last utterance makes us samesayers.)

We might abbreviate things by using a demonstrative in order to refer, not (surely) to my utterance (though this is what Davidson says), but to what was uttered. Thus:

The earth moves.
Galileo said that.

It is important to note that my utterance and Galileo's need only to share their content. Galileo's utterance was an *assertion* (and that is why he got into so much trouble), but those who reported Galileo to the church authorities were, according to Davidson, making an utterance with the same content, but they were not asserting the sentence (which is why they did not get into trouble). So the utterances need not share the same force.

Failure of substitution is explained because the utterance reporting the same-saying will now change truth-value. So let us change the example slightly. We may have:

(i) Scott is the author of *Waverley*.
     George III said that.
(ii) Scott is Scott.
     George III said that.

Here the first utterances in these pairs are both true and thus alike in truth-value. But the second utterance, while true in (i), is false in (ii).

7.4 Compositionality and extensionality

A Davidsonian truth-theory is purely extensional. So, as we have noted before, a true truth-theory may include a clause of the following form:

(T) "Snow is white" is true iff grass is green.

Now it may well be that a sentence of this form will not issue from a truth-theory that is sanctioned by the Principle of Charity. But we shall need to do a little more work to explain this. After all, the evidence in terms of what a speaker holds true would seem to support (T) since we shall have:

(E) *X* holds "Snow is white" true iff grass is green.

What Davidson says is that a holistic constraint imposed through the insistence that our theory is compositional suffices to rule out cases like (T). How does this work?

The term "white" will occur in many sentences other than the one above. So, for instance, we might have the sentence "That is white", where the demonstrative is interpreted as referring to a sample of snow. Now presumably the sentence (T) will emerge from the inclusion of a clause such as the following in our truth-theory:

(S) x satisfies the predicate "is white" iff x is green.

When we put this together with our clause for the demonstrative, we are likely to infer something like the following:

(T') "That is white" is true as uttered by X at t iff the object demonstrated by X at t is green.

And now this will collide with the evidence (collected by observing X's judgements about the truth of the sentence "That is white" on occasions when the demonstrated object is, e.g., a sample of snow) that

(E') X holds "That is white" true at t iff the object demonstrated by X at t is white.

So the sentence (T) is ruled out as a theorem of an interpretative T-theory because the compositional nature of the theory entails that the clauses from which such a sentence is derived will give rise to other T-sentences that are contradicted by the evidence.

7.5 Davidson and Foster

Foster (1999) begins by noting that the best way to read Davidson's programme is as an attempt to characterize the knowledge that would suffice to interpret the utterances of speakers of our target language. That is, we are not interested in claiming that the theory of meaning is in some way known and deployed by speakers themselves. This would be a difficult claim to make because it involves attributing to speakers knowledge that they deploy only unconsciously; it is, in the current terminology, tacit or implicit knowledge. In opting for only this very rough modelling of speaker's capacities, a Davidsonian theory of meaning forsakes many of the constraints that render the theory of meaning a more interesting philosophical project than that of translation. Davidson largely avoids the sceptical consequences of the indeterminacy of translation[13] only by adopting a different attitude to the Principle of Charity. For Quine the latter is a pragmatic aid to translation; for Davidson it is a necessary condition for the possibility of interpretation.

The first complaint raised by Foster cannot really be read as a genuine complaint against Davidson, as Foster readily admits. However, it is worth laying out because it sets the scene for the discussion.

His complaint is very simple. It is just this. The truth-theory is purely extensional, so provided we have an adequate truth-theory that interprets a certain predicate as P, then the theory will still be adequate if we interpret the predicate by another coextensional predicate P_1. But clearly P and P_1 might differ in meaning. So the truth-theory will not be interpretative. As an example, he suggests that the right interpretation of a predicate might be as meaning the same as "x is a part of y". But if this interpretation was part of an adequate truth-theory, then so would be an interpretation that interpreted the predicate as "x is a part of y and grass is green". The reason for this is that, since grass is green, "x is a part of y" and "x is a part of y and grass is green" have precisely the same extension. Moreover, it is quite clear that both schemes of interpretation would function in a compositional truth-theory. So we cannot appeal to compositionality here as we did in the previous section when we ruled out the putative T-sentence: "'Snow is white' is true iff grass is green".

The answer to Foster's point is obvious. We do not want just any truth-theory; we want a truth-theory that is interpretative, that is, loosely, a theory that offers *interpretations* of sentences in the target language. Of course we cannot appeal to the notion of translation here because that begs the question, and Davidson knows this. So what he does is to spell out constraints on how the truth-theory is to be arrived at, via the process of interpretation. If these constraints can be stated without appeal to the notion of meaning or translation or synonymy and so on, then they will characterize an interpretative truth-theory, which we shall call a T-theory (since it gives sentences, T-sentences, that satisfy Tarski's Convention-T). Now so far this is all familiar stuff. The constraints are, of course, Davidson's attempt to marry a truth-theory with the evidence of speakers' use of language via the Principle of Charity. So far, Davidson and Foster are marching in step.

The next step is again one that both of them take. It is this. Obviously it is not enough for an interpreter to know the facts stated by a T-theory. She could not use this to interpret since, even though she would get it right if she did so, she would not know she was getting it right. In other words, since there are many possible truth-theories, simply to be in possession of the knowledge stated in the right truth-theory is not enough to interpret. In addition, one has to know that this knowledge is stated by the right truth-theory, that is, by a T-theory. So, knowing that a given truth-theory is a T-theory, we can treat its deliverances as characterizations of meaning: we can move from "s is true iff p" to "s means that p". Thus *if we know that a truth-theory is a T-theory*, then we can treat it as a theory of meaning. But the proviso is all-important.

How do we characterize what an interpreter knows? We might say that the interpreter knows that a T-theory for L states that .... This, claims Foster, is problematic because it introduces the intensional idiom "states that" and if that is all right we might as well have stuck with the "means that" idiom. We shall come back to this option in a little while. However, we might think that we can do without the intensional idiom by characterizing the knowledge thus: S knows what T states and S knows that T is a T-theory. Foster quickly shows that this will not do since it factors the knowledge into two components, which can be decoupled. How? Well imagine that we have a T-theory for Shona stated in English, T_E. I learn this T-theory but do not realize that it is a T-theory. Now I also know a little German and am told by my German friend that a certain German theory, T_G, is a T-theory for Shona. My German is not, however, good enough for me to grasp the theory (or perhaps just to work out that what T_G says is the same as what T_E says). And now it is true that I know what T_G states – since I know T_E and these theories state the same thing – and I know that T_G is a T-theory; however, I cannot interpret Shona-speakers.

Now the debate continues, with Foster and Davidson discussing the analysis of statements such as "Galileo said that the earth moves". The relevance is obvious since we are thinking about a statement of a similar form, namely "T states that …". We can, however, delay that discussion because Davidson has a more direct response to Foster. He totally rejects Foster's attempt to decouple the two pieces of knowledge since obviously he is thinking of a case where one arrives at the T-theory through a process of interpretation and so one cannot but know that the resulting theory satisfies the relevant constraints and is therefore a T-theory. So he accepts the intensional characterization of the knowledge (i.e. S knows that a T-theory for L states that …). Why is this acceptable? For two reasons: first, Foster has misstated Davidson's aims. He is not trying to construct a theory of meaning in a purely extensional mode (as Foster suggests in the final section of his paper, this does not seem like a *problem*; it seems like an *impossibility*). We have already seen, for instance, that he uses the notion of belief in the context of holding a sentence true. Rather, he is trying to give a theory of meaning that does not take for granted any linguistic notions such as meaning, translation, synonymy and so on. And using certain intensional notions is no bar to that project.

Let us focus on one interpretational T-sentence, our old pal: "Snow is white" is true iff snow is white. What we want to characterize is a sentence of the form: "T states that 'Snow is white' is true iff snow is white." Now we might think of T as a set of sentences. Then what we want is: T includes a sentence that is synonymous with my utterance of "'Snow is white' is true iff snow is white". Obviously synonymy is just the relation we need. We cannot require that the theory include the particular sentence "'Snow is white' is true iff snow is white", since the theory might be in another language or there might be different ways of conveying just this information. But hang on a minute, have we not just been told that we cannot use notions like synonymy? Yes indeed we have. These notions cannot be used unanalysed in the theory. But Davidson takes himself to have already characterized synonymy in characterizing, in a non-question-begging way, to be sure, the constraints on an acceptable T-theory: that is, the constraints placed on a truth-theory in order for that theory to be interpretative suffice to characterize synonymy. So we can then use that notion in explaining what it is that an interpreter must know in order to interpret the language.

7.6 Dummett on Davidson

Consider Foster's characterization of the restrictions on Davidson's project:

> The essential, methodological vocabulary is independent of the particular interpretations which the theory offers: it holds constant through other theories of the same type dealing with other languages of the same grammatical structure. The accidental vocabulary is what adapts the general method to a particular object language: it provides descriptive resources to match the resources of the language to which that method of interpretation is applied. Such restrictions on vocabulary as we think appropriate (the avoidance, for example, of such terms as "meaning" and "necessity") fall only on the methodological sector. For it is from the method of the theory that we hope to gain insight into the nature of meaning. To impose restrictions on the vocabulary of the translations is to get entangled in a different problem, namely how concepts employed in the object language can be analysed into ones that are philosophically more basic. This is an interesting problem, but not one that here concerns us. (1999: 7)

What Foster is saying is that we need to distinguish two different projects. One is that of conceptual analysis and the other is that of interpretation. If one were interested in conceptual analysis, then one would insist that the concepts used in the analysis were, in some sense, philosophically more basic than those being analysed (as Quine insists when he considers putative analyses or definitions of "analytic"). However, Davidson's interest is not in analysis; it is in interpretation. The goal of interpretation is to provide adequate interpretations of expressions in the object-language. In order to do this we are entitled to assume that the expressive power of the meta-language mirrors that of the object-language. We throw light on the concept of meaning just by considering how this project of interpretation might proceed. In order to make the project an interesting one we need to restrict the concepts it is able to presuppose. So Foster makes a distinction between the essential vocabulary and the accidental vocabulary of the meta-language. The essential vocabulary is the vocabulary that governs how the interpretations are framed, for instance that these are specifications of truth-conditions. The accidental vocabulary is the vocabulary used in stating the interpretations, that is in specifying the truth-conditions. We make the interpretative project interesting by restricting the essential vocabulary.

The project is supposed to differ from and to be more interesting than that of translation. Translation simply pairs expressions of one language with synonymous expressions of another language, and this only yields an interpretation of the one language if we are able to presuppose an understanding of the other. So no account is given of what it is to understand a language; from the philosophical perspective, the account is thus worthless. But one might wonder whether, in allowing the meta-language simply to mirror the expressive power of the object language, we have not developed a project of no more interest than that of constructing a translation manual. This is the brunt of Dummett's[14] first worry about Davidson: if we assume that the resources of the meta-language simply reproduce those of the object language, then we seem simply to presuppose a grasp of the concepts expressible in the object language. But part of what it is to understand a language is to grasp basic concepts that are expressible in it (in addition one would need to grasp those concepts *by* understanding appropriate expressions in the language). Thus the account would not offer a full explanation of what it is to understand a language: that is, of what one knows when one knows a language.

Dummett (1993: 5) calls a theory of meaning that, in this way, presupposes a grasp of certain basic concepts a modest theory of meaning and he contrasts it with a full-blooded or (in later writings) robust theory of meaning. So his question is this: is a modest theory of meaning more interesting than a translation manual?

To be sure, a Davidsonian truth-theory, which issues in clauses of the form, "'Snow is white' is true iff snow is white", has all the appearances of being modest. Whether it is so or not will have to be assessed in relation to Davidson's account *of what it is to know such clauses*. So one of our main aims is to try to clarify this somewhat opaque, but crucial, aspect of his programme (see the debate between Davidson and Foster).

According to Davidson, we can treat an interpretative truth-theory as a theory of meaning. So we can move from a T-sentence "'Snow is white' is true iff snow is white" to an M-sentence "'Snow is white' means that snow is white". When the object and meta-languages are distinct, this is clearly informative. "'La neige est blanche' means that snow is white" gives us the interpretation of the French sentence in the English meta-language. However, when the meta-language is the object language, the M-sentence appears to be completely unexplanatory since it uses the very sentence that is supposed to be interpreted. However, it must equally be admitted that the M-sentence precisely captures the interpretation of the object-language sentence. So someone who knows the M-sentence knows the interpretation of the object-language sentence. Dummett certainly does not dispute this; however, he does insist that it is not sufficient to know that the M-sentence is true; in addition one needs to know what the

M-sentence expresses. There is an important distinction between knowing that a sentence is true and knowing the proposition expressed by the sentence. The point is obvious if we take into account knowledge by testimony. I might well know that the statement "Entropy tends to increase" is true, because my reliable neighbourhood physicist informs me of this. But I might have little or no understanding of the sentence. So I certainly do not know the proposition the sentence expresses.

Dummett's point is similar. Given that "Snow is white" is a grammatical English sentence, I may well know that "'Snow is white' means that snow is white" is true simply on the basis of my understanding of "means that". Thus I shall not be able to interpret if all I know is the truth of the M-sentence. I also need to know what the M-sentence expresses. And the question is: what piece of knowledge will get me from knowing the truth of the M-sentence to knowing what it expresses? It seems that nothing other than an understanding of the sentence "Snow is white" will do. And this explains why the Davidsonian theory appears to be uninformative.

Let us just run through things a little more carefully. In the cases where one knows the truth of a sentence but does not know the proposition it expresses, one has arrived at one's knowledge by a kind of short-cut: either one has judged something to be true on the basis of testimony or one has relied only on the form of the sentence and one's understanding of a component. But Davidson has something to say about how the interpreter arrives at knowledge of the truth of M-sentence. Rather than simply judge the M-sentence to be true on the basis of its form, one has to *derive* the M-sentence from axioms of a truth-theory. The axioms will specify the satisfaction conditions of predicates and the denotations of singular terms. So one knows the proposition expressed by the M-sentence (i.e. one understands the sentence thereby interpreted) because one derives one's knowledge of the truth of the M-sentence from the axioms governing the meanings of words. And this idea is certainly plausible. But then Dummett's question resurfaces in relation to the axioms.

The above account is plausible only if we think that interpreters know the propositions expressed by axioms such as "'London' denotes London" rather than simply knowing them to be true; one could know the truth of the axiom simply on the basis of knowing that "London" is a singular term in English and an understanding of "denotes". In order to move from knowing that the sentence is true to knowing the proposition it expresses, one would have to know the meaning of the word "London". So the interpreter must grasp the concepts expressible in the basic vocabulary of the language and must grasp these as the meanings of terms in her meta-language: that is, the account of what it is to understand the object language proceeds under the presupposition that one understands the meta-language and thus is no real advance over a translation manual.

It is worth pausing to clarify the state of the debate. Davidson distinguishes a theory of interpretation from a translation scheme by claiming that a translation scheme only gives a theory of interpretation if we assume an understanding of one of the languages. Of course, he admits, a theory of interpretation is given in some language and, thus, that language must be understood in order to understand the theory. But this is simply a feature of theories in general. Now the first hint of a worry is that a theory of interpretation is not just like other theories because the language of the theory needs to expand to mirror the language being interpreted. So it is not simply that in order to construct a theory we need to speak a language, but that the theory seems only to function through being parasitic on that ability. That this is so emerges when we think about what the interpreter needs to know. At the basic level the interpreter needs to know the propositions expressed by the axioms. But she can know this only if she understands a term of the meta-language synonymous with the relevant object-language term. So, unless Davidson can say more about what this knowledge consists in – if his theory remains modest – then his theory is, from a philosophical point of view, no advance on a translation manual.

Now the knowledge that the interpreter has (as emerged in the debate between Davidson and Foster) is knowledge that the axioms and T-sentences are axioms of an interpretative truth-theory – a truth-theory meeting Davidson's constraints. Now there are two ways of conceiving this. Let us take Davidson's constraint of maximizing the number of sentences held true. The interpreter might know just that the theory satisfies this constraint (for a speaker or community of speakers) *or* the interpreter might know that in applying this constraint the theory has to maximize truth amongst *a specific set of a sentences* (those observed to be held true). The first way of reading this is to treat the actual set of sentences held true as evidence for the correctness of the theory of truth. The second way of reading this makes those sentences internal to the content of the theory: they form part of what the theory states. At first Dummett thinks that the first reading is bound to correspond to Davidson's intentions since Davidson talks about the set of sentences held true as evidence for the theory. In the appendix to the paper he revises this opinion, suggesting that Davidson is better read in the second way.[15]

But both readings are problematic. The first simply involves knowledge of a T-theory and knowledge that it is a T-theory. So it factors the knowledge into two components, which the discussion of Foster revealed to be muddled. The response there was that we needed to think of the interpreter as constructing the theory through the methodology of radical interpretation. But then we adopt the second reading and, so conceived, the account is radically implausible. We are surely incapable, even in principle, of determining an assignment that maximizes truth among this large set of sentences. And, if we focus on an individual's holdings-true, then there will be many terms for which she fails to hold true a sufficiency of sentences in order to determine a reference. But, if we focus on communal holdings-true, then it is implausible to suppose that an interpreter will have access to these sentences.

Now, we have noticed that the theory does not say what knowledge of the axioms and theorems taken individually consists in. Rather, it claims simply that in both knowing a truth-theory and knowing that it is an interpretative truth-theory, the interpreter is in a position to interpret utterances in the language. That is, the knowledge of the theory and that it is a correct theory issues simply in an ability to speak the language. No effort is expended (nor can it be expended) in trying to show how the elaborate structure of the theory mirrors the structure of speakers' linguistic capacities. Dummett calls such a theory holisitc.

Now, if we could assume a perfect fit between the truth-conditions that the theory attributes to sentences and speakers' judgements about the truth-values of those sentences, then we could, in effect, ignore the holistic character of Davidson's constraint (of maximizing agreement). We could read the interpretative T-sentences simply as corresponding with speakers' capacities to recognize the truth-values of individual sentences; a clause such as "s is true iff p" will hold just in case speakers hold s to be true when and only when p. But we cannot take this option because many sentences – such as "There is intelligent life somewhere else in the universe" – are such that speakers need not be able to recognize them as true when they are true. So the clause "s is true iff there is intelligent life elsewhere in the universe" may be right but it may not be possible to justify its correctness in terms of speakers' holding the sentence s to be true in recognizable circumstances.

Also this would leave no room for the notion of a mistake; it is because speakers make mistakes that we have to aim at *optimizing* agreement. Davidson thinks that because agreement can never be guaranteed to be perfect, we need the notion of *belief*. We are forced to see speakers as holding true some sentences that, on the optimal scheme of interpretation, we would not hold true. So we are forced to see them as being committed to the truth of certain sentences despite the fact (judged by our own lights) that those sentences are not true. And this is to conceive of a state of *believing*. Now a speaker's beliefs will contribute to determining the meanings of her sentences since the theory of interpretation is built on a holistic constraint: aiming to maximize agreement.[16] This means that there is no real distinction between a change in a speaker's beliefs and a change in her meanings. A change in belief may, because of the requirement of the holistic constraint, result in adoption of an alternative scheme of interpretation, but it also might not. The only thing driving us one way or the other is the effort to satisfy the holistic constraint. And, other than this, there is no explanation of the distinction between changing one's meanings and changing one's beliefs. Similarly there' is no explanation of what is involved in making a mistake, of holding a sentence true when in fact it is false. The natural thing to say is that a speaker is in error just in case, given the meaning of the sentence, it should, in such-and-such circumstances, be judged to be true, whereas the speaker judges it to be false. Of course Davidson can *say* this, or roughly this. But for him, saying this is just to say that the speaker judges incorrectly according to the scheme of interpretation that satisfies the holistic constraint. And that is just to say that his judgement cannot be seen to be correct according to a scheme of interpretation that is successful at meeting the holistic constraint. This is not to explain the notion of a mistake; rather, it is simply to import it to explain the fact that we cannot guarantee a perfect fit between speakers' judgements and the interpretation scheme.

Dummett's complaint is essentially this. All Davidson considers is speakers' judgements about the truth-values of sentences. But what a theory of meaning should do is explain how speakers go about forming such judgements on the basis of their knowledge of the sentences' truth-conditions. Were we to do so we could explain what it would be for them to make mistakes in this undertaking. On Davidson's account an interpretative theory of truth satisfies a holistic constraint, and knowledge of such a theory gives rise to the ability to speak a language. But one might ask: why, when we operate, as speakers, with such theories do we not achieve perfect agreement? And the answer is obvious: because we make mistakes. But again that is just to make the programme seem plausible by appealing to a notion that it cannot explain.

The inability to give substance to the notion of a mistake is a consequence of constructing a scheme of interpretation – that is, fixing meaning – by imposing a holistic constraint on evidence that is the combined product of meaning and belief. Once we do so, any decision to count a piece of evidence as a product of a mistake will be made purely in terms of this holistic constraint. But that is not to explain what a mistake is; nor is it, as Davidson claims, a congenial position. It is to reveal, no doubt, that the attribution of mistakes arises in the operation of the holistic constraint. However, to think that this *explains* the notion of mistake is to ignore the fact that the constraint was (rightly) chosen, from the first, so as to allow for mistakes. So what *is* fundamentally revealed is that the constraint relies on a notion that the very methodology of radical interpretation inevitably expunges. The radical interpreter, because she is radical, cannot dissect her pieces of evidence to determine how they reflect on meaning and how on belief. Nothing is left to her but to sort the pieces of evidence holistically. Moreover, once the theory is constructed there can be no attempt to marry it with a dissection of the evidence; rather, the ability to speak the language is mirrored *in toto* in the theorist's deployment of the theory. Because of this, the theory never throws out a description of speakers' capacities against which they can be measured. If we knew what capacities a speaker ought to have exercised in relation to a given sentence, we could determine whether or not she had failed in one or another way. But with no such account we can simply say that the evidence provided by her performance fails to mesh with our favoured theory. So the account renders mysterious a fact that it rightly recognizes. Nor can we supplement the account by appealing to epistemology or the philosophy of mind to explain false belief. Here we run up against the same problem: since we cannot distinguish those pieces of evidence that are products of false belief, we cannot exploit such an account in explaining what a mistake is.

The notion of mistake that we have been operating with here is quite undifferentiated: it includes both false belief and performance errors in speaking a language. In Chapter 8 we consider the notion of a mistake in more detail. We consider a reading of Davidson that would deny that there are such things as linguistic mistakes. Then, in Chapter 9, we consider more recent arguments that claim that, although language has, what might be called correctness-conditions, there are no linguistic norms, no obligations governing speakers' use of language.

8. Linguistic norms, communication and radical interpretation

In his later work in the philosophy of language Davidson analyses communicative exchanges and arrives at the startling and weighty conclusion that linguistic norms and conventions are entirely inessential to linguistic meaning. I argue that this inference is flawed: if we place the account of communication against the backdrop of Davidson's own views about radical interpretation, then it becomes evident that linguistic norms *are* an essential feature of the Davidsonian picture.

Let us begin by clarifying. In claiming that there are *linguistic norms* I am claiming that, if a speaker means something by a certain term, then there are ways in which she ought or ought not to use it. Quite how we characterize those ways is a tough question but not one that matters for the basic claim. In claiming that there are *linguistic conventions* I am claiming that there are linguistic norms that, in some sense, apply within a community and are instituted and/or sustained by interactions within a community. Again, how we think of a norm as applying within the community and how we think of it relating to speakers' behaviour towards one another is another tough question but not one that needs to be addressed in making the basic claim. Davidson, in later work, denies both of these claims. Here I argue that he is committed to the former claim about linguistic norms and speculate that he may be committed to the latter claim also. In claiming that there are *linguistic rules* I shall be claiming that there are conditions of correctness that apply to speakers' use of language. There is a distinction between the notion of a linguistic norm and that of a linguistic rule: it is not patently false and may indeed be true to claim that there are facts about whether or not one's use of a term is correct in the absence of facts about how one ought or ought not to use it.[1] The distinction will be of paramount importance in Chapter 9 but will not be important here since we shall focus on the claim that there are linguistic norms, which entails that there are linguistic rules: if there is a fact about whether or not a use coincides with what I ought or ought not to do, then there is a fact about whether or not the use is correct.

8.1 Davidson on communication

Davidson launches an attack on traditional, convention-based conceptions of language by focusing on the communicative situation, a situation in which a speaker and hearer succeed in communicating via language. He identifies linguistic ability with the ability to use language to communicate.[2] Thus, if there is no role to be played by the notion of knowledge of norms, rules or conventions in explaining our ability to communicate, such knowledge plays no role in explaining linguistic competence.

We should supply some background to the argument before we turn to its details. Davidson's concern is *literal* meaning, which, of course, he refuses to identify with conventional meaning. Part of the point of having a conception of literal meaning is that Davidson, reasonably enough, wants a distinction between speaker-meaning and word- or sentence-meaning, and hopes to deploy the former in accounts of non-literal uses of language such as metaphor. He calls literal meaning "first meaning" and allows it to be fixed in Gricean fashion thus: the first meaning of an utterance is fixed by the primary Gricean communicative intention with which the speech act is performed – that is, it is the basic communicative intention on which the other intentions in performing the act depend.

Let us move now to the account of the communicative situation. Davidson thinks of this in terms of the speaker and hearer, each of whom deploys two interpretative theories: a prior and a passing theory. He supposes, in brief, that the speaker and hearer will each bring to the situation beliefs – encapsulated in theories of interpretation – about how the other will interpret the words spoken; these are the prior theories. During the conversation these beliefs may prove unworkable for one or another reason and so may well be modified. Davidson thinks of the results of so doing as passing theories. The prior and passing theories need to be characterized differently depending on whether we are focusing on the speaker or the hearer. To focus first on the hearer, what we have is:

Prior theory: the hearer's theory about how to interpret the speaker.
Passing theory: the theory the hearer uses to interpret the speaker.

And for the speaker we have:

Prior theory: that theory she believes to be the hearer's prior theory.
Passing theory: that theory she intends the speaker to use.

These theories aim to interpret *first* meanings. "As we mentioned communication succeeds when the speaker is interpreted according to the theory she intended the hearer to use and so '[w]hat must be shared for communication to succeed is the passing theory'" (LePore 1986: 442).

The meaning of the utterance is set by the manner in which it is interpreted by the (convergent) passing theories. So, somewhat perplexingly, its meaning now seems to be fixed in *two* ways: by the passing theory and by the primary communicative intention. But these two determinations are bound to come together because the relevant communicative intention needs to be informed by a systematic theory for it to be a *linguistic* intention and the passing theory precisely informs the speaker's speech acts.

In Davidson's view, *both* passing and prior theories are systematic theories modelled by truth-theories. So he does not think of the passing theory as an ad hoc qualification of the prior theory; rather, it is an entire systematic theory in its own right. As we have mentioned, theories of this sort are not literally known by actual speakers and hearers; rather, if we, theorists of language, are to describe the capacities of actual speakers we shall need to do so by means of recursive truth-theories. So the account, in this sense, provides a model of how conversation functions. But, once we allow for this element of modelling, the account is then supposed to be a straightforward explanation of conversation. As a hearer one has (systematically interrelated) beliefs about how to interpret a given speaker and then adapts those beliefs, if need be, during conversation. Similarly, a speaker will have beliefs *and intentions* about how she will be interpreted.

The crucial move in Davidson's rejection of linguistic norms arises from his view of how these theories are arrived at – specifically, his dismissal of any suggestion that there is a distinctive method involved. But in order to appreciate that point we need a sense of the origin of the view.

8.1.1 Davidson's motivation

Davidson is fascinated by the phenomenon of malapropism. Suppose Frank returns from his day trip, reporting as follows:

We took the table car up Cable Mountain.

In all likelihood one would not have too much trouble in arriving at the correct interpretation of these words as

We took the cable car up Table Mountain.

Before the conversation you would, no doubt, have been inclined to interpret Frank's utterance of "table" as meaning *table*, his utterance of "Cable Mountain" as meaning *Cable Mountain* and so on but, in the particular situation, adopting that scheme of interpretation fails to make good sense of his utterance. So, using your general knowledge and your nous, you adapt your interpretation of Frank's words to arrive at a more successful interpretation. Davidson describes this in terms of moving from a prior to a passing theory. Apart from talk of theories here this *seems* uncontroversial; in effect the hearer moves from one interpretation to another. For Davidson this is a matter of moving from one interpretative scheme to another, but this need not be so.

Consider the following alternative account. Failing to make sense of Frank's remark, you realize that it is likely (for a variety of reasons, given the meanings of the words he uttered, context, similarity between the sounds of words, etc.) that in uttering "table" he either intended to utter or should have uttered "cable"; in uttering "Cable Mountain" he either intended to utter or should have uttered "Table Mountain" and so on. Thus what he intended to utter or should have uttered is the second sentence. You can then interpret that sentence according to your standard scheme of interpretation to make sense of his remark. Note that on this second mode of description there is only one mode of interpretation in play – what I, somewhat tendentiously, called "the standard mode" – the movement from one interpretation to the other is a matter of moving from one utterance, the utterance Frank made, to another, the utterance he intended to make or should have made.

Let us make the two accounts explicit. The utterance we have to interpret is:

Utterance$_M$: "We took the table car up Cable Mountain."

Let us suppose, as seems plausible, that the right interpretation of **Utterance$_M$** is:

Interpretation: Utterance$_M$ is true iff the speaker's party took the cable car up Table Mountain.

There are then two possible routes from **Utterance$_M$** to **Interpretation.**

Route 1 (Davidson):

PRIOR THEORY

Axioms
The referent of "Cable Mountain" is Cable Mountain
The referent of "Table Mountain" is Table Mountain
x ^ "is a table" is true iff the referent of x is a table
x ^ "is a cable" is true iff the referent of x is a cable
...

Theorem
Utterance$_M$ is true iff the speaker's party took the table car up Cable
Mountain

Since the interpretation offered by the theorem is implausible, we modify the
prior theory to arrive at

PASSING THEORY

Axioms
The referent of "Cable Mountain" is Table Mountain
$x \wedge$ "is a table is true" iff the referent of x is a cable
$x \wedge$ "is a cable" is true iff the referent of x is a table

...

Theorem
Utterance$_M$ is true iff the speaker's party took the cable car up Table
Mountain

Route 2:

1. Utterance$_M$ is true iff the utterance the speaker intended to make or
    should have made is true
2. The speaker intended to utter or should have uttered "We took the cable
    car up Table Mountain" – call this Utterance$_I$ ($\neq$ Utterance$_M$)
3. Utterance$_I$ is true iff the speaker's party took the cable car up Table
    Mountain (standard theory of interpretation = prior theory above)
4. Utterance$_M$ is true iff the speaker's party took the cable car up Table
    Mountain

Here (1) holds because, if we want to understand the speaker – rather than
mechanically offering a literal interpretation of her words – we should, in
general, aim for interpretations of this form.

There is this crucial contrast between the two accounts. There is no logical
reason not to accept that Davidson's account offers a universal account of
communication. At the moment, to be sure, there is no reason to accept it *as
such* and your sense that malapropisms are an exceptional linguistic occurrence might cause you to have some qualms but nonetheless there is no bar
to universalizing the account. The "ordinary" cases will simply be cases where
the prior theory is identical to the passing theory but there is no reason to
suppose that these are statistically common or even, at the extreme, that they
occur at all. But things change dramatically if we consider the second account.
Accordingly, malapropism is not just an exceptional occurrence; it is necessarily

exceptional. For it cannot *generally* be the case that the utterance made differs from the one intended to be made; speakers' use of language must be taken as a reliable guide to their intentions to use language. (Necessarily, in general, **Utterance$_M$** = **Utterance$_I$**.) So occasions where **Utterance$_M$** ≠ **Utterance$_I$** *must* be exceptional.

Of course Davidson knows that malapropisms are an exceptional feature of our use of language. But he takes it that this is an accidental, although no doubt practically important, fact. An account of our use of language must be able to explain its function in situations such as those of malapropism, and if such an account can be applied in other areas too then, arguably, this account reveals the essence of communication. The interplay between prior and passing theories promises just this. In contrast, the opposing account would stumble at the first hurdle here, for on that account malapropism is not just exceptional but necessarily exceptional. Thus communication despite malapropism must be parasitic on another mode of communication. What other mode? That which involves successful deployment on the part of speaker and hearer of the standard mode of interpretation.

Having noted this contrast between the two approaches and having registered a reservation that Davidson's approach is not compelled, let us move on to some of the consequences of the Davidsonian scheme. As we said, successful communication consists in convergence in passing theories, and passing theories, we now learn, are completely ephemeral – perhaps having an application in only a single case – and are arrived at on the basis of intuition, luck, skill, taste and sympathy; as Davidson says, "[t]here is no more chance of regularizing, or teaching this process than there is of regularizing or teaching the process of creating new theories to cope with new data in any field – for that is what this process involves" (LePore 1986: 446). Thus we arrive at the crucial contention: communication relies neither on any established, shared knowledge nor on knowledge of a method for interpreting. Successful communication need only be the product of our skill at interpreting one another; and the assignment of meanings to a speaker's saying is just a way of interpreting it, so meanings are not established rules for the use of terms.

The argument against linguistic norms thus runs as follows. Linguistic competence has been described in terms of speaker and hearer deploying prior and passing theories. So we need to consider each sort of theory in turn in an effort to determine whether deployment of either can be seen as deploying knowledge of linguistic conventions. On the one hand, the passing theory is ephemeral, focused on the interpretation of a specific utterance. Because it may be constructed to deal with quite exceptional uses of language, it is, by its very nature, unsuited to form a fixed body of linguistic knowledge. It thus cannot be construed as formulating knowledge of linguistic conventions. On the other hand, prior theories need not be, indeed usually are not, shared. Moreover, there is no requirement for there to be *any* shared element between prior theories in order for there to be successful communication. So shared prior theories cannot be essential to language, nor can shared components of such theories play any essential role. Additionally, it is wrong to conceive of prior theories as constituting a speaker's linguistic knowledge. A prior theory is *doubly* relative since each needs to be conceived as X's prior theory for interpreting/speaking to Y, for some X and Y. Thus the prior theory cannot be identified with any one speaker's idiolect. So neither prior nor passing theory characterizes a language that a speaker knows; nor does either characterize linguistic competence, which is better seen in terms of deploying a multitude of theories for different audiences and developing them to suit particular cases – that is, as the ability to construct convergent passing theories on the basis of one or another suitable prior theory. But, crucially, *that* ability cannot be reduced to knowledge of rules; rather, it is the product of wit, luck and wisdom, of our general capacities for theory-construction. Thus linguistic competence, the ability to use language to communicate successfully, is not knowledge of any system of rules.

What is, of course, startling and distinctive in Davidson's account is that it finds no place for conventionally established meanings in the account of the essence of communication. And our sense that malapropisms are exceptional (or necessarily exceptional) is probably linked closely to some sense that established meanings play (or must play) a large part in successful communication. Davidson does not however, deny the existence of linguistic conventions, or better, he does not deny the existence of shared regularities of linguistic usage; indeed, he insists on the importance and practical indispensability of such regularities in our day-to-day conversation. But for him these shared regularities simply render massively more convenient the business of interpreting our fellows. Given the existence of such regularities, we are able to construct prior theories that, in general, require little or no modification in arriving at passing theories. So, given the existence of these regularities, the process of interpretation is easy – indeed often effortless – and quick – as a flash. The regularities are thus only a practical necessity: we do not want every chat to your neighbour to become a task akin to the decipherment of Linear B.

8.2 A non-normative conception of meaning?

Davidson's account of linguistic meaning takes the process of interpretation to be paramount. Meanings, construed as rules for use, are entirely mythical; instead, meanings are simply an interpreter's theoretical posits used to explain a speaker's behaviour.

I shall argue that this view is mistaken, and mistaken by Davidsonian lights. What we should have learned from Davidson's earlier work on radical interpretation is that the interpretation of a term is intimately bound up with regularities of use for that expression. More accurately, a scheme of interpretation should be seen as grounded in a speaker's regular use of language. But interpretations are not just the constructs of radical interpreters and hearers; *speakers* are guided in their use by interpretations. In being guided by a scheme of interpretation a speaker *intends* to uphold patterns of use: those patterns that would ground the interpretative scheme. Because these patterns of use are objects of the speaker's intentions they are not *mere* regularities, but regularities to which she intends to accord, regularities to which she is bound by her linguistic intentions. Her use is thus subject to standards, in the absence of which it is mere babbling. So the argument is very simple. It depends on the radical interpreter to make plain the primacy of regularities of use and then uses the fact that interpreters (or hearers) are speakers too in order to show that these patterns of use acquire normative significance.

8.2.1 Radical interpretation and regularities

Let us begin fleshing out the argument with the following observations. Our sketch of Davidson's argument revealed the following as pivotal points. First there is the interplay between prior and passing theories in the business of interpretation. Secondly, there is the vanishing of a univocal theory of interpretation that encompasses a speaker's linguistic knowledge; this becomes fragmented into sets of abilities relativized to different audiences. We shall return to the structure of prior and passing theories soon but I want to pause to consider the second point first. It seems to me that it if we are unimpressed by the first phase of the attack, this final pass should not intimidate us. After all, any account will have to make sense of the phenomenon of speakers adapting their use of language to what they know about different conversational situations. If my knowledge of English enables me to negotiate most of my mundane linguistic commerce, there is no obvious difficulty in explaining how knowledge of particular conversational situations might cause me to adapt, to supplement or to select from that knowledge as required. So I want to put this point about fragmentation aside in what follows.

The startling conclusion that knowledge of linguistic norms is unnecessary for communication might well strike one as a blatantly obvious consequence of the methodology of radical interpretation. If a radical interpreter, by definition unversed in the conventions governing her target language, is able to arrive at successful interpretations, then knowledge of those conventions must be unnecessary for communication. So what does the intricacy of prior and passing theories add? And why is it only then that we learn of the redundancy of linguistic conventions? What is added, it turns out, is *precisely* the dropping of the methodology of radical interpretation and it is this that facilitates Davidson's rejection of convention. The radical interpreter has to construct her theory on the basis of evidence collected of sentences held true in given circumstances.

So the radical interpreter interprets on the basis of considerable knowledge of the regularities of use among speakers of the language – and these, note, are regularities of use whether or not we think of knowledge of them as amassed over time. In this sense her interpretation is made on the basis of access to regularities operative in speakers' use of the language. Because radical interpretation is thus based on regularities of use, one might thus claim that, although radical interpretation begins from a naivety about linguistic norms*,[3] what it achieves *is* knowledge of those norms*. So interpretation is inseparable from knowledge of the norms*; for the radical interpreter, history[4] is essential to the construction of meaning. But in Davidson's account of communication, radical interpretation simply drops away: there is no regularized method by which the interlocutors arrive at the right passing theories. Luck, wit and general knowledge combine to yield a workable theory on a given occasion; the theory need not be informed by knowledge of the regularities of use exhibited by one's interlocutor. As Davidson says, history gives way to intention in the construction of meaning.

If this is so, it raises questions about the status of radical interpretation. Elsewhere Davidson is unequivocal: meanings are open to public determination and what is meant by "publicly determinable" is determinable by the radical interpreter. As he says,

> A speaker who wishes his words to be understood cannot systematically deceive his would-be interpreters about when he assents to sentences – that is, holds them true. As a matter of principle, then, meaning, and by its connection with meaning, belief also, are open to public determination. I shall take advantage of this fact in what follows and adopt the stance of a radical interpreter when asking about the nature of belief. *What a fully informed interpreter could learn about what a speaker means is all there is to learn*; the same goes for what the speaker believes. (LePore 1986: 315, emphasis added)

Radical interpretation is thus important to Davidson not so much because it follows from an insistence on the publicity of meaning but because it is what he means by publicity: meanings are public because an external observer can access them by using a method based only on evidence plausibly available to her – that is, radical interpretation.

As Foster (1999) points out – eliciting agreement from Davidson – it is not enough for the interpreter to be in possession of a truth-theory that is interpretative – a T-theory – rather, the interpreter needs to know that she has a T-theory; she needs to know what the T-theory states and has to know this in a way that ensures she also knows that these are facts stated by a T-theory. As we saw, Foster's concern is then that there is no non-question-begging conception of this knowledge. Davidson's answer to Foster is that the interpreter needs to know the facts stated by the T-theory *by* implementing the method of radical interpretation. We need, I think, to take this seriously; what it is for the theory to be correct *is* for it to be a theory that would emerge from the process of radical interpretation.[5]

Now Davidson had claimed to have given us the essence of communication in his description of arriving at agreement in passing theories, and importantly there was no role for radical interpretation in that description: "importantly" because, as we saw, radical interpretation does not move us away from the idea that interpretation involves latching on to linguistic norms*. But what it is for a passing theory to be correct is explained in terms of radical interpretation; the passing theory is correct if it agrees with a theory that would emerge from applying the method of radical interpretation (to a sufficiently rich sample of speech). So a full account of communication needs to bring in radical interpretation and with it the notion of linguistic norms*. Linguistic norms* drop out of Davidson's scheme only because grasp of these norms* fails – in the cases he is interested in – to play a role in interpretation but, when successful, what the interpreter achieves is what would be achieved via grasp of the linguistic norms*.

The point is apt to be lost when one reads Davidson on communication because he simply assimilates successful communication to the case where a speaker is interpreted as she intended: that is, where the two passing theories converge. The effect of this is to make it seem, first, that radical interpretation is irrelevant, because, secondly, all that matters is agreement in interpretative schemes. This is, I think, mere illusion for a number of reasons. Being able to interpret a speaker (correctly or not) is not merely to have a truth-theory that applies to her words; one needs some grounds for supposing that the theory one wields is an interpretative theory, otherwise one would have no grounds for treating the theorems of the theory *as* interpretations. What it is for a theory to be interpretative now might be taken in two ways: (i) for it to be what would be produced by a process of radical interpretation; or (ii) for it to agree with the scheme intended by the speaker. I am arguing for the first conception, whereas it seems that Davidson is contenting himself with the second. The second without supplementation allows that meanings might fail to be public. In order to guarantee publicity we need to ensure that a legitimate scheme adopted by a speaker will always be one that a hearer can knowingly converge on. Nothing has been said on this score except that the scheme must be such that implementing the method of radical interpretation to a sufficiently rich sample of use would bring about convergence (at least at the level of theorems interpreting sentences).[6] Secondly, we have focused mainly on the hearer here but we should also bring in the speaker and her intentions. The speaker intends to have her words interpreted in a certain fashion. This intention is empty unless it feeds into her use of language since this is the only way she can affect how she will be interpreted. Thus the scheme she intends the hearer to use must, in some sense, guide her use. In other words, in intending to be interpreted according to a given scheme she must intend to use her words so that the radical interpreter can interpret her according to such a scheme. Thus interpretative success according to (i) and (ii) will coincide (unless the speaker fails in her linguistic intentions – see the next paragraph). Thus from either perspective the determinant of what counts as a correct interpretation will be that given by radical interpretation.

The alternative to this conception is a crude account that fails to discern an essential role for use of language. Although the speaker's use might fail to be guided by her passing theory – let us suppose there is a slip of the tongue – speaker and hearer might still succeed in communicating if the hearer chances on the right passing theory. Although in some sense speaker and hearer may have communicated in these circumstances, this is hardly what we want to think of as *linguistic* communication. To resolve the situation Davidson needs to amend the account so as to retain an essential link between use and interpretative scheme. This is just what the radical interpreter's methodology achieves and, if we think of correctness in interpretative scheme as that which radical interpretation *would* deliver, then the account of communication can borrow the link from the radical interpreter.

What we have discovered is that by Davidson's lights meaning that p by (uttering) s is to be radically interpretable as meaning that p by (uttering) s. And to be radically interpretable as meaning that p by uttering s it is necessary and sufficient that one exhibit (actually or potentially)[7] a regularity from a family of regularities of use. Note that we cannot say that there is just one particular regularity that is both necessary and sufficient for being so interpretable; rather, the regularity in the use of an expression has to be seen holistically in the context of the speaker's use of other expressions and interpreted in that light. When so interpreted, any of a number of regularities will legitimate a given scheme of interpretation. We shall probe the reasons for this in slightly more detail soon.

8.2.2 Regularities and norms

In one sense, then, using an expression with a certain meaning is a matter of adherence to norms* of use. But nothing we have so far managed to establish shows that this notion of norm* carries any genuine normative weight at all. Meaning that p in one's use of s is a matter of exhibiting (actually or potentially) a certain regularity of use, but there is no clear sense in which that regularity constitutes a *standard of correct use*. It might seem to do so because, if exhibiting one of a family of regularities *is* to mean that p (or is entailed by what it is to mean that p by s), then if one is to mean that p by s, then one ought to use s with one of the regularities of use. But this notion of *ought* is not the normative *ought* we were seeking. To see this, note that we might well say that if X is magnetic, then X ought to attract iron filings. And here it is quite clear that all we mean is that if X is magnetic, then X would attract iron filings. Similarly, all we might mean by using "ought" in the case of meaning is that if one means that p by s, then one will and would use s according to one of a number of regularities.

A speaker's use of an expression with a certain meaning is linked to her intentions so to use it; the behaviour of a magnetic body is not linked to its intentions so to behave. How does this alter matters? Well, according to Davidson, if X uses s to mean that p, then X intends her use of s to be (radically) interpretable as meaning that p.[8] So – because interpretation must be possible from the remove of a radical interpreter – fulfilment of X's intention requires satisfaction of a certain regularity of use. If fulfilment of X's intention to φ requires that X ψ, then I claim that if X has the intention to φ, X ought to ψ. Of course there are apparent counter-examples to this. On distinct grounds it may be the case that I ought not to ψ, or it may be the case that I ought not to φ, or both. Either or both of φ or ψ might be morally reprehensible or impolite or contravene some other norm. So the inference should be allowed to stand but understood so as to have established only *prima facie oughts* that might be trumped by other *oughts*. In the linguistic case we are considering it is hard to see how *in general* there might be *oughts* that play the role of trumping;[9] of course there would be, if the *oughts* dictated what one *says*, but they do not – they dictate what one *holds true*. It suffices anyway to have established a *prima facie* obligation. The inference, in this case, entails that if X intends her use of s to be interpretable as meaning that p, then X ought to adhere to a certain regularity of use. And thus, by logic alone, if X uses s to mean that p, then X ought to adhere to a certain regularity of use. Here the *ought* is genuinely normative because X can be criticized for failing to fulfil it; in so doing she is failing to do what needs to be done to fulfil her intention.

As I suggested, I think this introduces the requisite notion of normativity. We need, however, to do a little more work because we need to show that the *ought* we have managed to introduce is not simply the product of prudential desires the speaker might have, desires such as to succeed in communicating or to agree in one's use with one's fellows. If the intention we mentioned were a consequence of such a desire, then the normativity we would have discovered would be an unsurprising consequence of the nature of intention and these extraneous desires; the normativity would thus be accidental and not essential to linguistic use. It is quite clear, though, that the intention we have focused on is simply an intention that must accompany any meaningful use of language: if one uses a term with a certain meaning, then one must intend to be interpreted appropriately. This is a feature of Davidson's account of meaningful language use. Thus the normativity arises purely from what it is to make meaningful use of language. One communicates successfully when one is interpreted as one intends, so one's intention to communicate successfully is a second-order intention to be interpreted as one intends. It is the first-order intention to intend to be interpreted thus and so that is the intention we have been focusing on. It is an intention distinct from and prior to that of intending to communicate successfully. Thus the norm is a norm that is essential to meaningful language use – just what we had set out to discover.

Another concern is this. The *ought* that we have discovered is an *ought* that emerges from the business of practical reasoning. And it may seem that this *ought* is not sufficiently robust. What I want to resist is the idea that it is intelligible that X means that p by uttering s, yet it be the case that X does not attempt to conform her use to a certain regularity. And my problem is that in the general case of practical reasoning such failures seem all too intelligible. Consider the case of a medieval alchemist attempting to convert lead to gold. The change that the alchemist is attempting to bring about requires, so modern science tells us, physical action on the sample of lead. However, our alchemist – ignorant of the details of atomic theory – attempts to bring about the change using only chemical action. Her intention is completely intelligible despite the fact that she utterly fails to attempt to do what she ought to do: that is, what is required for fulfilment of the intention. If similar reasoning could be applied in the case of meaning, then the *ought* we would have discovered is simply too feeble. Fortunately I do not think the reasoning can be transferred. The reason is that the case of the alchemist depends on ignorance: the alchemist does not know what she ought to be doing. But in the linguistic case, attribution of similar ignorance undermines the attribution of the relevant intention to the speaker; one could not intend to mean that p by using s, were one ignorant of the use required to mean that p. For, to grasp the content of one's intention – a necessary condition for having the intention – one must understand what it is to mean that p. And one cannot understand this if one cannot appropriately *interpret* a speaker's use of an expression as that of using it to mean that p. So to have the appropriate intention the speaker must grasp the relevant facts about use. Ignorance cannot provide a reason for divorcing what the speaker ought to do from what she attempts to do. We thus bring in intention by focusing on the *speaker's* use of language and then relay that intention to an intention relating to a pattern of use by focusing on the speaker as *interpreter* in order to eliminate ignorance of the relation of meaning to use. Thus in the linguistic case the *ought* is one that requires the speaker to aim at conformity. Thus, to sum up, the form of the inference is:

1. X intends to mean that p by uttering s. (X's intentions as speaker)
2. Meaning that p by uttering s requires using s according to pattern r. (From radical interpretation)
3. X knows that meaning that p by uttering s requires using s according to pattern r. (From (1), given that X is also an interpreter)
4. Therefore X intends to use s according to pattern r.

To repeat, (3) is guaranteed by (1), given that the speaker is also an interpreter, since having that intention requires that one be able to interpret a use of s as meaning that p, which requires knowing the pattern r that would sustain this interpretation. And the form is an instance of the following scheme, which is a good principle of practical reason:[10]

1. X intends to φ.
2. φing requires ψing.
3. X knows that φing requires ψing.
4. Therefore X intends to ψ.

8.3 Norms and mistakes

Let me voice and then try to allay a worry that might seem pressing. The account I have presented has the following odd consequence. Meaning that p by s requires that one ought to fulfil a certain regularity of use, namely, that regularity which enables one to be radically interpreted as meaning that p. So one aims to use s according to a certain pattern of usage, but that pattern may include mistaken uses, since radical interpretation is based on a body of use that may include mistakes. So the odd consequence is this: in using s to mean that p one aims to use it according to a certain pattern that includes mistakes. Thus, in a sense, one aims at making mistakes, although, of course, the mistaken uses need not be described *as* mistakes. There is no getting away from it: the consequence appears odd indeed.

We need to consider the nature of the mistakes. The sort of mistake we are considering can be narrowed down to two cases: first, where the speaker's use is prompted by a false belief; and, secondly, to mere slips. In the former case there is a clear sense in which, from an objective point of view, the use is mistaken but, from her own epistemic position it is also clear that the speaker's use is a good one. She cannot aim at more than using the expression in such a way that, judged from the perspective of her beliefs, the use is correct. Of course she can learn that some of her beliefs are false and with this knowledge she can revise which sentences she holds true. In light of this general feature she can make the distinction between the way things seem to her and the way they are objectively. But she cannot aim directly to make her use cohere with the way things are objectively, rather than with how things seem to her. So she cannot aim at a correct pattern of use that goes beyond the correct pattern encapsulated in those patterns that include objective mistakes. What we must be able to do, however, is to make sense of the *notion* that some of the uses in the pattern being aimed at are objective mistakes. But, as we have said before, this may be possible, provided one can make sense of the notion of false belief. So we require an answer to Dummett's question reported at the close of Chapter 7.[11]

To put the point another way: when, in the light of new information, a speaker comes to correct a false belief, she will not take her previous use of language as having been incorrect or as having been spawned by a different understanding of her terms. Quite the reverse: she will acknowledge that, had she those beliefs now, she would make the same uses as she did then.

Let us turn now to slips. What we need to win through to here is a way of making the uses that emerge from slips irrelevant to those patterns of use that determine correctness. There are two ways of doing so – we contrasted them in discussing Davidson on malapropism.[12] There are two drawbacks with applying Davidson's strategy to slips. On such an account the word would, in effect, become ambiguous: Frank's term "table" would mean *cable* in its slippage use but *table* in most other uses. The first problem is that the tactic of treating the word as ambiguous means that we have to suppose that a word, as used in the context of a slip, gains a whole set of systematically related uses spawned by its interpretation in the slip. Such uses will be a consequence of the word's systematic relations with other words under its given interpretation. But it is thoroughly implausible to suppose that in making a slip a speaker acquires a propensity to make all these other uses. Slips are by their very nature exceptional. Secondly, the tactic of attributing ambiguity is dangerous. If the gambit of ambiguity is available in these cases, why not consider a word to display as rich a manifold of ambiguities as is required to make all uses of it count as correct? There need to be much tighter constraints on when attribution of ambiguity is legitimate.[13]

Another way of making these uses irrelevant is the second option we canvassed earlier. We can simply say – to be sure most likely in the light of having interpreted the word – that in such cases the speaker intended to use a different word and then interpret the utterance according to the interpretation of the word she intended to use.[14] The mistake would then be in failing to realize one's linguistic intentions but, in the light of one's meanings, there would be no fault in one's intentions.

For our purposes we do not need to resolve this debate here. If we adopt the Davidsonian view, then the slip is incorporated as an ambiguity, and if we have stomach enough for that claim, then there is nothing untoward in factoring in the relevant sets of use as those that the speaker intends to uphold. On the second view the slip is dismissed from those uses involved in interpretation. So it does not figure in the uses a speaker intends to uphold.

We have not mentioned idiosyncratic (mis-)understandings since these precisely will alter how the speaker is to be interpreted. Such uses are not to be regarded as mistakes from the perspective of the interpreter – whose perspective thus differs from that of the schoolteacher.

The conclusion I have been urging is this. Davidson's conception of meaning necessarily involves a conception of patterns of use that constitute standards of (subjectively) correct use. So conceived, the machineries of radical interpretation, interpretative schemes and intendings to be interpreted combine in elucidating a normative conception of meaning that is at odds with Davidson's stated position. That it emerges unbidden from fundamentals of the Davidsonian position is a consequence of two mistaken aspects of Davidson's thinking. The first, as I have mentioned before, is his wont to ignore the basic role performed by the radical interpreter when he turns to look at the business of communication. This allows him to ignore history or practice (actual and potential) in favour of intention in the construction of meaning. The second is his claim that the *oughts* that accompany our use of language are all external and can be accounted for in terms of prevalent but inessential intentions accompanying our use of language – such as the intention to communicate successfully or to cohere in one's use with that of others. This is false. Once we think of ourselves not merely as interpreters but as speakers of language, it becomes clear that the regularities – now seen to be necessary by reinstating the position of the radical interpreter – are the objects of our linguistic intentions. Not only is language use necessarily intention involving, but some intentions are necessarily involved in the use of language and some of the latter intentions are directed to conforming one's use to certain regularities and thus, merely as a speaker of language, one aims to uphold a pattern of use. The upshot is a picture of speakers binding their own use of language; we need to conceive of speakers as rule-followers.

It is worth noting and speculating on just how this picture involves history, or at least practice. First, as already mentioned, the intentions involved in meaningful use of language are intentions to uphold a pattern of use. Secondly, and more speculatively, Davidson often plays down the role of history and practice because he supposes that every case of linguistic communication might be modelled on what occurs when malapropism is involved. That is, each linguistic exchange might involve fresh linguistic intentions that are peculiar to that particular exchange.[15] However, it is dubiously coherent to suppose that a speaker might have intentions to uphold patterns of use, none of which survives into other exchanges, none of which is therefore ever acted on. Of course there might be cases, indeed many cases, where this occurs; but it wants powerful argument to show that the phenomenon might be pervasive, and that we have not had.

Finally, whether it is coherent to think that speakers bind their own use without some help from their community and, if it must be seen in terms of a community, quite how conventional the binding thereby becomes are weighty matters that cannot fully be tackled here. However, it is worth noting that Davidson himself has his doubts about the ability of a speaker to hold herself to account (see e.g. Davidson 2001b: essays 8, 14).

8.4 A generalization of the argument?

Although the argument focuses on the details of Davidson's philosophy and aims at a parochial conclusion – that is, that elements of that philosophy do not cohere – I think there is a more general conclusion in the offing. The argument proceeds by establishing two claims: first, that meaning something by an expression must be seen in terms of sustaining (even if only potentially) a pattern of use; secondly, that a speaker intending to mean something by an expression must intend to sustain a pattern of use of which she is, in some sense, apprised. Our route to the first claim was via the role of the radical interpreter. And our route to the second claim hinged on thinking of speakers as using terms intending to mean such-and-such and as knowing the link between that meaning and the relevant use (the latter because speakers are interpreters too). The peculiarly Davidsonian element in the argument is thus the appeal to the radical interpreter. However, the radical interpreter is, as we remarked, Davidson's way of ensuring the publicity of meaning and what it secures is the role of history and practice in the construction of meaning. But *any* conception of the publicity of meaning will make use essential to meaning something by a term. Where one conception will differ from another is in how it conceives of use and (thus) to whom meanings are viewed as publicly available. On the Davidsonian scheme, use is seen in terms of holding sentences true in a variety of publicly available circumstances. And this gives rise to a particular conception of linguistic norms. But we can change our conception of the publicity of meaning, argue for a link between meaning something and sustaining a use (construed in some appropriate fashion) and then feed that into the second phase of the argument. Thus it seems that any conception of meanings as public will give rise to a corresponding conception of linguistic norms. Well, so it *seems*; we cannot quite endorse the argument in this abstract form because we would need a supplement that varies from one case to another. Just as we supplemented the argument here with an attempt to validate the norms we had discovered as coherent and plausible norms, we would need to supply a supplement in these other cases. So, at present, we do not have a fully general argument for linguistic norms; rather, we would need to develop a sustained argument for each proposed conception of publicity. But there is little reason to think that this would not be possible and probably good reason for thinking that a conception of publicity for which this task proved impossible would not be plausible.

Our task in the next chapter aligns with that in this: once again we are interested in the notion of linguistic norms, that is, of *oughts* governing usage. The obvious differences are these. Here we have used publicity to motivate the idea that to mean something by a term will be a matter of sustaining a use and we then focused linguistic intentions on that use. In Chapter 9 we begin from a conception of meaning as involving correctness-conditions. We shall then consider how correctness-conditions figure in practical reasoning in a way that delivers linguistic *oughts*. On the one hand the task seems easier because, unlike here, we begin from a normative conception of meaning. But on the other it seems harder because we lack the link between meaning and a sustained use. However, these differences are not as stark as they seem because the normative conception is allowed to be very minimal indeed; for instance, the correctness-condition of a predicate may be given simply by the fact that it applies to some objects and not to others. What will do our work for us is just the fact that correctness-conditions, through being swept up in practical reasoning, are thereby held to be conditions of which speakers are apprised and that thereby connect with use of an expression or, better, intentions to use an expression. So whereas in this chapter we worked to establish these facts by appeal to the radical interpreter (in effect, to publicity) and to the dual roles of speaker and interpreter, in Chapter 9 we shall begin largely from these facts as given in some minimal sense. We then attempt to derive and justify certain norms. Thus it *may*[16] be possible to see Chapter 9 as arguing for the supplement, mentioned in the previous paragraph, for a *minimal* conception of the linguistic situation. As it happens, the norms we reveal are likely to be of little interest to the philosopher of language attempting to explain meaning in terms of norms; one might say that they are minimal norms. But this is not the important point at this stage of the debate. The question before us is whether we should think of the use of language as being an essentially normative phenomenon and, if the arguments of this chapter and Chapter 9 are sound, the answer to this question is yes.

9. Linguistic normativity

9.1 Norms and prescriptions

Linguistic items are meaningful and most of our uses of them are meaningful too. In order for this to be the case, language is bound by a set of correctness-conditions according to which uses of language can be categorized as either correct or incorrect – that is, there are linguistic rules – or so it is at least plausible to suppose. Our question now is not whether or not language is meaningful and normative in this sense but whether those correctness-conditions normatively bind *speakers' use* of language: does this normativity of language entail the normativity of linguistic usage? Ought speakers of a language to abide by its correctness-conditions? Do linguistic rules entail linguistic norms, or, more pithily, do linguistic rules rule? I shall argue that provided we focus on the appropriate correctness-conditions – correctness-conditions framed at the level of sense rather than that of reference – these do indeed deliver *oughts* governing use.

The question before us is not whether this or that conception of meaning is committed to the normativity of language use, but whether any account of meaning should be so committed; or rather, whether any account that links meaning with correctness-conditions is so committed. We shall also make very few assumptions about how correctness-conditions are to be conceived; these may simply be application conditions of a predicate or denotation conditions for a name. Thus, in effect, we shall be asking whether *any* theory of meaning should be committed to the normativity of language use. I shall call anyone who believes this – that is, who believes that correctness-conditions bind use by yielding *oughts* – a "prescriptivist".

Both Paul Boghossian (2005) and Anandi Hattiangadi (2006)[1] have recently attacked prescriptivism by denying the inference from correctness-conditions to *oughts* governing use. Their arguments are similar. Each concedes that there is a correctness-condition for, say, the English word "hadeda"[2] that entails that "hadeda" is correctly applied to an object only if it is a variety of large dirty-grey ibis with a wont to screech annoyingly. But each argues that this imposes no obligations on speakers who use the word "hadeda" to mean *hadeda*. The nub of the problem is that the correctness-condition that "hadeda" applies correctly only to hadedas incurs an obligation on speakers' use of language only if we suppose that speakers are using language with desires and intentions that transcend the mere intention to use a word with a particular meaning. For instance, we might think that such a speaker is obliged to use the term "hadeda" to apply to hadedas; but this is false since she might well use the term to mean *hadeda* but apply it (incorrectly) to an egret in an attempt, say, to deceive or to be funny. Thus we generate the obligation, the *ought*, only if we suppose, in addition, that the speaker intends to speak truly. But this is to ascribe an intention that is extraneous to meaningful use of language and generates a hypothetical, not a categorical, obligation. Boghossian writes:

> Of course, we can say that, if you mean addition by "+" and have a desire to tell the truth, then, if you are asked what the sum of [68 and 57] is, you should say "125." But that is mere hypothetical normativity, and that is uninteresting: every fact is normative in that sense. (Compare: if it's raining, and you don't want to get wet, you should take your umbrella.) (2005: 207)

Given the right set of background conditions – in terms of wants and intentions and in terms of the way the world is – then one can construe any fact as yielding, via practical reasoning, a corresponding *ought*. No doubt that is true. However, the observation does not suffice to render all hypothetical *oughts* uninteresting. Provided we can fix a restriction on the background conditions, then it may well be the case that facts about correctness yield *oughts* that are indeed interesting. If, for instance, it follows from those intentions that are intrinsic to speaking a language that conditions of correctness yield *oughts*, then this should not be dismissed; that was one of the lessons that Chapter 8 aimed to teach. To suppose that the prescriptivist needs to conjure *oughts* that are more substantial than this is simply to attack a straw man; in this sense it would be crazy to argue that one ought to apply "hadeda" to hadedas. Why should this *ought* engage speakers of Malagasy?

Alex Miller seems to make this mistake. In considering whether a norm entails any obligations he writes:

> The reason why it does not follow [that one ought to do such and such] is that it is not enough that [the norm] (N*) is "in force". We also require some additional consideration which implies that (N*) expresses a norm that we ought to subscribe to: a requirement that in this case is plainly not satisfied. (Forthcoming: 9)

We do not need to support the *ought* derived from a norm by a claim that we ought to subscribe to the norm. Such a position threatens a regress – at least if *oughts* go along with norms – but, more importantly, it is blatantly false. Having missed my two serves I ought to concede the point to my opponent. Why? Because it is correct to do so when playing tennis and I am playing tennis. Ought I to be playing tennis? The question is absurd in many circumstances and anyway irrelevant to the question of who ought to get the point.[3] So the question is not whether one *ought* to subscribe to the norm but whether one *does* subscribe to it. In the linguistic case, it is surely absurd to suggest that one ought to speak English, say. Perhaps one ought, if one wishes to converse with friends and family, but then, rightly, that will be dismissed as a hypothetical *ought* arising out of extraneous desires. The question though is whether, *qua* speaker of English, the correctness-conditions of that language deliver any *oughts*.

Hattiangadi spends rather more time on the point. First, contrasting prescriptivity with mere endorsement of the normativity of language, she argues:

> according to Prescriptivity, a speaker who means something by a term ought to apply it correctly, where "applies correctly" stands in for "refers to", "is true of", "denotes", and so forth. Thus, Prescriptivity makes it a necessary condition of meaning something by a term that a speaker ought to speak the truth. But this requirement is too strong to be a purely semantic requirement. It implies that on occasions when someone ought not to tell the truth, she does not mean what she ordinarily means by her terms. (2006: 227)

That seems right: it is no part of meaning something by one's terms that one ought to use them to speak truly. Hattiangadi then considers the weaker claim that the prescriptivity of language emerges not from an *ought* governing speaking truly but from a desire to speak the truth. She then writes as follows:

> Hypothetical means/end prescriptions are conditional prescriptions in which the consequent and antecedent bear a relationship of means to end. An example of an ordinary hypothetical means/end prescription is this: "If you want to get from Oxford to Cambridge by noon, you ought to take an early morning train". Taking an early morning train is a means of getting from Oxford to Cambridge by noon. A categorical prescription, in contrast, is not contingent on an end. This distinction is not just about form: categorical prescriptions can have a conditional structure so long as the antecedent and consequent are not related as end to means. Hence, "If you are a moral agent, you ought to aim to maximise happiness" is a categorical prescription: aiming to maximise happiness is not a means to being a moral agent; it is a condition of your being one.

> The distinction between categorical and hypothetical "ought"s is difficult to draw. Nevertheless, the distinction is decisive, since many hypothetical "ought"s pose no difficulty for naturalism. The reason is that on our usual, normative interpretation of "ought", hypothetical "ought"-statements seem to be plainly false. How can it be that some-one's desire or intention to do something makes it the case that she ought to do it? It is clearly not the case that just because George W. Bush wants or intends to invade Iraq, he ought to do so. Hence, as R. M. Hare suggested, the force of many hypothetical "ought"-statements must be descriptive, rather than prescriptive. …Thus, it is important that the "oughts" foisted on the naturalist are not hypothetical oughts, and thus descriptive.
> (*Ibid.*: 228)

Hattiangadi's points are as follows: (i) true hypothetical *oughts* relate the ante-cedent to consequent as means to end; (ii) such hypothetical *oughts* should be treated merely descriptively, as saying that a way (or perhaps, more strongly, the only or the most effective way) of achieving the end is to do the action spelled out in the consequent; and (iii) *oughts* framed in terms of conditionals where the consequent is not related to the antecedent as means to end are not true hypothetical conditionals. I think all these points are good but they do not quite support Hattiangadi's conclusion that "[i]f meaning is normative … then the fact that an agent means something by an expression must amount to the fact that she ought to use the expression in accordance with its meaning *quite independently of what she wants to do*" (*ibid.*, emphasis added). What we cannot allow, to be sure, is the following to count as genuine normativity:

(1) S means F by s → (if S intends to φ then S ought to use s thus and so)

The reason is that the *ought* here is contingent on S's possession of the inten-tion to φ and, it seems, that using s thus and so would just be a way to achieve, or a requirement on achieving, φ; the *ought* drops out in favour of something merely descriptive. If, on the other hand, S's intention to φ was constitutive of her meaning F by s, then, *given this fact*, we could dispense with the bracketed conditional and have

(2) S means F by s → (S ought to use s thus and so)

All of this should be granted. However, it does not follow that the *ought* should be independent of what the speaker wants or intends, for the content of the ought might perfectly legitimately include wants and/or intentions. In other words we might have something of this form:

(3) S means F by s → (S ought (to use s thus and so, if S intends to φ))

or (4) *S* means *F* by *s* → (*S* ought (to use *s* thus and so, only if S intends to
φ))[4]

Now what we would require is a filling out of the bracketed statement in the
consequent that is related to the antecedent other than as means to end.

The prescriptivist thus might respond to the objection in the following ways:
(i) she might settle for something of the form of (2) but argue that such intentions as the intention to speak truly are not extraneous to meaningful language
use; or (ii) she might accept the argument that one derives hypothetical *oughts*
only from norms taking the form of (2) but then offer an alternative conception
of norms taking the form of either (3) or (4). I shall accept that the first strategy
fails since it will inevitably have to appeal to extraneous intentions such as the
intention to speak truly. So I want to investigate the second strategy.

9.2 Correctness-conditions, practical reasoning and norms

The problem for the prescriptivist seems to arise in this way. The correctness-
condition is formulated in terms of the application of a term to worldly items.
We then note that this generates an obligation on the speaker's use of language
only if she intends to achieve a certain sort of semantic success, for example,
speaking truly. However, this sort of semantic success transcends any intention we have a right to ascribe as part of speaking meaningfully. So the fault is
that a correctness-condition formulated in terms of semantic success generates
an obligation that itself entails semantic success and that is thus thoroughly
implausible, unless we supplement the account by attributing an intention to
achieve this level of semantic success. But so doing converts the obligation into
a merely hypothetical obligation or implausibly requires that we factor such an
intention into those intentions intrinsic to meaningful language use. The solution might thus be to tone down the nature of the correctness-condition from
one involving semantic success to one involving semantic purport.[5] To put the
matter differently, we might say that the fault we have discovered arises from
formulating the correctness-conditions at the level of reference. If instead we
formulate the correctness-condition at the level of sense, we may develop a corresponding obligation that is sustained purely by one's intentions, as a speaker
of the language, to mean something by one's use of language. The aim would
thus be to discover an obligation that would be incurred no less in cases of lying,
deceit, irony and the like than in cases of straightforward truth-telling. How
would we fill in such a story?

My aim is simply to uncover *an* obligation on speakers' use of language that
accrues through a plausible correctness-condition on language. That aim will be
achieved if I can spell out the outlines of an account for any sort of expression
in language. So I can choose to look at sentences.[6]

To adapt Hattiangadi's (2006) account to sentences we would have something like the following, first at the level of reference:

Correctness$_R$: In c, S means that F by $s \rightarrow$ (S asserts s correctly in c only if F)[7]

And that correctness-condition generates the implausible obligation:

Prescriptivity$_R$: In c, S means that F by $s \rightarrow$ (S ought (to assert s in c only if F)).

But now consider this correctness-condition, framed at the level of sense:

Correctness$_S$: In c, S means that F by $s \rightarrow$ (S asserts s correctly in c only if S intends to assert that F)

And this generates the obligation:

Prescriptivity$_S$: In c, S means that F by $s \rightarrow$ (S ought (to assert s in c only if S intends to assert that F))[8]

The manner of generating the prescription from the correctness-condition is worth comment. *Prescriptivity* is, in each case, generated from *Correctness* by assuming that S ought to do what is correct. But the failure of the transition from *Correctness$_R$* to *Prescriptivity$_R$* shows that this principle is not, in general, valid. What we are looking for is versions of *Correctness* and *Prescriptivity* that are independently plausible. If they have the right relation to one another, then this fact justifies the view that, in this instance, S ought to do what is correct. Such is the claim with *Correctness$_S$* and *Prescriptivity$_S$*. I shall look at the plausibility of these claims in due course. But first there is another, rather different route to *Precriptivity$_S$*, which itself aids my claim about its plausibility.

Glüer and Pagin (1998: 218), although hostile to the notion of linguistic norms, offer a careful examination of the way in which such norms might engage with practical reasoning and, in so doing, help my explanation of *Prescriptivity$_S$*. How the norm engages will, of course, depend on how it is conceived. We are concerned here with what might be called constitutive – since not means–end-related – rules or norms and Glüer and Pagin consider two such conceptions: the "counts as" version of constitutive rules (which they discover in Midgley's and Searle's writings); and the conception of such rules as being "in force". The first account will not be significant to our discussion since both they and I regard the second conception as more plausible. So let us move directly to that account.

Glüer and Pagin recommend seeing constitutive rules as rules that must be "in force" for practitioners if a certain practice is to be possible. Arguably correctness-conditions for linguistic terms function in just this fashion. So rationalizing one's use of language, one might have (cf. Glüer & Pagin 1998: 224):

(PA′)   I intend to say that *F*.

(R′)   Saying *s* is correct iff *F*.

(PA″) So, I intend to say *s*.

Note that here the function of (R′) is insensitive to one's intent to speak truly;[9] indeed, we could (as Glüer and Pagin suggest) replace (R′) with the premise (M) to get:

(PA′)   I intend to say that *F*.

(M)   *s* means that *F*

(PA″) So, I intend to say *s*.

And from this they infer that even if meaning is *established* by rules for correct use, it is meaning rather than those rules that *guide* use. They conclude: "Some rules [those recently described] can be regarded as determining meaning ... but they cannot be said to guide speakers in ordinary usage" (*ibid.*). So we do not have an *ought* that actively governs speakers' use. This conclusion is both premature and lacks motivation.

Let us just be clear about the status of the practical inference. The inference renders one's intention to say *s* reasonable. It does not obligate it because there may be other sentences with that same meaning and, indeed, other sentences that may be more apt to use on this occasion. But, given (M) (or (R′)), one ought to fulfil the intention in (PA″) only if (PA′) holds; since otherwise one will be acting to fulfil an intention that one does not have.[10] Of course, it may well be the case that one ought not to fulfil either or both of the intentions in (PA′) and (PA″); either might, for instance, be morally reprehensible or impolite. So the practical inference establishes a *prima facie ought* captured in:

If (M) then I ought [to say *s* only if (PA′)]

And that is just a rewriting of *Prescriptivity*$_S$. So *Prescriptivity*$_S$ can be derived without having to invoke *Correctness*$_S$; in effect we assume no more than *Correctness*$_R$. In addition, we do not make the questionable assumption that speakers ought to do what is correct; as I hinted previously, that assumption seems to apply in this case *because* the correctness-condition and its associated prescription are independently plausible.

Does this derivation of the prescription bring the normative theorist to endorse prescriptivism? Although I think it does, more needs to be said. What the believer in mere normativity will say is that here we simply have a case of practical reasoning based on meaning-facts; other facts are normative in this sense too, as follows:

(PA*)   I intend to φ.

(F*)   ψing is an (efficient) way of φing.[11]

(PA**) I intend to ψ.

This then yields the (*prima facie*) prescription:

If (F*), then I ought [to ψ only if (PA*)].

But although this is all true, there is, to my mind, this crucial difference. Let us call the first inference linguistic practical reasoning (LPR) and the second practical reasoning (PR). An essential feature of PR is that its second premise relates the action one intends to perform to something else: either an efficient means of performing it or to something that counts as doing it, depending on the nature of the case. Nothing like this occurs in LPR.[12] The analogous premise here assigns a content to a linguistic item. What then sustains the practical inference in the linguistic case are particular features about the structure of locutionary (or perhaps phatic) and illocutionary (or perhaps rhetic)[13] acts – acts of saying and of saying that – determined in turn by the structure of linguistic meanings. So the *ought* that is developed is not merely one that parallels the involvement of just any fact in practical reasoning; no, it is one that depends on the special properties of meanings. Thus the reasoning in LPR cannot be reduced to anything of the form PR. So, although any fact can potentially be associated via practical reasoning with a range of *oughts*, meaning-facts have a distinctive relation to the *oughts* they are associated with. Glüer and Pagin's point would hold if it were the case that the meaning-fact plays a role in practical reasoning that resembles any other (non-normative) fact. But this has not been shown. Quite the reverse: it appears that meaning-facts are swept up in practical reasoning in a manner delivering *prima facie oughts* that is quite distinctive. It may well be that correctness-conditions of the form (R′) do not feature significantly in practical reasoning governing speakers' use of language, but they do deliver *oughts*, which are embedded in practical reasoning, and they do so in a distinctive fashion. In that sense meanings essentially have a distinctive range of normative *consequences*[14] and so meaning might be said to be essentially and distinctively normative.[15]

9.3 Non-literal uses of language

We need, however, to justify *Prescriptivity$_S$* as being both a plausible and a substantial prescription. Those tasks will, respectively, be the business of this and the next section.

The notion of assertion used in the prescription is not that of sincere assertion. So when I lie in saying that you are in full remission from your terminal illness I still assert (although falsely) that you are in full remission from your terminal illness. Thus the obligation applies and is complied with in cases of lying.

A more taxing problem concerns non-literal uses of a sentence, *s*. Our norm states that if *s* means that *F*, then one ought only to assert *s* if one intends to assert that *F*. However, if an assertion can be non-literal then one may well assert the sentence without intending to assert the content. So here it seems that one flouts the norm and, I would argue, does so problematically, since we need an account that allows for non-literal uses of language rather than one that dismisses these as *mis*uses. Ideally what we want here is a solution that does not commit us heavily to a particular approach to non-literal uses of language. However, my hunch is that it is impossible to have a view about the nature of linguistic prescriptions that does not depend on a particular way of understanding non-literal uses of language. The reason is that such uses press our conception of linguistic prescriptions to the limit and so the nature of the prescriptions that we hang on to will depend on how we construe the non-literal uses. We can, however, make some progress on behalf of the prescriptivist, provided that we ensure that prescriptions survive any plausible treatment of non-literal uses of language, even though the precise nature of the prescriptions will vary depending on how one conceives of the non-literal. We can divide treatments of the non-literal into two camps: those who treat the meaning of a sentence used non-literally as differing from its literal meaning – meaning-shifters[16] – and those who treat the meaning of sentences used non-literally as identical with the literal meaning – meaning-retainers.[17]

Let us consider the meaning-shifters first. We had conceded that non-literal uses of language counter-exemplify my proposed prescription precisely because here we have an assertion of a sentence *s*, *whose content does not change*, but whose speaker does not intend to assert that *F*. Without the emphasized qualification, which a meaning-shifter will precisely not grant, it is difficult to see how the counter-example would worry the proposed prescription. So, on the meaning-shifting proposal, we have no counter-example to deal with.

Now consider meaning-retainers. Here undoubtedly we do have a counter-example; however, I think that the prescription can be revised adequately. Consider the following:

Prescriptivity$_S$*: In *c*, *S* means that *F* by *s* → (*S* ought (to say *s* in *c* only if *S* intends to say that *F*))

Here I am using "say" as meaning simply to utter – so saying s is, in Austin's terminology, a merely phatic act – and "say that" is performing an act with a certain content (here, that F) but one that does not involve asserting that content – *saying that* is thus a rhetic act, in Austin's terminology.[18] In asserting s, I may well be both saying that F and asserting that F; and, in addition, I also say that F in asserting that F. Now because *saying that* is, as it were, *merely* a rhetic act, accomplished merely by uttering a sentence with a given meaning, and since, on the meaning-retainer's proposal the meaning of the sentence does not change, the relevant rhetic act must be involved in the non-literal use of s. Thus we have no counter-example on the revised conception of the prescription.[19] So, to sum up, either the meaning of the sentence changes in the non-literal case, in which case the original prescription stands, or it does not, in which case the speaker intends to take up the attitude of *saying that* towards the original content and the revised prescription holds.

9.4 Are the norms substantial?

What needs more attention is the nature of the proposed prescriptions. Is the prescription close to what a prescriptivist might have hoped to reveal? Part of the answer to this question lies in the manner in which the prescription engages with different cases: cases such as deceit and non-literal uses of language. We have discussed those above. But, assuming that discussion was cogent, we should now ask whether the prescription is substantive. It might seem that the *ought* is indeed redundant; for does it not follow merely from the fact that S means that F by s that S asserts s only if S intends to assert that F? I do not think it does. Consider slips of the tongue. S might mean that the cable is on the table by "the cable is on the table" and that the table is on the cable by "the table is on the cable", but, intending to assert that the cable is on the table, S might mistakenly utter, "the table is on the cable". S *ought not* to have done so, but that is what S did. So the obligation developed is not trivial. Moreover, if we were to derive *oughts* in the form "(S intends to speak L) & (In L and c, s means that F) → (S ought (to assert s in c only if S intends to assert that F, in c))" (see note 4) then the norms would count against idiosyncratic understandings that diverge from commonly accepted meanings. The norm we develop is thus a substantial norm that engages with what we might call performance errors – slips and idiosyncratic (mis)understandings.

A further question is whether we should include intentional in addition to performance errors. Let it be the case then that S means that F by s. Now what we want is for someone to flout the relevant prescription and this she might do either by making an inappropriate utterance or by forming an inappropriate intention. The former gives rise to performance errors; the latter, potentially, to a variety of deliberate errors. But cases are going to be rare because it is hard to imagine someone meaning that *F* by *s* but who intends not to use *s* to say that *F*. Compare with Wittgenstein's example of saying "It's cold here" and deliberately meaning "It's warm here" (1958: §510). But cases are (just) imaginable. Take Humpty Dumpty's assertion that "glory" means *a nice knock-down argument*. Humpty Dumpty's confidence here is built on a false theory of meaning: "'When *I* use a word,' Humpty Dumpty said, in rather a scornful tone, 'it means just what I choose it to mean – neither more nor less'" (Carroll 1982: 184). Dumpty may well intend "glory" to mean *a nice knock-down argument* but intending that it be so does not make it so; Dumpty mistakes the relation between meanings and intentions. So we have:

Dumpty means that there's glory by "There's glory" → (Dumpty ought (to say "There's glory" only if Dumpty intends to say that there's glory))

Although the antecedent is true (*contra* Dumpty's theory of meaning and his intentions), Dumpty flouts the *ought* since he says "There's glory" but intends only to say that there is a nice knock-down argument. Although it may smack of desperation to elicit the support of a fictional character from an absurd tale, it is worth noting that Alice initially and justifiably reprimands Dumpty for misusing language – "But 'glory' doesn't mean 'a nice knock-down argument', Alice objected" (*ibid.*) – and, more importantly, *readers'* reactions will jibe with Alice's; in fact, she weakens her case by engaging with Dumpty's view of meanings. Dumpty clearly does not intend to flout the prescriptions that govern his use of language; rather, labouring under a false belief about what those prescriptions are, he intentionally flouts what are his language's actual prescriptions. Under these circumstances we could construct other examples. Another set of examples may well, depending on one's view of things, arise from speakers who intentionally "misuse" their words in order to compensate for idiosyncrasies or inadequacies in their hearers' understanding – for example, the speaker who means that there's glory by "there's glory" but who uses it with the intention of saying that there is a nice knockdown argument because she is talking to Humpty Dumpty. My conclusion thus is that the prescription is both substantive – it admits of performance and (some) intentional errors – and has no counter-examples.

Of course the linguistic obligation that we have discovered is stated in contentful terms: one ought to use a sentence only in order to assert *that* such and such. So the notion of use is much richer than that of simply applying a term to an object or set of objects; it necessarily conceives of use in the context of a speaker's intentions in relation to certain contents. The norms for use are thus norms that cannot be used to *explain* content. But whether or not we are intending to elaborate norms for use as part of that explanatory enterprise is a further question. McDowell, who advocates the normativity of language *use*, but rejects an account of that use in content-free terms, is an example of a prescriptivist who *could* simply accept the present account (see McDowell 1976, 1981, 1987, 1997). Other prescriptivists might want to find more informative norms of use underlying the ones we have uncovered. The main point, however, is that this is not a question that we need to face now. The aim was simply to uncover norms for use from the normativity of language and that we seem to have done – no matter whether or not they serve other explanatory interests.

Our focus in the next four chapters is the notion of the publicity of meaning. We begin by questioning whether radical interpretation is the right way to conceive of publicity and then attempt to formulate and argue for an alternative conception. What we take to this discussion is the findings of the last two chapters, namely, the discovery that meaning is essentially normative.

10. Radical or robust?

10.1 The mysteriousness of language

I have argued that radical interpretation is an essential ingredient in Davidson's framework for three reasons. The first is that the broadly extensionalist approach of the radical interpreter promises to shed light on the intensionality of language. The point is worth reprising in the context of Dummett's (1993: essay 1) discussion of Davidson. Recall that, at a certain stage, Dummett complains about the triviality of a Davidsonian meaning-theory, which he takes to be modest and thus philosophically no more interesting than a translation manual. The complaint is surely just if you view a Davidsonian meaning-theory simply as the interpretative scheme given by the T-theory. But, as Dummett comes to realize, the complaint seems to miss its mark. Davidson hopes for philosophical illumination not simply from the T-theory but from the T-theory *given its mode of construction*, that is, given that it is the product of radical interpretation. When we look at things from this angle, the triviality of a homophonic T-theory is likely to be welcomed – given its clear correctness – as confirming the methodology of radical interpretation. Whether Dummett is right to factor in the import of the radical interpreter's methods in quite the way that he does – by making the precise set of sentences held true part of what the interpreter knows in knowing how to interpret speakers – is a question we can side-step for now; the fact remains that it is only when we wed a T-theory to the fact that it is the product of radical interpretation that Davidson manages to shed light on meaning.

The second reason is that radical interpretation is the embodiment of an insistence on the publicity of meaning. This reason links closely with the third reason, namely, that the theoretical account of radical interpretation defines what it is for a scheme of interpretation to be correct. For, since meanings are public, they are accessible to the radical interpreter, whose method is thus guaranteed to give definitive results.

155

Thus three important roles are performed by the notion of the radical interpreter, roles that should survive her demise. Any account of meaning should explain the publicity of meaning;[1] should be able to justify the correctness of a proposed account; and should be illuminating. Whether radical interpretation is well motivated depends on whether there are alternative approaches that promise also to satisfy these requirements. Let us begin with an alternative conception of illumination.

There appears to be no need for us to pretend to divest ourselves of our linguistic competence in order to understand how language works; rather, we might well exploit that competence in constructing an account that is genuinely informative or, as Dummett says, we want a robust, not a modest, account. But what might we require of "a genuinely informative" account? Dummett's thought is this. We want an account that details, in terms that do not presuppose grasp of our target language, what one needs to know in order to understand the language. Let us illustrate the point by relating it to Davidson. Let us say that the following is a correct account of what someone knows when she knows the meaning of "Yellingup": S knows that "Yellingup" refers to Yellingup. The problem, as Dummett sometimes portrays it, is that this account of S's knowledge uses the term "Yellingup" in the specification of the content of that knowledge. So, if I am to glean an understanding of what S knows, I need already to grasp the concept of Yellingup. Dummett's thought is thus that we need to specify not merely what it is that S knows; we need to explain what it is for S to have this knowledge; we need to be able to explain what S is able to do as a consequence of having this knowledge. One might conceive of this – as Dummett often suggests – in terms of giving an account that even a Martian could use as a way of understanding the language, provided, of course, that the Martian understood the language of the theory. The Martian shares the external perspective on language of the radical interpreter, but unlike the latter she is charged not with constructing a theory of meaning but just with being able to use one when it is presented to her.

However, there are problems with viewing the project in these terms. First, it may be possible to give an account of what someone who knows something is able to do without thereby possessing the knowledge oneself – without, that is, being able to do what they can do. As Price (2004) points out, it may well be that what the speaker is able to do depends on possessing sensory powers that we do not have – imagine that our speakers are sensitive to light in frequencies that we cannot detect by eye – but that would not frustrate the attempt to say what the speaker is able to do. Secondly, the form of the account will shift from one where we say that S knows that "Yellingup" refers to Yellingup to one where we say – somewhat lamely, let us admit – that S is able to recognize Yellingup when it is appropriately presented and marks that recognition through a willingness to apply the term "Yellingup". Now, although there may be much wrong with that account of what S knows, it is an attempt to say what S's knowledge consists in. But how does it advance the previous account? After all, if I am to understand what S is able to do I need to understand the term "Yellingup" – or some equivalent, if the theory is framed in, say, a Martian language. Thus the account does not seem to help our Martian any more than the obviously modest account. The Martian example is thus a deceptive way of illustrating the point of what it takes for a theory to be genuinely informative.

The point does not concern so much the character of the person who uses the theory; it concerns what we are saying about S, the speaker. On the modest account we are attributing an understanding of "Yellingup" to S on the basis of her possession of the concept *Yellingup*. The content of S's knowledge is explained as "'Yellingup' refers to Yellingup", that is, S knows a certain proposition. But in order to know that proposition, S needs to grasp its constituent concepts including the concept *Yellingup*. Thus, unless we supplement the clause in some way, we are explaining S's understanding of the term "Yellingup" on the basis of her possession of the concept *Yellingup*. Thus the difference between a modest theory of meaning and a robust one is this. On a modest theory of meaning we account for a speaker's understanding of a language on the basis of her possession of concepts expressible in the primitive terms of the language; in contrast, on a robust account speakers' understanding is accounted for without making any presupposition about their conceptual accomplishments. The modest theory is philosophically lacking because it explains possession of concepts only in terms of possession of other concepts and ultimately leaves the possession of certain concepts unaccounted for; the robust approach takes on the task of accounting for concept possession in terms of non-conceptual capacities. Modesty is thus silent on the ultimate question of the nature of concept possession; robustness attempts to speak (and write) volumes.

There are large questions waiting in the wings here. The philosophy of language acquired huge pretensions during the last century and a half. It came to be thought by many that the only approach to analysing the nature of thought was via the analysis of language and, since the central goal of philosophy was to be the analysis of thought, the philosophy of language came to assume a fundamental role: Dummett calls it "the foundation of the whole of philosophy" (1978: 309). The movement in this direction has been called "the linguistic turn" and is variously attributed to Frege, the early Wittgenstein and some of the logical positivists. Clearly, if you are convinced by the linguistic turn, that is, convinced both about the aims of philosophy and about the best way of pursuing those aims, then modesty is no option for you; robustness is the only game in town. However, many have questioned both the aim and the linguistic pursuit of that aim. This is too large an issue for us to take on here directly; rather, we should be bold and adopt the ambitious approach of robustness as a matter of methodology. We may as well see what can be achieved by the philosophy of language by pushing it to its limits. When and if we discover robustness to fail, we shall have discovered that the linguistic turn was ill conceived and why it was so.

The proposal is thus that we exchange being radical for being robust.[2] We can think of this move as one from hypothetical genealogy to theoretical philosophy; whereas Davidson's question is genetic: how would we come to be interpreters of a given community's speech? Dummett's is programmatic without being genetic: what form would an informative theory of meaning for a given language take? On Davidson's view we imagine an enterprise that results in a sensitivity to the meaning-properties of expressions; we thus account for the possible *origin* of our concept of meaning. On Dummett's account we begin with the relevant sensitivity – we have the concept of meaning, at least implicitly – and we use this sensitivity in making explicit the notion of linguistic meaning.

Davidson's second reason for needing radical interpretation – that it provides the definition of a correct interpretation – was, I noted, internal to his system. But it is obviously important for any approach to know when it has got things right. So what does the robust theorist say here? For her, although there may well be difficult cases, the issue itself is not vexed; as speakers of the language, our own informed reflection on the nature of our practice will be what determines judgements about whether an account is correct.[3] The method is not foolproof, nor is it likely to be regularizable, but there is every reason to think that if we can rely on our own linguistic expertise in making judgements about the adequacy of an account, then those judgements should be reliable – and if they are not, what would be? Questions about whether an account of language is a good one will often take us back from programmatic philosophy – for example, carrying out the radical interpreter's project – to the ordinary messy business of philosophizing. But importantly it is our ordinary selves, not selves with pretended incapacities, who will do the philosophizing.

What all this shows is that radical interpretation may well be dispensable. But are there reasons for thinking that we should dispense with it?

10.2 Doing away with radical interpretation

I am going to argue that radical interpretation fails, first, because it fails to account for the publicity of meaning and, secondly, fails to be adequately illuminating about meaning. So it fails in two of its major roles. But it fails in the third role too and that is why it fails in the other two. Essentially the problem is that radical interpretation sets too low a standard on an adequate interpretational scheme.

Let us consider publicity first. The worry emerges from putting together radical interpretation with the construction of interpretational truth-theories. What Foster points out is that if we have an interpretational truth-theory, T, that interprets a predicate, P, as follows:

x satisfies P iff x is thus and so

then the following will be an equally adequate interpretational clause:

x satisfies P iff x is thus and so and the earth moves.

The clause will play a perfectly satisfactory role in a systematic theory of truth, T'. Ramberg offers the following defence on behalf of Davidson. He claims that the deviant clause could be satisfactory only if the target language did not include resources for "talking about the earth and movement":

> If we already have L-speakers talking about planetary motion, then we would have structural roles assigned to those words of L that we trans-late as "earth" and "moves" and so on. This would make it possible to deny, in L as interpreted by T, that the predicate $[P]$ also implies that the earth moves. (Ramberg 1989: 79)

Let us say that the sentence S is translated by T as "The Earth moves". Then T will acknowledge no good inference from something's satisfying P to S, whereas T' will acknowledge the goodness of this inference. Ramberg's defence is thus that the two schemes can be distinguished if we allow for the indefinite exten-sibility of natural language. I want to question both whether Ramberg succeeds in making the distinction he seeks and whether he satisfies the requirements of publicity, if we concede that the distinction can be made good.

To start, Ramberg's point is not completely clear. On the one hand it is not obvious that the inferences he mentions should not be counted as good. Given that S is true (since it is translated by "The earth moves"), the material condi-tional taking an ascription of P as antecedent and S as consequent is true. Thus the inference is good, and will come to be counted as such – by T – provided the language includes a material conditional. So, given his own willingness to count extensions of the language as allowable in determining its current properties, we should be prepared to count the inference as good. If, on the other hand, we know that the language has come to include a connective for a stronger condi-tional than the material conditional – strict implication,[4] say – "$\Rightarrow$" then T will count "$Px \Rightarrow S$" as false, but T' will count it as true. But this assumes that we have interpreted "$\Rightarrow$" correctly as strict implication and since the connective is inten-sional it is not clear quite how it should be interpreted given only the evidence of speakers' holdings-true. To sum up, we cannot allow Ramberg's point about inference to be made by focusing simply on sentences held true because this assumes that we have interpreted components of those sentences appropriately, for example, that "$\Rightarrow$" is to be interpreted as strict implication. We might, on the other hand, make the point by referring to speakers' inferential practice. But this tactic faces two problems. First, the methodology of radical interpretation does not seem to allow us to make use of this sort of evidence. We are constrained simply to the evidence of the circumstances in which sentences are held true.

That meagre evidence does not permit us to discern a sentence as held true *because* another is, that one sentence *is derived from* another. These judgements can be made only by imposing an interpretational scheme. So Ramberg is right to point out the relevant difference between schemes but wrong to think that this difference is one on which the evidence will allow us to base a choice. In addition, speakers' inferential practice may well fall short of acknowledging every inference to which they are committed. And, indeed, it may well be that a reason for this is that the language lacks expressive resources: introducing logical vocabulary enables us to come to see certain inferences as valid, which we may have been unable to do hitherto. Thus, setting aside the worry about whether it is admissible, it is likely that this second tactic of focusing on infer-ential practice will be indecisive and that we need to consider something akin to the first tactic, which I argued was question-begging.

The second worry brings out an important characteristic of the publicity of meaning. Were Ramberg's proposal successful, what we would have is a way of deciding between different interpretational schemes. That is, given rival such schemes we could imagine a development in the language that would enable us to decide between the schemes. Or, to put it another way, we would always have a way of discounting an incorrect scheme as incorrect. Thus meanings would be public in the sense that a difference between a speaker's meanings and those ascribed to her by an interpreter is always capable of being revealed. So, although there will always be a way of determining the incorrectness of an interpretative scheme, we cannot finally confirm an interpretational scheme as indeed correct. Meanings are therefore public only in the sense that diver-gences in meaning can be revealed; we cannot, however, confirm convergence in meaning. Many would argue that this is insufficient: publicity of meaning does not simply require that divergences in meaning can be brought to light; in addition we need to be able to *know* that we agree on meanings. For all any two speakers know it is always a possibility that they are failing to communicate. So they can never know that communication is successful. If this is so, it is hard to see how speakers can ever have good reason to suppose that they do com-municate. For if the totality of their use up to a given point can be accounted for without the assumption that meanings are shared, then what in that use would justify the claim that meanings are in fact shared?

10.3 Indeterminacy of reference

A second source of dissatisfaction with radical interpretation arises from a consequence that Davidson acknowledges and even embraces: that is, inde-terminacy of reference. We should thus be careful about how indeterminacy of reference constitutes a complaint against the radical interpreter. In brief, the point will be that accepting indeterminacy of reference is a source of tension with pre-theoretic views about meaning and that there is no need for us to accept it. I shall start with the latter point first and approach it by raising an apparent riddle about the robust meaning-theorist's approach. But, first things first, what is the indeterminacy of reference?

The indeterminacy of reference is the thesis that numerous incompatible reference schemes for a language are compatible with all the relevant linguistic data. Of course, large questions will hinge on what one regards as the relevant linguistic data and the plausibility of the thesis will largely depend on what sort of answer one gives to those questions. For Davidson the answer to that question is, however, easy: the relevant linguistic data include the empirical data that fund the project of radical interpretation. Thus the relevant data include information about which sentences speakers hold true and the circumstances in which they are held true. It is also easy enough to see why, on such a construal of the thesis, it holds. Let us suppose that φ is a non-trivial permutation of the objects in our domain of discourse. That is, φ assigns an object b to each object a and never assigns the same object to distinct objects. Moreover, suppose that φ is not the identity mapping. In these circumstances the following reference schemes are empirically equivalent but incompatible:

Scheme 1: the referent of "a" is a
$(x)(x$ satisfies "F" iff $Fx)$

Scheme 2: the referent of "a" is φa
$(x)(x$ satisfies "F" iff $F\varphi^{-1}x)^5$

We then assume that each scheme is subject to the same compositional rule determining truth-conditions of each sentence on the basis of the referential values of its components:

"F" ^ "a" is true iff the referent of "a" satisfies "F"

According to Scheme 1 we have:

"F" ^ "a" is true iff the referent of "a" satisfies "F" iff a satisfies "F" iff Fa

According to Scheme 2 we have:

"F" ^ "a" is true iff the referent of "a" satisfies "F" iff φa satisfies "F" iff $F\varphi^{-1}\varphi a$ iff Fa

Thus the two incompatible referential schemes yield precisely the same attributions of truth-conditions to sentences. Thus one will be adequate to the empirical data just in case the other is.

To illustrate, consider this adaptation of Davidson's account (1984: 230). Suppose every object has one and only one mother and no two objects have the same mother. Consider a referential scheme that assigns "Wilma" the reference Wilma, and "tall" the extension of tall things. Then "Wilma is tall" is true under this scheme just in case Wilma is tall. Consider now the scheme that assigns "Wilma" the reference the mother of Wilma and "tall" the extension: the mothers of tall daughters. Then, under this scheme, "Wilma is tall" is true just in case the mother of Wilma is the mother of a tall daughter. Again, the attributions of truth-conditions under both schemes are equivalent.[6]

There is no doubt that the thesis of the indeterminacy of reference is apt to strike one as an insignificant logical shuffle, but it makes a serious semantic point that should not be missed. It might strike one as reasonable to suppose that the empirical data that are relevant to the determination of reference concern the use of whole sentences ("Only in the context of a sentence does a word have any meaning"; "Only ask for the meaning of a word in the context of a sentence"), yet also suppose that these facts combined with structural features of the way a sentence's truth-conditions are determined by the referential values of its components suffice to determine reference. The thesis of the indeterminacy of reference shows these suppositions to be incompatible; indefinitely many relations of words to wordly items suffice to explain these facts.

Davidson's way of assimilating the lesson is to say that Schemes 1 and 2 apply to different languages. What the empirical data fail to determine is which of these languages a given speaker is speaking, provided of course that the data support attribution of one of the languages.

Let us spell out the argument in a little more detail. This is worth doing for our own purposes and, since arguments about indeterminacy have been prominent in recent literature,[7] it is worth doing for its own sake.

1. The empirical evidence concerning speakers' use of whole sentences is compatible with indefinitely many mutually incompatible schemes of reference.
2. What is understood by speakers, that is, meanings, must be fully displayed in their capacities to use linguistic expressions.
3. An expression has a use only in the context of using whole sentences.
4. What is understood by speakers must be fully displayed in their capacities to use whole sentences.
5. Therefore what is understood – meaning – fails to determine a unique scheme of reference: attributions of meanings to sentences, in particular the attribution of truth-conditions to sentences based on their structures, fails to determine a unique referential scheme.
6. If anything determines reference then it is facts about the attributions of meanings to sentences.
7. Nothing determines reference; reference is indeterminate.

There are four premises in the argument: (1), (2), (3) and (6). Premise (1) is supposedly a consequence of the argument from permutations; (2) is an insistence on the publicity of meaning; (3) is an endorsement of some version of the context principle; and (6) denies that a relation such as a causal relation between words and things in the world can be relevant to the determination of reference. However, a fifth assumption is built into the argument. Our brief reprise of the permutation argument suggested that the attribution of truth-conditions to sentences is compatible with indefinitely many mutually incompatible schemes of reference. So we seem to be assuming that the meaning of a sentence is given by its truth-conditions and that the use of a sentence is accountable in terms of its truth-conditions. The latter is plausible in light of the former, since if truth-conditions fail this explanatory burden, then truth-conditions have a poor claim to determine a sentence's meaning. But we might want to deny that a sentence's meaning is given by its truth-conditions. So it might well seem that a way of rejecting the argument might be to reject truth-conditional accounts of meaning. I do not want to press this objection; it appears plausible only because of a weakness in the way we framed the permutation argument, which made it both simple and particularly pertinent to Davidson. But, as Putnam shows, the argument can be strengthened to apply to almost any conception of use. So provided (2) and (3) hold, the argument will go through.

Premise (6) has proved to be a popular target of attack for those wishing to rebut the argument. Davidson considers and rejects this move. As he points out, a causal account of reference claims that words stand in a certain causal relation to objects in the world and that this relation is (or at least constrains) the reference relation. But if words do stand in such a relation to objects in the world, then they stand in a certain relation to the images of those objects under the permuted relation and now there is a good question to answer as to which of these relations constitutes (or constrains) the reference relation. To illustrate by means of our previous example, uses of "Wilma" are CAUSED by Wilma if and only if uses of "Wilma" are CAUSED* by the mother of Wilma, where x is CAUSED* by y just in case x is CAUSED by the daughter of y. The causal response claims that x refers to y just in case x is CAUSED by y, but if that claim is available then so too is the claim that x refers to y just in case x is CAUSED* by y. And our question is whether we can have any grounds for preferring the CAUSAL account over the CAUSAL* account.[8] We cannot answer that question without being able to say what the reference relation is. So, rather than underwriting a refutation of the argument, the objection depends on such a refutation.

The point might be made rather differently. Facts about the causal relations of words to objects in the world will be answerable to facts about speakers' use of those words and, if the context principle holds, these will be facts about speakers' use of those words in the context of whole sentences. So the causal relation itself is constrained only by facts that constrain the reference relation. Thus it cannot provide any sort of additional constraint.

There is, however, a possible equivocation between the first and second premises. Whereas the first premise talks of "the empirical evidence concerning speakers' use of (whole) sentences", the second premise talks of "capacities to use whole sentences". The empirical evidence concerning speakers' use of whole sentences is, let us grant, evidence that a radical interpreter will have access to. The notion of speakers' capacities to use whole sentences is a much less definite notion and will vary depending on one's conception of publicity. Let me illustrate by introducing two notions of publicity. I do not wish to endorse either notion but it will help to understand the third alternative if we begin with these two. The first notion might be called radical publicity and the second modest publicity:

Radical publicity: A competent speaker is able to display her understanding to a radical interpreter by exercise of capacities that can be characterized in "broadly" extensional terms.
Modest publicity: A competent speaker is able to display her understanding to other competent speakers by exercise of capacities that can be characterized only by utilizing the relevant concept within a content specifying "that" clause.

Note that each of these notions of publicity is two-dimensional, one dimension marking the nature of the capacities that are exercised in displaying one's understanding and the other marking the nature of the character to whom the understanding is displayed. We have already said a good deal about radical publicity so let us put that notion aside for the moment, simply noticing that, on such a construal, the argument for indeterminacy of reference seems compelling: no gap opens up through an equivocation between first and second premises.

What is modest publicity? On McDowell's view (1981; 1987), one's entry into language brings about a perceptual access to facts to which one would not, before that accession, have had access. So, once you learn the meaning of the sentence "Snow is white" you are able to perceive a particular action as the action of asserting that snow is white. That action thus becomes a publicly available feature of one's use of language that is germane to one's ability to display one's understanding. Thus McDowell's thought is that one displays one's understanding in such actions as using a sentence to assert that thus and so, and that, in doing so, one displays one's understanding to those who understand the sentence. McDowell's view of publicity is unashamedly reconcilable only with modest ambitions in the theory of meaning. The sort of use constituting one's understanding cannot be characterized except in terms that require attribution of the relevant concept; that concept is used within a content-specifying "that" clause. Thus there is no characterizing speakers' abilities – the nature of understanding – from a perspective that does not presuppose conceptual competence. Although there is obviously room for debate on whether anything more than modest ambitions are appropriate – and McDowell argues that they are not – the approach obviously opens itself up to accusations of not offering a sufficiently illuminating account of linguistic competence. But let us skirt that debate and return to the argument for indeterminacy of reference equipped with grasp of this new notion of publicity.

There is now a clear equivocation between the first and second premises. For the empirical evidence of speakers' use is now quite distinct from our conception of the capacities of speakers to use sentences. The former evidence is taken to be characterizable "broadly" extensionally, that is, without begging any questions about content, whereas on McDowell's view the latter can be characterized only from within content. Thus on modest publicity the argument fails by committing the fallacy of equivocation.

So far we have two notions of publicity, each of which may seem problematic. The first sustains the argument for indeterminacy of reference; the second will not support that argument but frustrates what might appear to be legitimate philosophical ambitions. Is there a conception of publicity that frustrates the argument for indeterminacy of reference without at the same time frustrating our explanatory ambitions? There may well be. Our diagnosis of the equivocation in the argument from the McDowellian perspective depended only on the first dimension of the characterization of publicity, namely, the characterization of the nature of the relevant capacities. We might thus hope to diagnose an equivocation by focusing instead on the second dimension – the nature of the character who can detect a display of capacities – without thereby frustrating our explanatory ambitions. Consider then this notion of publicity:

> *Robust publicity*: One displays one's linguistic competence to those with relevant linguistic competence by exercise of capacities that can be characterized "broadly" extensionally.

Clearly such a notion of publicity does not frustrate our explanatory ambitions because it insists that linguistic competence be explained in terms that do not presuppose a grasp of content. So it can make a legitimate claim to have explained what it is to grasp the concepts expressible in the basic terms of the language. The explanatory programme is different from that of Davidson because, whereas he insists that the account of linguistic competence must be recognizable as such from the radical interpreter's perspective, this view allows that the account may only be recognizable as an account of linguistic competence to someone who possesses the relevant linguistic competence. I illustrate this difference in some detail below. Our question now is whether robust publicity sustains or frustrates the argument for the indeterminacy of reference.

As it stands, however, the contrast between robust and radical publicity makes use of a dimension that is not factored into our premises. The first premise speaks simply of empirical evidence of speakers' use and does not mention to whom that evidence should be available; the second premise speaks simply of understanding displayed in speakers' capacities to use sentences and does not mention to whom it should be displayed. Of course, we can introduce the second dimension into the second premise and do so as robust publicity would require. That is fine because the job of that premise is to introduce the relevant notion of publicity into the argument, although we would obviously have further work to do in explaining that notion as motivated (see below). But what we need to show is that the argument requires that the first premise needs to framed in terms of the empirical evidence being available to a radical interpreter, or that the premise is false if we read it as insisting only that the evidence be available to a competent speaker. We shall then be able to say either that the argument commits a fallacy of equivocation or, if not, that it is unsound.

For the sake of argument we may assume that the facts of usage are characterized in the same way on either the radical or robust view of publicity. What differs is that robust publicity allows that these facts are apprehended by an observer who understands the relevant terms. What difference does this make? In broad terms it may obviously be the case that one appreciates the significance of a set of facts only given a certain expertise. For instance, one may be able to appreciate the significance of the fact of making a certain mark on a document as a commitment to pay such and such for a house only if one is aware of the contractual laws governing the buying and selling of houses. The mere description of the act of signing may be neutral about its legal significance; nonetheless someone who is aware of such possible significances may be able to see the act, thus described, as having a certain legal significance. Note too that the act might from a certain perspective be indeterminate as to its legal significance: it may be possible to reconcile the neutral description of the act with a multitude of legal practices and thus significances. The indeterminacy is resolved by bringing to bear an appropriate ability to appreciate its significance. And the situation might be closely analogous in the case of the facts about linguistic usage. The facts themselves might admit of a neutral description, but it might take a certain linguistic competence to appreciate the linguistic significance of those facts. Moreover, it may well be that bringing to bear the appreciation of the linguistic significance of those facts will resolve linguistic indeterminacies that remain so long as we settle on the mere neutral description of the relevant facts. Given this broad possibility, the argument for the indeterminacy of reference must be regarded as unsatisfactory and possibly the move from radical to robust publicity renders it unsatisfactory. It is difficult to demonstrate that this quite generally holds because the argument is framed so as to be neutral on its conception of meaning. The next paragraph tackles the demonstration in the restricted case of a Davidsonian referential account of meaning, arguably the most difficult conception of meaning on which to build such a demonstration.

The claim of such theories is that we can give the meaning of an expression such as "Wilma" by specifying its reference:

"Wilma" refers to Wilma.

The clause specifies the meaning of "Wilma" when taken as part of an interpretative scheme, T, for the language as a whole. Similarly, the following clause specifies the meaning of the same word when taken as part of an empirically equivalent interpretative scheme, T'.

"Wilma" refers to the mother of Wilma.

The question is which interpretative scheme captures the meaning-determining facts. As long as we adhere to radical publicity there is no answer to this question: the one scheme stands on all fours with the other. But that does not mean that the schemes *are* on all fours; it might simply mean that *from the perspective of the radical interpreter* there is no recognizing which scheme captures the meaning-determining facts. The radical interpreter may well be apprised of these facts, since she may be in possession of a scheme such as T, but she cannot recognize these facts for what they are. Realizing this, she has no choice but to embrace indeterminacy (of reference). But if we reject radical in favour of robust publicity, the fact that T captures the meaning-determining facts might come into view. And surely it does so since a competent speaker of the language will have no trouble in preferring and in justifying her preference for T over T'. She needs simply to appeal to her understanding of the term "Wilma" (among others) in order to do so.

When we attempt to model radical and robust publicity theoretically, what we get is, respectively, the radical interpreter and robust theorist. So the theories presented by the robust theorist and the radical interpreter *might* not differ. The difference between the two theorists will lie in their respective abilities to justify their preferred theories. The radical interpreter will not be able to justify her preference over indefinitely many alternatives; the robust theorist will. *If* we concede that indeterminacy of reference is to be rejected, then this shows that the robust theorist is able to recognize her theory for what it is – the account of reference on which meaning is based – while the radical interpreter is unable so to do. Thus – our first conclusion – the "broadly" extensionally describable facts relating to language may be accessible to a radical interpreter but, divested of her understanding of the target language, she may be unable to appreciate their significance. Our second conclusion is simply that from the perspective of a robust theorist the indeterminacy of reference is only the semblance of a problem admitting the most trivial of solutions. I know that "cat" refers to cats and not to cherries since, being a competent user of English, I know that when I use the term "cat" I use it to refer to or to talk about cats and not to refer to or to talk about cherries; my statement is rendered true or false by how it is with cats, not by how it is with cherries. It would simply be crazy to suggest otherwise.

167

10.4 Arguments for robust publicity

Our conclusion thus far is that if robust publicity is the right notion of publicity to adopt, then we can reject the approach of radical interpretation and hence reject the indeterminacy of reference. We need to supplement the argument in a number of ways. We need first to show that robust publicity is to be preferred over radical and modest publicity, secondly, to show that publicity is well motivated and thirdly, to show that we should object to the indeterminacy of reference. Chapters 11–13 will take up the general issue of privacy and publicity, and the next section of this chapter will discuss indeterminacy of reference. In this section we shall consider whether robust publicity is well motivated.

Dummett himself places two constraints on acceptable accounts of meaning and understanding that for him implement the requirement that meaning and understanding be public. In the literature these constraints are dubbed the manifestation and acquisition constraints. If we go along with Dummett and accept these as plausible implementations of the publicity requirement, then, I shall argue, robust publicity is the consequence. This may seem like an insignificant accomplishment (if Dummett is right, then Dummett is right), but recall that robust publicity has not been culled directly from Dummett's writings. Rather, the motivation for calling the relevant notion of publicity, in deference to Dummett, "robust" stems from the argument I am about to give, which justifies it in terms of the manifestation and acquisition constraints.

Dummett claims that one's understanding of an expression must be capable of being fully displayed in one's capacity to use it in publicly observable ways. For, if not, then that two speakers share an understanding of an expression can never be definitively substantiated. Any agreement in use, no matter how extensive, will fail to constitute an agreement in meaning since the speakers may diverge in the unmanifestable ingredient of understanding. Such a notion of meaning is repugnant to any conception that essentially locates meaning in its social role of facilitating communication. Communication requires not merely a sharing of meanings, but a sharing of meanings that is capable of being known.

Speakers gain an understanding of language through being inducted by other speakers into a practice of use. What speakers learn cannot go beyond what can be made available to them to learn. So what speakers learn must be available in publicly accessible uses of language. Linguistic competence must be seen as being acquirable on such a basis.

We have not here provided any strong reason for either of these constraints; rather, I have loosely motivated and explained them. Our task is not to assess, at least not yet. What we need to do is to see how robust publicity is a consequence of accepting them. Let us begin with the manifestation constraint. The constraint functions between competent speakers of the language: one speaker must be able to manifest her understanding to another if the two are to be able to communicate. So clearly the constraint motivates nothing stronger than robust publicity, and arguably it requires nothing more than modest publicity. The acquisition constraint is a rather different matter. Here one might think that what we need is something stronger than either robust or modest publicity. For does acquisition not require that the capacities constituting understanding be available to a learner and so available to someone who does not have the relevant linguistic expertise? Thus the capacities should both be describable independently of content – that is, in broadly extensional terms – and should be recognizable by someone who is linguistically innocent. So radical publicity would seem to be a consequence and, since it is the only form of publicity that can be reconciled with *both* manifestation and acquisition, its claims will carry the day.

Tempting though this thought is, I think it is mistaken. To be sure, acquisition requires that the relevant capacities be available to the linguistically uninitiated and thus characterizable independently of content. So modest publicity is out of the running.[9] But this does not mean that the capacities that constitute understanding are recognizable *as such* by the learner. Quite the reverse may be possible; although the capacities are recognizable independently of grasp of the relevant content, it may well be that they are only recognizable as constituting understanding once one has oneself gained the relevant understanding. If this were the case, then robust publicity would be the consequence.

What reasons do we have for this view? There are two. First, it seems entirely unmotivated to require any more than this. The learner is exposed to the evidence of speakers' usage of an expression. There is no need to suppose that in acquiring these capacities she needs to be able to isolate that set of capacities constitutive of understanding of the target expression. Why should she have this clarity about the task that lies ahead? Plausibly the learner is in a fog that gradually clears; knowing what it is to gain clarity might well be something that simply cannot be anticipated. Perhaps a tendency to think otherwise stems from assimilating first-language to second-language learning. Secondly, Dummett (1993: 94–6) argues that the very distinction we are considering separates purely practical from not purely practical knowledge. His claim is that, since what it is to understand an expression cannot be anticipated in advance of gaining the relevant understanding, linguistic knowledge is not purely practical. He makes the point by reference to an episode in a P. G. Wodehouse novel, which amply bears repeating. A character, on being asked whether she can speak Spanish, replies, "I don't know, I haven't tried". Dummett diagnoses the humour in the remark as stemming from an absurdity. In some cases there is obviously no absurdity in a similar remark: just imagine that the character had been asked whether or not she can swim or ride a bicycle. In cases such as these one can have a clear conception of the capacity in question in advance of possessing it but in the linguistic case it makes no sense to suppose that the character can conceive of what it is to speak Spanish in advance of speaking it. Similar remarks would of course apply, and for the same reasons, to understandings of particular words: imagine she had been asked whether she can understand the word "brittle". Dummett's thought is that the absurdity arises from the fact that in the linguistic case the knowledge is not purely practical: grasp of meaning does not simply issue in a capacity to use an expression appropriately but in an ability to have one's use guided by the meaning and for that knowledge to be at the service of an indefinite variety of extra-linguistic ends. Of course there will be occasions where one can know what is involved in understanding an expression without being able to use it appropriately. One example would be cases where a word is interpreted in another language. Here one would understand the relevant term (provided one understands the interpretation), but what would prevent one from using it would be other capacities that one lacks (an inability to understand other expressions in the language to which the term belongs). So, for instance, I know that "imbwa" means *dog* in Xhosa, but, that being the extent of my knowledge of Xhosa, I am unable to use the word. Another set of examples is provided by Price (2004): here one can say what speakers are able to do without thereby possessing the capacity that speakers have. His example is that of expressions whose use involves making sensory discriminations that we are unable to make. There is obviously some scope for phenomena of this sort. We can easily enough imagine terms for colours that lie in regions of the spectrum that we cannot detect. But in this case our conception of the capacity is dependent on a conception of similar capacities that we do in fact possess; we conceive of the capacity in question as an understanding of a colour term and this conception depends on us having an understanding of certain colour terms. Could we have a conception of something's being a colour term without being masters of some colour terms ourselves? This seems doubtful. Price's point is that in some cases it may be possible to conceive of the capacity to use an expression without thereby possessing the capacity. His examples are restricted and we have noted a few reasons for why they might be restricted. The important thing for us here is that a movement beyond robust publicity would require a globalization of Price's claim: that is, in all cases it is possible to conceive of the capacity in question without thereby possessing the capacity. Moreover, if the point were to be relevant to the appraisal of acquisition, we would need to think of the relevant conception of the capacity as being available to the linguistic initiate.[10] No reason for such a global claim seems in the offing, and against the possibility of such a claim we have Dummett's thought that there is a non-practical element to linguistic knowledge that, in general, frustrates it. Dummett sums up as follows:

> Explicit theoretical knowledge consists in the capacity to formulate the relevant propositions … Such knowledge presupposes mastery of some language within which to frame those propositions; hence knowledge of that language, or at least of one's mother tongue, cannot be of that

kind. At the other extreme is simple practical knowledge of how to do something which has to be learned: it consists in the ability to do in practice what, even before one learned how to set about doing it, one knew what it was to do. Between these comes knowledge of a language, which falls under neither of these heads: it is an acquired ability to engage in a practice of such a kind that *one cannot know what engaging in it consists in until one has acquired the ability to do so.*

(1991b: 94, emphasis added)

In general we have no reason to insist, and indeed it would be mistaken to insist, that learners can conceive of what it is they have to learn in learning a language.

To conclude, there is no reason to think that acquisition requires more than robust publicity and some reason to think that it *cannot* require more than robust publicity. Thus, if the right way to conceive of publicity is in terms of manifestation and acquisition, then robust publicity is well motivated.

10.5 Rejecting indeterminacy of reference

The indeterminacy of reference arises because numerous referential schemes are compatible with assignments of the same truth-conditions to sentences and therefore beliefs. It is, however, grossly unintuitive. That it is so emerges from the way it conflicts with our pre-theoretic sense of aboutness. One thought is this. According to the indeterminacy of reference, there is no fact of the matter as to whether a speaker who holds true "Wilma is tall" has a belief about Wilma or about Wilma's mother. Or, more precisely, there is no such fact of the matter if we take it that what a sentence or belief is about depends on what its constituents refer to. However, it seems strange indeed to suppose that someone who has perceptual contact with Wilma but not with Wilma's mother manages to acquire beliefs about Wilma's mother but not about Wilma herself. But the indeterminacy-theorist can easily accommodate such examples; she needs simply to restrict the permutations she considers in such a way that each is the composition of permutations, each of which permutes objects *within* a perceptually salient set. Permutations are just too easy to construct for any such response.

The real worry about indeterminacy of reference must be much more basic. What the thesis asks me to accept is that there is no fact of the matter as to what my beliefs are about. Intuitively we rebel against such a conception. The response might be to place some distance between the technical notion of reference and the intuitive notion of aboutness. But this is surely a dereliction of our obligations as philosophers of language; we should be attempting to explain aboutness, and the notion of reference has its role as a technical explication of that notion. We arrive at the indeterminacy of reference by thinking of the

171

notion of reference as having its content purely determined by its role within an interpretative theory. But, provided we retain its link with aboutness, it also has another role: that is, in maintaining a conception of ourselves as talking and thinking about worldly items. Why should we forsake that self-conception without compelling argument?

Where does this leave us? We had located the motive for radical interpretation in radical publicity. Thus if radical publicity is unmotivated, radical interpretation will be so too. Furthermore, radical publicity sustains the argument for the indeterminacy of reference whereas robust (and weaker versions of) publicity frustrates it. So the indeterminacy of reference is also unmotivated. The indeterminacy of reference is repugnant to our pre-theoretic conception of meaning, so unless there is strong theoretical motive for adopting a position that commits us to it we should avoid it. Radical interpretation commits us to indeterminacy of reference but is unmotivated, so it lacks the theoretical weight necessary for counteracting its unintuitive consequence. We should thus reject radical interpretation. Adopting a robust approach has, in contrast, been shown to be well motivated on an unpacking of publicity in terms of manifestation and acquisition, and it has no unintuitive consequence, as far as indeterminacy of reference is concerned; so, at this stage of enquiry the robust approach has everything to recommend it and nothing against it. Our argument has, however, been predicated on an insistence on publicity. We need to examine the aptness of that insistence and whether our reading of publicity in terms of manifestation and acquisition can be justified. So we need to examine the notion of publicity itself more thoroughly. Chapters 11–14 pursue this aim by examining the communal nature of language.

11. Language and community

There are a daunting number of deep and difficult questions lurking in the area of the relations between language use and its communal setting. Some we shall need to look at; others will take us too far afield into issues lying at the intersection of epistemology and the philosophies of language and mind. Some questions concern natural language: in what sense is natural language a communal phenomenon? Must it be understood in its communal context? In what sense is natural language a private phenomenon? Must it be understood in terms of private acts of conferring meanings on signs? Can it be so understood? Other questions concern hypothetical languages: could there be a private language, a language that can be understood only by a solitary user? Can there be a language that incorporates some signs only understood by a solitary user? The questions are, of course, interrelated and bring us to further questions about the nature of self-knowledge, of avowals, of ascriptions of capacities, of sensations and private objects. The issues are inherently interesting and important, so we shall be tackling them for their own sake, but we are also trying to find an approach to the philosophy of language and so our aim will be to motivate a certain conception of publicity.

11.1 Natural language is essentially communal: semantic externalism

In what sense does one's use of a public language such as English depend on one's membership of a community? Must we understand the phenomenon of English as an essentially social phenomenon or is English merely a product of similarities between the idiolects of particular speakers? In this section we shall look at Putnam (1975: 215–71), who makes natural-kind terms the focus of his attention. His first example indicates a phenomenon that is analogous to those Kripke highlights in relation to names. Very often a speaker will succeed in effecting a reference by use of a term although the knowledge she has about the term's bearer(s) will be inadequate to distinguish that (or those) thing(s) from others. So, for instance, Putnam unashamedly admits that his botanical knowledge is so weak that he is unable to distinguish an elm from a beech. Nonetheless he is able to refer to elms by the use of the word "elm" and to pass on useful information about, say, a copse of beech trees to botanically more informed acquaintances. The reason why his use of "elm" succeeds in referring cannot be found in anything that informs Putnam's use of the term but rather rests on the facts that, first, his community contains experts who are able to distinguish the one sort of tree from the other and, secondly, Putnam defers to these experts in his use of the term. So, Putnam argues, we must acknowledge a division in linguistic labour. If this view is right, then the idea that a public language should be seen as an overlapping of idiolects is simply false; the language spoken by an individual owes its character to that spoken in her community. In terms of the notion of sense, Putnam fails to grasp the sense of "elm" completely but his reference succeeds because his community includes members who do grasp this sense completely (and Putnam defers to them). So the example fails to trouble the general thought that reference is mediated by sense, although the community will be the primary locus of attention rather than the individual.

If Putnam is right about our actual use of natural-kind terms, then it is certainly true that our language has a distinctively social dimension. And, even if our language is, as a matter of fact, not best described in this way, Putnam seems to have shown that a language could be such as to have a distinctively social dimension. But, of course, none of this demonstrates that a language *could not* be purely idiolectical. And surely considerations of this sort must fail to demonstrate this. Imagine that the speaker of the idiolect possesses all the knowledge that the experts in Putnam's example possess. It is implausible that such a speaker exists but by no means impossible. In essence, since the notion of sense still survives, it is possible to think of the language as one in which a single speaker fully grasps all senses.

Putnam, however, pushes the point further since he wants to show that not only does one's social setting affect the language one speaks, but one's causal embedding in the world does so too. Although this question is not directly concerned with the nature of the community's role, my response to it will help bring out elements of that role. He asks us to consider a twin earth that is atom-for-atom identical with the earth, other than the fact that on Twin Earth the chemical composition of the stuff that has all the phenomenal characterisitics of common table salt (it tastes like salt, can be used for preserving and pickling, dissolves easily in water, etc.) has some other chemical composition. Now since Twin Earth replicates Earth it possesses a doppelgänger of Putnam. Both Putnam and his twin would seemingly attach the same sense to the term "salt" since (apart from the fact that they are physically qualitatively identical, we could stipulate that) they use precisely the same features to apply the term "salt" to stuff in their respective environments. However, Putnam contends that his term refers to sodium chloride whereas his twin's term refers to some other stuff. So the sense one has attached to a term does not determine its reference; if reference is a feature of one's language, then the language one speaks depends on one's causal embedding in the world.

Now Putnam thinks that this example will work no matter how sophisticated or primitive his and his twin's communities are in matters chemical. So even if the two communities lack any notion of chemical composition, it is still the case that his and his twin's terms differ in extension. However, were Putnam to encounter the stuff that goes by the name "salt" on Twin Earth, he would call it "salt" and, given that there is no chemical knowledge to which he holds his use responsible, there is no sense in insisting that he would be wrong to do so. Alternatively, if the knowledge that this stuff differed in chemical composition from what he normally calls "salt" came to light, it is simply undetermined whether we would say that salt has more than one chemical composition or that the other stuff was not salt. A decision on the meaning of the term "salt" would be called for (see Dummett 1978: essay 23). So Putnam's point does not seem to have quite the generality he claims for it.

If, however, we consider twins whose communities have a fairly extensive battery of chemical tests for determining the composition of a substance, then we approach something akin to the elm/beech case and the phenomenon of the linguistic division of labour. The only difference would be that in this case the experts might not have exploited the tests in distinguishing the two sorts of stuff. But the community would possess a clear notion of the manner in which the reference of their respective terms would be determined.

Yet another scenario is, however, conceivable. For, although there may be no precisely circumscribed set of tests for determining the nature of a sort of stuff, we may, nevertheless, have enough chemical sophistication to have a notion of sameness of stuff, a notion that depends on similarity of underlying chemical composition. In such a case we might introduce a term by means of a sample, determining its extension by insisting that it apply to the same stuff as the sample. In so doing we would be holding our use of the term responsible not to a particular way of determining the reference (unanticipated advances in chemistry may render it quite obscure precisely how the reference of the term will, in fact, be determined), but to the nature of the stuff itself. And, in this case, it would seem that Putnam and his twin might be relevantly similar – might agree with respect to any conceivable ingredient of sense – yet their respective terms differ in reference simply because of the nature of the stuff in their environment.

The case now resembles that of the name "Gödel" in our discussion of Kripke on names. In both cases it is a feature of our use of a term that we hold our use responsible to something other than expertise possessed within the community.

175

In the present case this is because we allow our use to be responsible to the findings of future scientific investigation whose form cannot now be anticipated. In the "Gödel" case this is because we hold our use responsible to features about how past speakers introduced a term. So, although in both cases we have some conception of what would determine the reference of a term, what actually fixes that reference is some fact or facts of which we, *qua* speakers, may not be apprised.

Dummett claims that "In using words of a language a speaker is responsible to the way that the language is used now, to the presently agreed practices of the community; he cannot be held responsible to the way people spoke many centuries ago" (1978: 430), or, he might also have said, to the way we might come to use language. So Dummett thinks that the Fregean doctrine needs to be modified only to take account of the social aspect of language use. However, Putnam's point seems to be that the way we presently use language incorporates responsibilities to aspects of the way the world is, aspects whose mode of discovery need not be (expicitly or implicitly) factored into the conferral of meaning.

Dummett wants to assimilate Putnam's cases to that of indexicality.[1] For in those cases we have a feature of present linguistic practice that involves the world yet is not regarded as a problem fundamentally affecting Frege's notion of sense. Certainly the manner in which we envisage a term being introduced – that is, salt is the same stuff as *this* – suggests that something very akin to indexicality is in play. Consider an ordinary case of, say, introducing a name by saying, for example, "Fido is that dog" (using the demonstrative to pick out the appropriate dog). In so doing we set up a way of identifying the dog (presumably by its appearance) that correlates with the sense of the name as thus established. Similarly, when we say "Salt is the same stuff as this", we set up a way of identifying salt (presumably by its distinctive phenomenal qualities). We have a criterion of identity for dogs, or, less controversially, we have a notion of sameness of dog. Now no matter what method of identification we use in conjunction with the name "Fido", it may be that it fails: Fido's appearance may change drastically, or the place may suddenly become awash with Fido lookalikes. Were we to find ourselves in such a position we would attempt to determine the reference of Fido by applying our notion of sameness of dog and attempting to discover whether a given dog is the same dog as that originally demonstrated. What considerations may count in this investigation and whether, in any given case, it will be successful cannot be prejudged. So in this sense we hold our use responsible to facts about the world.

Does this case challenge Frege's notion of sense? One would think not. For one way of seeing that doctrine is as the idea that if one understands a term, one knows how to determine its reference. There is no sense in which I fail to know how to determine the reference of "Fido" even if I cannot be guaranteed to determine that reference (infallibly and in all circumstances) and even if what collateral information may aid that determination cannot be circumscribed. In so far as it impinges on the notion of sense, Putnam's case appears to be entirely analogous to the present one.

It remains true that two introductions of the name "Fido" might be relevantly similar, yet the term might be introduced with a different reference on each occasion (there might be two dogs bearing the name "Fido" who are uncannily similar to one another in appearance and, perhaps, character). So two speakers who acquire an understanding of "Fido" in these circumstances might be psychologically identical (in relevant respects). What this shows is that knowledge of sense cannot be characterized in narrow psychological terms. What a speaker needs to be able to do is to set about determining whether a certain presentation of an object is a presentation of the same object made on another *particular* occasion: the determination of reference is made relative to that particular occasion, which therefore must figure in the account of a speaker's knowledge of sense.[2] The general point would be that knowledge of sense comprises a certain set of capacities with respect to objects or sorts of objects in one's environment. So the nature of one's language in general depends both on one's environment and on one's community. But one might be competent in a language with the same expressive power as those Putnam describes, without having the relevant social setting. We need simply to suppose that one is extremely well versed in the nature of one's world. So natural languages are likely to be distinctively social phenomena but, as far as this argument goes, could exist in the absence of that dimension. The role of the environment is, however, ineliminable.

11.2 Communication requires publicity of meaning

It is often held that communication requires shared meanings. A speaker succeeds in communicating with her audience when that audience interprets her as she intends. So, to that extent at least, each party to a successful communicative interchange must agree with the other about meanings. This conception of successful communication thus requires that meanings be public in the sense that they are shareable. But this is a very weak constraint: almost any ingredient of one's private world is shareable in the sense that there is no reason to suppose that another subject might not enjoy qualitatively similar ingredients of her private world. Any pain, tickle, idea or impression that you have might, for all we know, be qualitatively identical to some pain, tickle, idea or impression of mine. Of course there may be a concern here about what sense we can attach to these comparisons when the comparisons cannot, in principle, be made. But we probably do better to sidestep that broad issue and consider whether there is any ground for thinking that in the case of meanings successful communication requires not merely shared meanings but the capacity to *know* that we share meanings.

If agreement in use constitutes or conclusively establishes agreement in meanings, then agreement in meanings is, in the required sense, knowable. So let us suppose that agreement in use – in other words, complete coincidence in propensities to use language – is consistent with a divergence about meanings. Now one worry you might have about such a position is that it is entirely obscure what one would require such a notion of meaning for; so construed, meanings are explanatorily redundant; since here the notion of meaning goes beyond use, it cannot be required simply in order to explain linguistic behaviour. Maybe so; but maybe there are other explanatory roles for meanings, relating them not to use but, perhaps, to thought. At any rate the assumption here that meanings must explain use is too close to our conclusion for the argument to be of much interest. The question to ask is this: how in such circumstances could we have any reply to the sceptical thought that there is massive failure to communicate? Dummett puts the thought very directly. On his view the position makes it always an act of faith that we communicate and he takes it that such a position is absurd, presumably because if one's faith can be misplaced on occasion, it can always be misplaced, in which case, scepticism about our success in communicating is in order.

Obviously there is, at the very least, an awkwardness in responding to this challenge because all the evidence of the nature of speakers' meanings comes in the form of their use of language, and the hypothesis we are contemplating precisely allows that agreement in use fails conclusively to establish agreement in meaning. So none of the evidence available to us will warrant the claim that communication succeeds. The thought is a little too quick because it seems to assume that what we want here is a deductive inference from agreement in use to agreement in meanings and hence to communicative success. Dummett sometimes suggests that it cannot be at most a hypothesis that agreement in use justifies ascribing agreement in meanings because, if it were so, that hypothesis could have no justification; our belief in communicative success would collapse into a mere act of faith. But it is not obvious that Dummett's complaint is well taken. For might we not substitute the deductive inference with an abductive inference – that is, the best, in the sense of simplest, explanation of agreement in use is agreement in meanings? Well, certainly this is an explanation of sorts – if speakers agree about meanings they will agree in their use – and it is a simple explanation of agreement in use. However, since the abductive inference is always available – we shall *always* be justified in inferring agreement in meanings from agreement in use – it is not clear why one would distinguish the one from the other: why not simply say that agreement in use *constitutes* agreement in meanings?

The reason can only be that some other explanatory interest forces us to make the distinction. It may be, for instance, that we think there is a scientific theory that explains what constitutes understanding in terms of ulterior capacities of which ordinary speakers may have no knowledge. Or it may be that one wants to explain some feature of understanding that requires that grasped meanings be seen as private *sources* of use. For instance, one might be struck by the authority that speakers have about the nature of their own understandings and one might think that locating meanings in a Cartesian inner world is the best explanation of this fact of how we go about ascribing understanding or of the phenomenology of understanding. Given a view of either of these sorts, it seems one might accept the abductive inference as always valid but reject the assimilation of meaning to use.

A great innovation introduced by semantic externalism was the idea that scientific, empirical investigations can uncover essences or constitutive properties. The question is whether such a view might be used to support empirical investigation into the constitution of understanding. The question is no doubt highly debatable but, in the light of our discoveries in the previous section, the prospects look bleak. We had supported a modest form of externalism, one in which we hold our use responsible to the underlying nature of a thing when it is introduced by means of samples and an associated criterion of identity that determines the relevant underlying properties. But we do not introduce ascriptions of understanding in this way and consequently it is hard to see ourselves as holding our use of such ascriptions as responsible to the underlying nature of understanding. Given the background of a culture with sophisticated chemical or physical knowledge, there is a sense to what we mean by "same chemical or physical stuff" but there is not a corresponding sense to the notion of "same psychological state". Indeed, what intuitions we have seem to push in the opposite direction; ascriptions of understanding are responsive purely to facts about speakers' usage. The criterion for ascribing understanding of an expression is manifestation of a capacity to use it appropriately; the criterion is not supplemented by any allusion to sameness of the underlying structure that issues in the relevant capacity. It is unlikely that differences in underlying structure that failed to manifest as differences in use would be taken to constitute differences in understanding. At any rate, even if one rejects modest semantic externalism in favour of something more ambitious, advocates of this response will have to motivate the thought that linguistic understanding is a natural kind. We await news on this front. The complaints thus are that: the relevant notion of sameness is thoroughly obscure; there is scant evidence that we invoke any such notion; and there is little reason to think that understanding is itself a natural kind.

In contrast to this, the purely philosophical drive towards privacy has found many adherents, appears to be tolerably clear and to perform some explanatory work. We can, it seems, explain the peculiar relation that each of us bears to our own meanings by placing them in a realm to which the subject has a peculiar access. So, if there is an argument for publicity from the need to account for success in communication, then it needs serious supplementation in the form of an argument that shows that the explanatory value of the story about a private realm of meanings is completely bogus. That is a hugely weighty supplement;

if indeed it can be provided, it constitutes in its own right a powerful argument against privacy. For what it would have to show is that the conception of the inner, on which the putative explanation is based, is deeply muddled. Wittgenstein, it is widely agreed, assumes the burden of showing this in his various remarks on the possibility of a private language, although quite what his objection is and how efficacious it is are widely disputed. We thus conclude this chapter by claiming that there is no independent argument from the possibility of successful communication to publicity and turn to what seems to be a more profound question of whether a private language is so much as possible. We need to put ourselves in a position to tackle that question and, in order to do so, we shall need to have in mind Wittgenstein's remarks on the nature of following a rule.

12. Rules and privacy: the problem

12.1 The problem of rule-following

In sections 172–242 of his *Philosophical Investigations* Wittgenstein considers the nature of following a rule. We shall concentrate on Kripke's (1982), now classic, exposition of this argument.

Consider the following, natural enough, train of thought. There are many addition sums that I have never performed – let us, following Kripke, assume that 68 + 57 is among them. Now one normally supposes that, given what I have always meant by "+", there is just one correct response to this addition sum, namely: 125. In other words, if asked what the sum of 68 and 57 is according to the way I have understood addition, I *should* respond with a numeral denoting 125. Or, to call on thoughts about compositionality, one supposes that we have succeeded in conferring a meaning on the signs "68", "57" and "+" such that the complex sign formed from them – "68 + 57" – has a determinate meaning and thus refers to a determinate number, namely, that number that is the correct answer to our addition sum.

The first thing to note here is that, if this is indeed a very natural train of thought, then the meaning of a sign such as "+" – that is, what you understand when you understand that sign – sets up a standard of correctness against which your future use is measured. It is *right* to respond with "125" to the query, "What, given your past understanding of '+', is 68 + 57?", wrong to respond with "5". Similarly, the meaning that the sign "+" has for you *justifies*, at least in part, your answer of "125". So the meaning of a sign provides one with a rule for its use: meaning is essentially *normative* over use. This is why Wittgenstein is interested in the general question about what it is to follow a rule: that is, what it is for one's practice to be subject to standards of correctness.

12.1.1 The sceptical challenge

Wittgenstein undertakes a probing examination of our "natural train of thought" and Kripke pursues this by imagining a sceptical challenge. If one's understanding of "+" requires one to respond to our question with "125", then there must be a feature of one's mental history and previous use of the term "+" that determines this. But to what past fact, asks Kripke, can you point that *justifies* your answer of "125" rather than, say, "5"? The sceptic will motivate his challenge as follows. Your previous use of the term "+" can consist only in a finite set of uses. There must therefore be some sums that you have never performed and, by hypothesis, 68 + 57 is one of them. Since we have only a finite set of uses to go on, indefinitely many rules are compatible with the history of your use of the term. If, say, you have performed addition sums only with numbers less than 57, then your use of the term can be reconciled with "+" meaning standard addition or with "+" meaning the following:

$$x + y = \begin{cases} \text{the sum of } x \text{ and } y, \text{ if } x \text{ and } y \text{ are both less than 57} \\ 5, \text{ otherwise} \end{cases}$$

Let us call this quaddition or quus. Then Kripke's sceptical question is this: what in your history of your use of the term "+" determines that, if you intend to accord with your past use, you now should mean addition (the plus function) by it – and should respond "125" – rather than that you should now mean quaddition (the quus function) by it – and should respond "5"?

Before we elaborate the discussion with the sceptic, we should note a few points about the challenge. First, obviously if we have no response to the sceptic, then we cannot justify our belief in the normativity of meaning and, since meaning is essentially normative, our notion of meaning will be undermined.

Secondly, the only thing that might conceivably determine correct use must be something in my past use of the term. For the question is this: what, *if I am to accord with my past use of the term*, determines that this rather than that is the correct response? So, for the sake of the argument, Kripke is not questioning whether we *now* mean addition by "+"; rather, he is questioning whether there is any fact of the matter about what we meant by it in the past. If there is such a fact of the matter – if, say, in the past it is a fact that we meant addition by "+" – then that fact will determine that, if we now aim to accord with our past meaning, then we should respond with "125" rather than "5". Of course, if there is no fact of the matter about what we meant in the past, then there can be no fact of the matter about what we mean in the present either. The reason for this is that the argument will not trade on any restrictions on our access to the past. So for the sake of argument we are assumed to have perfect recall of any aspect of our past lives and mental histories. There is thus nothing about the present that makes it disanalogous to the past. Hence, if in the past there was no fact of the matter about our meanings, then neither is there any such fact in the present. We could, indeed, frame the argument from the first in terms of whether we *now* mean addition by "+". Kripke does not do so for strategic reasons only: in setting up the problem he does not want to have his current use of language questioned. Thus he frames the challenge by raising a question about past meanings. Nothing of philosophical importance depends on focusing on the past because, as we have just said, we are assumed to have complete and accurate recall of past facts. Thus, if we are unable to answer the question about past meanings, this will not be a consequence of an inaccessibility of the relevant facts. And therefore, if we cannot answer the question about past meanings, we cannot answer it about present meanings either.

A third point, very closely connected with the last, is this. What is argued is *not* that *for all we know* there is no fact of the matter about what we meant in the past; rather, it is that there *is* no fact of the matter about what we meant in the past. In other words, the argument is not an argument for an epistemological scepticism – it is not arguing that there is a limit to what we can know about meaning – it is an argument for ontological scepticism – it argues that there are no meanings. The reason for this was made in the previous paragraph: the only facts that could be relevant to the determination of meanings are facts about my past use of the term and my past mental life. To all of these facts I am assumed to have complete access. So, if I fail to find a fact that determines what I meant by a term in the past, then it follows, not simply that for all I know there is no such fact, but simply that there *is* no such fact.

A fourth point concerns the difference between Quine's argument for the indeterminacy of translation (and hence meaning-scepticism) and this argument of Wittgenstein's. As we saw, the background of Quine's argument is his physicalism – his belief that physics describes the ultimate structure of the world, that all facts are determined by the physical facts – and consequent behaviourist stance. This means that Quine limits the facts that are available as candidates for determining translation to those facts that have a good physicalist pedigree. To many, this robs Quine's conclusion of much of its power; only if you share his physicalism can you find in his arguments a reason to be sceptical about meanings. Wittgenstein's argument is not premised on any such view and is thus, if successful, more general and more powerful. We are, for instance, able to appeal to facts about our past mental lives – feelings, intentions, images – without having to question whether these are physicalistically acceptable. One way this comes out is that Quine's argument is framed in the third person: how does the translator set about translating *their* – the foreigner's – language? Wittgenstein's question is framed in the first person: what did I mean in the past by "+"? So, for Quine, evidence for a translation scheme has to be available to an external observer. For Wittgenstein I can appeal to aspects of my own mental life.

Finally, note that Wittgenstein is not raising any kind of scepticism about how the present is determined by the past. He can allow that there is a fact of the matter about how I *shall* go on to use the term or about how I am now going to use it – after all, it is clear that I now answer the addition problem with "125" and clear too that I would have done so. But this is no help in responding to the sceptic: knowing that I shall say such-and-such is no *justification* for its being *right* to say such-and-such. Of course, given that I am trying to accord with a certain rule and given that I am, in general, reliable in succeeding at my attempt so to accord, it may be that my use is a good guide to what one ought to do if one is to follow that rule. But: (i) it is hard to see that this is the sort of fact one could cite in *justifying* one's use (do I reassure myself about my general competence in applying a rule to a novel case?); (ii) the response presupposes that in the past we have managed to answer our current question about how one ought to go on – how else would one come to the justified view about one's reliability? – and thus it begs the question; and (iii) this is not a fact that provides any *guidance*: it simply supplies a reason to trust one's own inclinations and, if this is all there is to which one can appeal, then how would one ever pick out that one had made a mistake? If, for instance, my inclination had been to respond to the addition sum with "5", then, according to this response, that answer is justified. But what we wanted was a way of validating or invalidating an inclination: and this account does not give us that.

We can thus summarize the argument as follows:

Premises:
1. However many addition sums I have performed, there will be only a finite number of these and these are compatible with indefinitely many ("deviant") extensions to new cases.
2. No fact about the history of my mental life and use of the term can *justify* an answer as that required if I am to accord with my previous meaning.
3. No other sort of fact could have any bearing on the issue.

Sub-conclusion:
There is no fact of the matter about what I meant in the past by "+".

Premise:
4. If there is no fact of the matter about what I meant in the past by "+", then there is no fact of the matter about what I now mean by "+".

Conclusion:
There is no fact of the matter about what I now mean by "+".

Premise (2) is clearly crucial: why are there no features of my past use of the term, including my mental history, that show that in the past I meant plus, not quus, by "+"?

12.1.2 *Previous instructions/definitions*

A first, obvious enough, suggestion is that I may have defined "+" so as to determine that I meant plus rather than quus or gave myself instructions for the use of "+" that similarly so determine what I meant. So, for instance, I might have given myself an algorithm to follow when presented with addition sums. I may have linked adding with counting thus:

> To work out "$x + y$", count out x apples then count out y pears, put the apples and pears together and count the number of fruit.

Or,

> Add the numerals in the singles column according to the following list $(0 + 0 = 0; 0 + 1 = 1; 0 + 2 = 2; \ldots ; 9 + 8 = 17; 9 + 9 = 18)$, put down the numeral in the singles position and carry the numeral in the tens position into the tens column. Add the numerals in the tens column according to our list, repeating the carrying procedure into the 100s column. Repeat the procedure until all columns in the sum have been exhausted.

But such an instruction will not help rebut the sceptic. It can do so only if the instruction is exempt from the sceptical challenge, but there is no reason why it should possess such immunity. So the sceptic simply asks, why, if I am to mean by "count" what I meant by "count" in the past, should I now count the apples and pears? How do I know that in the past I did not mean quount by "count", where to quount a collection, one counts it unless it contains more than 57 objects, in which case the answer is 5? In the second case, we can come up with deviant answers simply enough: imagine that by "carry" I mean quarry, where to quarry one carries unless the numbers in the sum are more than 57, in which case you ignore the numeral in the tens column from our list. (In this case 57 + 68 = 15, which is bad enough. A little more ingenuity and we could interpret our instruction so as to come up with "5" as the answer.)

Another suggestion is that we have completely defined addition, which we might do by means of what is called a recursive definition, as follows:

$$x + 0 = x$$

$$x + S(y) = S(x + y), \text{ where } S(y) \text{ stands for the successor of } y.$$

But again this assumes that by "*S*" we meant successor, whereas we might have meant quuccessor, where the quuccessor of a number is its successor unless the number is more than 124, in which case it is 5.

So the accusation is that importing the notion of an instruction or definition that you have previously given yourself either begs the question against the sceptic, since it presupposes that what you meant in the past by the instruction is unquestionable, or it simply sets off an infinite regress.

Besides this, it is perfectly clear that there are many expressions that I understand, for example "blue", which I could not define or for which I could not supply an informative instruction for its use. So understanding is not, in general, a matter of having given oneself a definition or instruction. (Ask yourself in what language you would have given the definition/instruction. And how did you come to understand this language? ...)

12.1.3 Dispositions

An apparently promising strategy is to appeal to the notion of a disposition. How does this help with our problem? Well, the sceptic had asked: how do I know that, if I am to accord with my past use, I should now respond "125" to the addition sum? And the answer might be the following. I know that I *should now* make that response because that is the response I would have made in the past, had I been asked. In other words, in the past I possessed the disposition to respond "125" and thus should now respond similarly. The sceptic's problem can be seen as emerging from a question about how past states determine a correct answer in the present. That is, how is one's finite use to be extended to this new case? The dispositional account can be seen as responding to this by saying that the answer in this new case was present in the past, although only dispositionally. So, in a sense, we see our problem as emerging from the limited nature of our past use and states of mind; we inflate the scope of those states by thinking of them dispositionally.

This can be seen very clearly in one aspect of the dispositionalist's thinking. Part of the problem with the addition case is that our finite set of uses can be extended in indefinitely many new ways to potentially infinitely many new cases. The dispositionalist thinks that she can overcome the finitude of our occurrent (non-dispositional) states by factoring in dispositions. And, in fact, this is mistaken. As Kripke says, we have only finitely many dispositions to respond to addition sums: at a certain stage the numbers become too big for us to cope with and we have no reliable disposition to give a certain response. But nonetheless we ordinarily think that even in these cases the meaning we have conferred on the plus sign requires just one answer as the correct one. Some think that we can get round this by thinking about the dispositions that we would have had had we been smarter, quicker thinking, longer lived and so on. But then Kripke says these are just hypotheses about what we would be disposed to say in these particular circumstances; we really do not know what dispositions we would have had in these cases. In essence here we trick ourselves by imagining that we had *whatever it takes* to perform this huge addition sum correctly. But then the dispositional account collapses into emptiness: it is not helping us to fix on a notion of correctness; it presupposes such a notion.

But let us set this worry aside and grant that, in the past, I had the disposition to respond "125" to the addition sum. Does this help in providing a response to the sceptic? Kripke argues that it does not, for a number of reasons:

(i) Our question was: how, if I am to accord with my past understanding of the term, should I now respond? The answer is that I *should* now respond as I was disposed then (i.e. in the past) to respond. But this will not help me unless I know that that disposition was correct according to the rule I was then and am now intending to follow – otherwise it fails to provide any sort of *justification* for that response. And what assures me that the disposition was correct? This is a legitimate question because speakers do misapply their terms and sometimes do so systematically. So how do I know that this disposition is not a disposition to misapply the term? Another way of putting the point is this. It makes sense to suppose that I can have a disposition that is incorrect. But from the dispositionalist's point of view, correctness is determined by the disposition so that that supposition cannot make sense. So if, for instance, in the past I had the disposition to respond "125" to the addition problem, that only helps me to justify that response (and thus to rule out the response "5") if I know that that disposition was correct according to the rule I intended to follow. But then I need to know that I was correctly following the addition rule and not mistakenly following the quaddition rule. In other words, we need to have answered the problem the sceptic had put to us. So, in the present context, the response is viciously circular.

(ii) A second problem is that we do not appeal to the nature of our past dispositions in justifying our answer. We do not have any secure and immediate access to what our past dispositions were, so it is only a hypothesis that we would have responded "125" in the past. But how can that hypothesis provide any kind of justification for my present use of the term? This radically misconceives what it is like to be a language-speaker: one simply does not test one's usage by reflecting on and hypothesizing about how one would have used the expression in the past. If anything, one takes one's present disposition/inclination to indicate what one's previous dispositions would have been. But this just means that my present inclinations need not meet any standard: as Wittgenstein says, "whatever seems right to me will be right", but this means only that we cannot talk about right and wrong.

It is tempting to think that there must be some confusion in the sceptic's challenge because we can build machines that automatically follow certain simple rules. If the machine can be so constrained, then why should we not be similarly constrained? We might think of the machine as churning out answers to applications of the rule and, if this were so, we could similarly think of ourselves as doing so. The mechanism of the machine grinds on to new cases according to its physical makeup. Since that makeup embodies the rule, the notion of correctness is incorporated in the physical processes at work in the machine. What is right about the example is that, *if the machine functions properly*, then it incorporates the rule. But what is it for the machine to function properly? Wires bend, components melt, gears stick … Is an instance of one of these happenings an instance of the machine malfunctioning or was it designed to take into account that after so many applications this part will become bendy? We cannot determine an answer to this question without knowing what rule the machine was designed to embody. So the machine cannot be taken to determine correctness; rather, the proper functioning of the machine is understood in terms of a prior notion of the rule. We might, though, consider an ideal machine made of ideally rigid, frictionless components. But then what we are considering is not a physical machine – something whose physical processes will extend it to new cases – but the *idea* of a machine. In fact we are thinking of the expression of a rule, perhaps in a particularly vivid or metaphorical way. But that just returns us to the problem – it does not solve it.

The essential problems with these views are that the appeal to dispositions attempts to explain what we ought to do in terms of what we actually do or would do. And this fails because these facts about what we would do (i) are finite, not infinite; (ii) are not the sorts of things to which we appeal in justifying a use; (iii) fail to take into account the fact that these descriptive facts about us do not provide a justification, which must be normative – the notion of a mistaken disposition makes this point; and (iv) address the normative question by eliminating the possibility of a mistake, but then beg the question – we have to appeal to *idealized* machines or to dispositions that *correctly* implement our intentions to carry out such-and-such a rule.

12.1.4 Feelings and images

No simple experience – a feeling such as a tickle, pain or sensation of green – can constitute your meaning one thing rather than another by a sign. Perhaps my understanding of the sign "+" consists in having a certain experience associated with my use of the sign; Kripke suggests that you have a certain characteristic headache. But the question is: how does the presence of this headache indicate that I should respond "125" rather than "5"? Perhaps one supposes that having the headache is characteristic of meaning plus rather than quus by "+". But what is the argument for this? This seems completely arbitrary. Perhaps one supposes that the headache accompanies correct uses of "+" in the past and now accompanies my response of "125" to the addition sum. The sceptic can happily concede this: the correct response to "57 + 68" given your current meaning of "+" is "125"; the question is whether you are now using it as you meant it in the past. That the headache always accompanies correct uses of "+" is consistent with the sceptic's hypothesis that in the past you meant quus by "+" and should now respond with "5" if you are to accord with that use.

Having a certain image cannot be taken as either necessary or sufficient for understanding but, more importantly, no image accompanying the use of a sign can determine its meaning since the image needs a rule of application. It might seem natural to think that a red image accompanying my use of the term "red" determines the application of "red" to red things. There are all sorts of problems here in thinking about just what shade of red my image is and why it then guides my application of "red" to red things of a different shade and why if, say, my image is in fact scarlet, I still mean *red* by "red" and not *scarlet*. What all this shows is that, even if there is such an image, it alone does not determine meaning. Rather we have to know how to *use* the image. But how are we to know this? By use of a further image that depicts the application of the first image? The regress that beckons is fatal to the proposal. The basic problem here is that the appeal to an image is the attempt to appeal to something that is intrinsically representational (i.e. represents what it represents because of its very nature rather than because of how it is [properly] used). This is the myth of a rule that interprets itself – a self-intimating rule. The proposal collapses as soon as one notices that there is more than one way in which the image can guide use. The image then ceases to be self-intimating and we set off on an infinite regress.

12.2 Kripke's sceptical solution

The upshot of the argument is scepticism about meaning. We can respond to the argument in one of two ways. First, we can point out one or another inadequacy in the argument and so refuse to accept its conclusion. This is what Kripke calls a straight solution to the argument. But, secondly, we might offer what Kripke calls a sceptical solution to the argument. A sceptical solution would accept the argument as a good one but then try to dispel the aura of paradox surrounding its conclusion. It would do this by accepting that conclusion but go on to explain how our talk about meanings and our attributions of understanding can still have a legitimate role. We shall look now at Kripke's sceptical solution. We shall then find fault with scepticism and the sceptical solution and thus it will be a task for us to find an approach to understanding language that avoids the sceptical problem.

The conclusion of the argument is that there are no facts about meanings: that is, factualism about meaning is rejected. So we cannot understand our talk about meanings as portraying facts. But this does not mean that such talk is illegitimate and should be jettisoned, since we might be able to explain such talk as having some function other than that of portraying facts. The general strategy here is not uncommon. Often a philosopher will find a reason to be suspicious about a putative range of facts. For example, these may be: moral facts (possible reason for suspicion: lack of convergence in moral judgements or lack of explanatory role for moral facts); mathematical facts (possible reason for suspicion: abstract objects such as numbers do not exist); or facts involving theoretical entities in science (possible reason for suspicion: theoretical entities cannot be observed). When the philosopher finds herself in this position, she may then reject talk that appears to be talk about those facts, so she may reject mathematical talk or talk in theoretical science. But this is usually an unpalatable option; more usually the philosopher will try to reinterpret the relevant discourse as not fact-stating. She may thus interpret moral discourse as expressive of our attitudes rather than as descriptive of the world. She may interpret mathematics as laying down rules rather than as describing a realm of abstract objects. She may buttress this position by pointing out the utility – the role played in our lives – by these expressions of attitude (morals) or laying down of rules (mathematics).

Kripke adopts a similar strategy in relation to our talk about meanings.[1] We learn from the sceptical argument that such talk cannot have the role of describing any aspect of the world – since its sentences are thus incapable of stating truths about the world, we shall say that it is not truth-conditional. This coheres, Kripke claims, with a reorientation in Wittgenstein's thinking about language in general. Wittgenstein's early work, the *Tractatus*, adopts a truth-conditional account of meaning – a sentence represents a possible state of affairs and is true if that state of affairs exists, false otherwise: the possible state of affairs thus gives the condition for the sentence to be true – but in the later work he examines the meaning of a sentence by looking at the conditions in which it is used. So, for declarative sentences we focus on the conditions in which the sentence is asserted. Thus Kripke says we have: (i) to look at statements about meaning in terms of their assertion-conditions rather than their truth-conditions; and (ii) to understand their usefulness as so used. He writes:

> All that is needed to legitimise assertions that someone means something is that there be roughly specifiable circumstances under which they are legitimately assertible, and that the game of asserting them has a role in our lives. No supposition that "facts correspond" to those assertions is needed.
>   (1982: 78)

Kripke's point will be that assertions about meaning and attributions of understanding play a fundamental role in promoting and maintaining agreement in use of language *across the community*. So it is essential for him that talk of meaning occurs in the context of a community's use of language.

Kripke's first point is that we unhesitatingly apply simple rules. One simply acts with confidence, without internal deliberation and, as the sceptical argument shows, one is unable to offer a justification for that use. And, again as the sceptical argument shows, no fact can be cited that determines the use as correct or incorrect. So, if we focus on an individual in isolation, all we can say is that she persists in her use: "whatever seems right to her will be right and that only means that it makes no sense to talk about right" (paraphrasing Wittgenstein).

But bring in the community and, according to Kripke, all changes utterly. We noted in our discussion of dispositions that a hypothesis about the character of one's previous dispositions just is not the right sort of thing to justify one's present use as being in accord with past use – one simply does not reflect on such facts to justify one's use. Similarly, one does not take samples of past usage to justify what one presently means. Rather, one offers explanations and, where these run out (as they will), one goes on without justification (but with confidence). From the third-personal perspective, though, things change radically: the teacher's attribution of understanding will be made on the basis of samples of sufficiently diverse use. So the first-personal statement "I mean addition by '+'" has no justification conditions – it simply expresses a certain kind of confidence – the third-personal statement "He means addition by '+'" has reasonably clear justification or assertion-conditions. The purpose of such statements is that they are used to bring people into the linguistic community, to mark them out as members whose practice we can rely on: not "rely on" in the sense that their terms genuinely express a given meaning, but "rely on" in the sense that we can depend on their use as being in agreement with our own. Of course there is no guarantee of our ability to rely on one another, but our whole lives together – what Wittgenstein calls our shared form of life – depends on this reliability and presumably there is some fact about our natural history that explains it.

12.3 Problems for the sceptical solution

12.3.1 Global non-factualism

An apparent problem for the account is that, unlike our other examples of non-truth-conditional or non-factual discourses, non-factualism about meaning explodes into non-factualism about everything. Why so? Well, take some sentence about anything that we are now inclined to treat as factual, for example "The earth is flat". Now the question of the factuality of such a sentence is the question of whether it is a matter of fact as to what its truth-value is. The sentence has whatever truth-value it has (false, in case you are wondering) as a result partly of what it means and partly as a result of the way the world is. But, so the sceptical argument tells us, there is no fact of the matter about what it means so there can be no fact of the matter about what its truth-value is. For if there is no fact of the matter about what, in part, determines something, then there can be no fact of the matter about that thing. If there is no fact of the matter about the size of your bank account, then there is no fact of the matter about precisely how wealthy you are. And now the worries are: (i) that if Kripke cannot distinguish talk about meaning and understanding as being non-factual in contrast to other factual discourses, then the claim that such talk is non-factual collapses; and (ii) that one cannot make sense of what it is to be a global non-factualist.

Clearly there is no general requirement that in order to make sense of a distinction one needs to be able to encounter instances of either term of the distinction. So it is not obvious that Kripke needs to distinguish a non-factualist discourse by pointing to factualist discourses. So the real worry is just whether one can be a global non-factualist. Given that factualism involves adoption of a truth-conditional account and non-factualism involves adoption of an assertion-conditions account, the question is just whether it is coherent to be a global assertibility-conditions theorist. The problem with that position is that the assertibility-conditions for a discourse are supposed to be *descriptive* of conditions in which making an assertion is taken as being warranted.[2] That is, assertion-conditions capture *truths* about the practice. So here at least a factualist construal seems to be called for.[3]

12.3.2 Goldfarb's objection

Goldfarb (2002) demonstrates a tension between Kripke's sceptical solution and his view that the sceptical solution rules out the possibility of a private or, as Goldfarb prefers to say, solitary language. As we have just noted, what Kripke requires is an assertibility-conditions account of talk of meaning and understanding: that is, an account that correctly describes just when practitioners permit one another to make ascriptions of meaning and understanding. Take the following clause from such an account:

(*)   It is licensed to assert that a person means addition by "+" when that person has responded with the sum in every case [or in some sufficient range of cases] so far attempted.   (*Ibid*.: 102)

Goldfarb points out that these are conditions relating purely to an individual language-user so there is no reason why they cannot be applied by the private or solitary linguist: there is a distinction between such a user's actually fulfilling the condition and her impression that she does so. What Kripke needs to do is to insist therefore that such specifications of assertion-conditions are illegitimate; instead we need to specify such conditions by appeal to such things as agreement with the community of speakers. But, the question is, what reason has Kripke for imposing this restriction?

Goldfarb makes the following suggestion on Kripke's behalf. Arguably the account of the assertion-condition given in (*) is illegitimate because it presupposes that we know what the sum of two numbers is. For without this understanding the statement of the assertion-condition makes no sense. Thus we should opt for a "thinner" account of the requisite assertion-condition in terms of similarity of response among practitioners. But Goldfarb goes on to argue that this suggestion falls to precisely analogous problems. Take the following suggestion:

(**) It is licensed to assert that a person means addition by "+" when that person has made the same response as those of her community in every case [or in some sufficient range of cases] so far attempted.

But this can only mean that the person's response and those of her community are all tokens of the same type. So the account of assertion-conditions presupposes the relation of type to token. However, the relation of type to token is "a case of the relation between the continuation of a series and the rule governing the series" (*ibid.*: 103). Thus this account of the assertibility-conditions is just as question-begging as our account in (*), focusing purely on the individual. So Kripke cannot both espouse non-factualism about meaning and understanding – in the guise of applying an assertions-conditions account – and use this to argue against private language. Is there a more direct rebuttal of the sceptical solution?

12.3.3 *Applying our concept of a rule-governed practice*

Wittgenstein's discussion of the nature of following a rule culminates in the following passage:

> This was our paradox: no course of action could be determined by a rule, because every course of action can be made out to accord with the rule. The answer was: if everything can be made out to accord with the rule, then it can also be made out to conflict with it. And so there would be neither accord nor conflict here.
>
> It can be seen that there is a misunderstanding here from the mere fact that in the course of our argument we give one interpretation after another; as if each one contented us at least for a moment, until we thought of yet another standing behind it. What this shews is that there is a way of grasping a rule which is *not* an *interpretation*, but which is exhibited in what we call "obeying the rule" and "going against it" in actual cases.   (1958: §201)

The paradox is our sceptical conclusion that there are no rules. Thus what appear to be rules and what appear to be rule-governed practices are not genuinely so. The resolution is to realize that there is a misunderstanding, which arises from thinking that grasp of a rule is always grasp of an interpretation. Instead we should realize that there is a way of grasping a rule "which is exhibited in what we call 'obeying the rule' and 'going against it' in actual cases".

Undoubtedly this resolution is dark, but let us start with obvious points. First, Wittgenstein here seems to reject the aim of giving a constitutive account of rules or of grasping a rule. We are told what *exhibits* grasp of a rule but not what such a grasp consists in. Secondly, the resolution depends on noticing that the practice of adjudicating whether or not something counts as according, or conflicting with the rule, the practice of policing our practice – the policing practice, for short – plays a crucial role.[4] However, it is at exactly this point that the obvious gives way to the obscure. Just why is the policing practice so crucial in Wittgenstein's solution? I shall present an argument that aims to show that once we see the pivotal role of the policing practice, we shall be unable rationally to adopt the sceptical solution.

Apparent rule-following: Let us begin by introducing the notion of an apparently rule-governed practice. The paradox recorded in the first paragraph of §201 is a sceptical conclusion about rules and rule-following: it denies that these are *genuine* phenomena. They are, however, apparent phenomena and much of Wittgenstein's discussion of practices that exhibit rule boundedness or normative constraint must be read, not as being about *genuinely* rule- governed practices, which would beg the question against the sceptic, but as being about the *apparent* phenomena. How should we best understand this? Retreat one section from our quoted one and we find Wittgenstein discussing outlandish distortions of the practice of playing chess. Chess is an apparently rule-governed activity in the sense that we would, sceptical worries aside, be inclined to apply the vocabulary of rule-following here. The outlandish cases are used to probe just what needs to be in place if such an application of normative locutions is thought to be appropriate. So it seems plausible to think of an apparently rule-governed practice as one in which our usual criteria would lead to an application of normative vocabulary. The sceptical challenge then effectively claims that the appearance of normative constraint that is promoted by the application of such vocabulary is not genuine. When the situation is examined, we come to see that all apparent rule-following is just that: *merely* apparent; the genuine article cannot be found. This sort of situation is typical of many sceptical challenges. The epistemological sceptic does not question whether there is knowledge as judged by our usual standards for ascribing knowledge. Rather, she argues that, on philosophical reflection, we can see that satisfaction of those criteria fails to deliver genuine knowledge, because, for instance, we find ourselves incapable of ruling out possibilities that we do not usually consider but whose actualization would be incompatible with our possession of knowledge. Just so here: the rule-following sceptic thinks that when we investigate our usual practice of discerning rule-following we find that we fail to detect the real thing because we cannot find a fact that ultimately justifies the way we go on.

The crucial thing for our purposes is that the dialectic requires that we distinguish the notion of practices that are in a substantial sense apparently normative – these count as normative by a correct application of our usual criteria – both from the notion of those practices that are only superficially apparently normative – these can be seen to result from a mistaken application of our usual criteria – and from the notion of those that are genuinely normative – these can be seen as normative even in the face of the sceptical challenge. So conceived, the task of rebutting the sceptic can be seen as one of showing that (substantially) apparently normative practices are genuinely normative. I think that we can give an argument to that conclusion by considering the role of the policing practice; so Wittgenstein's observation does provide the clue to ruling out the sceptical solution.

The practice and policing the practice: The first plank in the argument is the claim that the existence of an apparently rule-governed practice requires an associated policing practice. In other words, the policing practice is internally related to its apparently rule-governed practice. Witness these remarks of Wittgenstein's. Having dismissed the idea that grasp of an interpretation can ground rule-following (1958: §198), he asks himself the following questions: "What has the expression of a rule – say a sign-post – got to do with my actions? What sort of connexion is there here?" And he goes on to suggest the following answer: "Well perhaps this one: I have been trained to react to this sign in a particular way, and now I do so react to it." And then, importantly, the objection comes that this is merely a causal connection, that it is not an intrinsic connection of the sign to actions in accord with it: "But this is only to give a causal connexion; to tell how it has come about that we go by the sign-post; not what this going-by-the-sign really consists in." But, although he says nothing in answer to the constitutive question, he rebuts the charge of merely having given a causal account: "On the contrary; I have further indicated that a person goes by a sign-post only in so far as there exists a regular use of sign-posts, a custom."

The background of training and of customary use is thus not a contingent feature of rule-governed practices but an *essential* condition of them: "a person goes by a sign-post *only* in so far as there exists ... a custom" (my emphasis). Thus there is no taking a move as being bound by rules unless that move is situated in the context of a practice, a custom sustained by training. However, that is not to say that the rule-governed practice requires that there be practice of policing moves within it. However, there can be no institution of training unless there is a practice of instruction and of monitoring receipt of that instruction. We could not do so without a means of monitoring whether or not a move in the practice is or is not correct. "The words 'right' and 'wrong' are used when giving instruction in proceeding according to a rule. The word 'right' makes the pupil go on, the word 'wrong' holds him back" (Wittgenstein 1978: VII 39). So a practice cannot be taken to be rule-governed unless there is a system of training and there can be no system of training unless there is a policing practice.

How essential a feature of following a rule is training? Wittgenstein writes as if it is not:

> But couldn't we imagine that someone without any training should see a sum that was set to do, and straightaway find himself in the mental state that in the normal course of things is only produced by training and practice? So that he knew he could calculate although he had never calculated. (One might, then, it seems, say; The training would be mere history, and merely as a matter of empirical fact would it be necessary for the production of knowledge.) – But suppose now that he is in that state and calculates wrong? What is he supposed to say to himself? And suppose he then multiplied sometimes right, sometimes again quite wrong. – The training may of course be overlooked as mere history, if he now *always* calculates right. But that he *can* calculate he shews, to himself as well as to others only by this, that he *calculates* correctly.
>
> (*Ibid.*: VI 33)

Here, although Wittgenstein admits the contingent role of training, he does so in a very guarded way. The training may be seen as such only when our practitioner *goes on* to follow the rule correctly. Where his performance fails this optimal standard he stands in need of further training – of correction via the policing practice. However, even if we say that he does grasp the rule without training, we (and he) can do so only against an extended performance that has been monitored to be correct. So, although the training may have been dispensable, we can say so only in the light of performances that have been monitored as successful. So what is not dispensable is the monitoring of practice; what is not dispensable is the policing practice.

I have put these points in terms of what is required in order for us to take a practice as rule-governed, in other words, what is required for a practice to be apparently rule-governed. But perhaps this is not in Wittgenstein's mind in these passages; he may have been talking simply about what is required for a practice to be (genuinely) rule-governed. However, he follows the quoted section with this, in which he makes quite clear that his concern is the application of our phrase "obeying a rule": "Is what we call 'obeying a rule' something that it would be possible for only *one* man to do, and to do only *once* in his life?" And he comments, "This is of course a note on the grammar of the expression 'to obey a rule'" (1958: §199). The exploration of this question takes us into the next section, in which we are presented, as already mentioned, with two outlandish distortions of the game of chess. Wittgenstein seems quite clearly to be testing whether we would be inclined, by ordinary criteria, to classify these cases as cases of rule-following. In the first, what takes place resembles what takes place when we play chess but there is no background of playing games at all. In the second the superficial resemblance is lost; "play" takes place by means of stampings and yells and so on. Although he typically leaves us hanging on the question of whether we would say that these are games, the suggestion is that, although the superficial resemblance between the first case and our practice of playing chess might lead us to categorize this as playing chess, here we have a case that is only *superficially* apparent rule-governed activity. Why? Because in the case of the stampers our decision would be entirely dictated by the question of whether or not there is an appropriate background custom of game-playing – *this*, we reflectively discover, is the decisive criterion, not the extent of superficial resemblance between cases considered as isolated happenings.

To my mind this is the right reading of Wittgenstein here; he is probing the criteria that govern our usual use of terms such as "rule", "sign", "game" and so on, and nothing in these investigations involves the question-begging assumption that terms so used pick out the genuine phenomenon. I shall thus conclude that we cannot *take* a practice to be rule-governed if we cannot detect a practice of policing it. In my terminology the existence of an apparently rule-governed practice requires the existence of a policing practice.

The policing practice and the sceptic: The policing practice is a practice in which we make judgements about the correctness or incorrectness of actions intended to conform to a rule; we judge what counts as obeying or going against the rule. The sceptic claims that there are no facts about whether or not a move is correct or incorrect. So no such judgement could be true. Thus, if such judgements are, on occasion, true, then scepticism about the existence of rules is false. Therefore, if we could justify the application of truth to these judgements, we would be able to rebut the sceptic about rules. But all we have is a practice in which we appear to make certain sorts of judgement and it is open to the sceptic to deny – as Kripke's sceptic does – the status of these judgements as genuine. As we have seen, she replaces a truth-conditional construal of these statements with an assertions-conditions construal supplemented by an account of the instrumental value of such practices, of the role they play in our lives. The policing practice is consequently seen as having *merely* instrumental value in securing communal agreement in our use of language, which is essential to our lives with one another.

The crucial question now is this: can the sceptical solution cohere with our discovery of the internal connection between the policing practice and its apparently rule-governed practice? The internal connection consists in the fact that the existence of the apparently rule-governed practice requires the existence of the policing practice (and vice versa): the existence of the latter is a necessary condition for the existence of the former. Can we accept this and still see the policing practice as *merely* instrumentally valuable? Surely not; even if the policing practice performs an instrumental role and even if it necessarily *can* perform that role, still there is no guarantee that it *must* perform that role. If something else *can* perform that role, then it is *possible* that it *does* perform that role and thereby deprives the policing practice of its role. So, let us suppose with Kripke that the role of the policing practice is in promoting and sustaining agreement, then it is surely possible that a wonder drug or course of hypnosis is at least as efficient in promoting and sustaining agreement. It is possible too that the world is so constituted that we simply agree with one another without any need to enforce agreement. In such circumstances the policing practice would have no instrumental value: it would be entirely dispensable. Nothing here needs to hinge on the detail of the instrumental value accorded to the policing practice. The point is that if its value is instrumental, then there can be no reason for thinking that nothing else can fulfil that instrumental role, in which case there is only a contingent link between the apparently rule-governed practice and the policing practice. Thus the instrumental view cannot cohere with the necessary interdependence of the existence of the two practices.

That conclusion suffices to put the sceptic in considerable difficulty, if there is no other way than instrumentalism to avoid a factual construal of the policing practice. So what alternatives are there to instrumentalism? The obvious candidates are varieties of either error theory – a theory claiming that claims made in a discourse are all false since there are no facts of the kind to make such statements true – or some form of expressivism – a view according to which the statements in question are not the sort of statements that aim at truth, they aim at something other, for example, the expression of an attitude. The problem with these positions is not that in this context they are false – although they are – but that they are beside the point. These positions offer alternative construals of apparently fact-stating discourse; they do not explain the value that the discourse has under their preferred construal. It is tautological that their value so construed is not in stating fact, and mysterious what else it could consist in if not something instrumental. What role could be played by, say, expressions of one's attitude to moves in the practice if it is not that of cultivating agreement? But in that case we have not found alternatives to instrumentalism.

Another tactic would be for the sceptic to be entirely negative and thus to resist offering a sceptical solution. But this tactic simply makes her position worse. Such a character would have to view any practice as a mere set of regularities. Although some regularities may logically presuppose others – as presumably is the case of the policing practice presupposing the practice it polices – there is no other way for there to be an internal connection between regularities, and thus no way to understand the fact that the existence of the policing practice is necessary for the existence of the practice it polices.

The suggested conclusion is thus that a non-factualist construal of the policing practice cannot be reconciled with the existence of an internal connection between that practice and the apparently rule-governed practice. Thus non-factualism about the policing practice is false. The policing practice is factual and thus rules exist. In other words, a necessary condition for the existence of an apparently rule-governed practice is the existence of a policing practice. This fact entails that the policing practice is factual, which, in turn, entails the falsity of scepticism about rules. Apparent rule-following is thus genuine rule-following.[5]

Note that the argument never offers a constitutive account of rules – it never says what it is to follow one or another rule – but instead it infers their reality from revealing a necessary condition for their appearance. We cannot acknowledge the necessity of this condition consistently with a denial of the reality of rules. Thus we infer the reality of rules from facts about the necessary conditions for the appearance of rule-following. The position is distinctly Kantian in that the validatory inference is based on the necessary condition for an appearance. Here we validate our realistic view of rules by showing that alternative non-realist views cannot be reconciled, not with the necessary conditions for the appearance, but with the fact that those conditions are necessary.

The view thus is that the objectivity of rules emerges not from a connection of our practices with anything external but from a certain complexity in how our practices interlock. This interlocking of practices is sufficient for rationally grounding our non-sceptical belief that rules are real. Although Wittgenstein never puts the point in quite these terms, we do find him hinting at such a view: "If I have once grasped a rule I am bound in what I do further. But of course that only means that I am bound in my *judgement* about what is in accord with the rule and what not" (1978: VI 28). The reality of one's being bound by a rule requires no more than that one's use is subject to a policing practice.

How adequate is the argument as a response to the sceptic? It is tempting to see the response as falling short of anything the sceptic might require, which is to justify why, if I am to accord with my past usage of "+", I should now say that 68 + 57 = 125. Clearly nothing that has been said thus far offers such a justification. But there is a justification: in the past I meant addition (not quaddition) by "+" and thus "125" is the right response when asked what 68 + 57 is.[6] This response is non-reductive because it does not justify my claim about what I meant in terms of anything more basic and thus, although it points to a gap in the sceptic's argument, is apt to seem deeply unsatisfying. I do not suggest that the thoughts reviewed here exhaust what needs to be said in response to the sceptical train of thought – see Chapter 13 – but they do move us some way towards an acceptable non-reductive position. Why so? The reason is that the thoughts are validatory of our mundane realism about rules. The sceptic concedes the existence of apparently rule-governed practices and the argument given forces her to accept the reality of rules as a necessary condition for there being apparently rule-governed practices. And now, *given that realistic* outlook, there is nothing unsatisfying in the non-reductive reply unless we can explain why that realistic outlook is itself the source of some other philosophical puzzlement. In Chapter 13 we shall look at just that question: why is the phenomenon of rule-following puzzling and what response can we offer to this puzzlement?

Ultra-realism about rules: There is another Kantian aspect to our conclusion. The discovery of the internal relation between the apparently rule-governed practice and the policing practice is incompatible with non-realism about rules, but is equally incompatible with what we might call ultra-realism or Platonism about rules: the view that rules owe nothing to our practice. Wittgenstein has separate arguments against such a position: he thinks that such views launch the regress of interpretations (since we could internalize rules viewed in this way only as interpretations) and are useless (to put the point in Kripkean terms, we could allow that responding "125" now is according with the rule of addition but nothing shows that this is the rule with which we ought to accord, if we are to use the term "+" consistently with our past usages). These complaints against Platonism blame it for leading to scepticism and for offering no response to scepticism.

Another complaint against such views is that they precisely cannot recognize the internal connection between the policing practice and the apparently rule-governed practice. If rules are independent of our practices, then there need be no connection between practice according to the rule and our policing of that practice. If acting in accord with the rule is simply a matter of how one's actions stand in relation to the independent dictates of the rule, then practice that appears to be governed by the rule does not require the existence of a practice of policing it. In other words, if rule-following is a matter purely of aligning one's practice with the rule construed Platonistically, then the policing practice, although fact-stating, is a dispensable feature of our following a rule. Unless explication of the requisite alignment itself necessarily implicates the policing practice – and how could it? – there would be no way to see that practice as having anything but an instrumental value in bringing about that alignment. So our claim is equally efficacious against ultra-realism about rules.

13. Rules and privacy: the solution?

13.1 Can there be a private language?

At §201 – quoted above – Wittgenstein (1958) draws the paradoxical conclusion from his previous meditation on following a rule and then goes on to diagnose the error. The solution requires us to make two moves: first, to reject the view that grasping a rule is always a matter of having an interpretation and, secondly, to accept that there is a way of grasping a rule that is exhibited in calling particular uses either "obeying the rule" or "going against the rule". I want to focus first on the second, positive, movement. As we noted, Wittgenstein does not respond to the rule-following paradox by offering an account of what it is to follow a rule; rather, he says that there is a way of grasping a rule that is *exhibited* in what we call accord and discord. We thus discover not what rule-following is but an essential condition for there to be rule-following. That essential condition is that there must be a practice of regulating our practice; there is no mere practice of following a rule since, for there to be such a practice, there must also be a "second-order" practice of policing the practice. So rule-following is necessarily a reflective activity; rule-followers must engage not only in the practice of following a rule but in the practice of assessing performances as either in accord or in conflict with the rule: "Hence it is not possible to obey a rule 'privately': otherwise thinking one was obeying a rule would be the same thing as obeying it" (*ibid*.: § 201).

For the private linguist there cannot be two distinct practices, one of following the rule and one of assessing one's performance. For, from the private linguist's perspective there is no *current* monitoring of her practice. Her decision about whether or not to perform such-and-such a move *now* is indistinguishable from her decision about whether or not such a move is *now* correct. So the policing practice collapses into the practice it polices, or, better, there is no policing practice. Of course all this shows is that there is no private linguist in the specious present, not that there is no solitary user of language. There is no coalescing of such a speaker's past performance with her *reflection* on whether or not that performance *was* correct. So a solitary user of language has a policing practice in which she makes judgements about her past uses. But if we think through such a position we shall see that it is scarcely coherent. How is such a speaker to make judgements on her past uses unless she is able somehow to refer to them? How does she refer to them except by utilizing some linguistic or symbolic device? And how does she use such a device unless she is a rule-follower? So, yes, such a character might be a solitary rule-follower if we are prepared to concede that she is already a solitary rule-follower. There is thus no conception of such a speaker that is not based on vicious circularity.

Let us put this thought about first- and second-order practices aside – although it remains important. Here our aim is to understand the nature of rule-following and, in particular, in what way rule-following gives rise to a conception of the publicity of meaning. Two major themes obsess Wittgenstein in the next forty sections of *Philosophical Investigations*. One is the sense in which a rule points beyond itself and the other is the role of human agreement in constituting rule-following. There is an important connection between each obsession and the other. One is apt to see the rule as pointing beyond itself in Platonistic terms: the rule lays down a pattern of correct usage extending beyond any actual or potential uses of practitioners; it stands as an ideal standard against which those uses are to be judged. In recoil from this radical dislocation of the rule from the practice that sustains it, one is apt to see rule-following as no more than a matter of human agreement: what is correct is what the community agrees is correct. But then, of course, the community itself is not subject to any standard, so this position might, in turn, provoke its own recoil, ushering back in the Platonistic position. We need to understand both aspects aright if we are not to be frustrated by continual recoil from one inadequate position to another.

13.2 Platonism about rules

Let us begin with the Platonistic construal. Wittgenstein is concerned to expose this view of rules as mythological and moreover as a useless myth. In what sense is the pattern of use present in the mind of the rule-follower? If it is present, then how is it represented? And if it is represented, then is this not to have an interpretation? But we know that interpretations and justifications of one's performances soon give out. We know too that grasp of the rule cannot always be a matter of interpretation. But it *seems* that there must be something in the mind of the rule-follower that is not present in her actual use. Her actual use can be deployed to convey an understanding of the rule to a trainee, but it *seems* that, when so deployed, her use does not exhaust her understanding: it is up to the learner to "guess the essential thing" (1958: §210).

However, this is a distortion of the situation. We are tempted to say that the learner has to guess "the essential thing" because no demonstration of use is proof against misunderstanding. Thus it seems that what is understood is not fully displayed in the rule-follower's use. It is as if understanding is grasp of a pattern of use that transcends all uses. However, although the thought is quite natural, it is muddled: understanding is not a state that somehow incorporates the totality of uses – it could not be so because there is no way such a totality could be represented. Rather, the simple unembellished fact is this: the state of understanding is *not* to be identified with the capacity to make just any set of uses, which is not to say that it *is* a capacity to make any of an infinite set of uses.

Wittgenstein has his interlocutor ask, "Doesn't our understanding reach beyond all the examples?" and he comments: "A very queer expression, and quite a natural one!" (1958: §209). Both queer and natural: "natural" because we want to distinguish understanding from a capacity for a limited set of uses; "queer" because we are apt then to see it as a capacity for an infinite set of uses, as grasp of a rail to infinity. The limited sets of uses, given as part of instruction, are thus accompanied by the qualification "and so on", or the like. Wittgenstein rejects the idea that "and so on" functions as an abbreviation, as a gesture towards some set of uses that we cannot actually perform. Rather, the phrase means that we should go on in the *same* way. But, as he points out later, notions of sameness and of fit cannot be used to explain the notion of rule: they are precisely coordinate with it. What counts as continuing in the same way will depend on the nature of the rule; there is no intrinsic notion of sameness that can determine what will count as continuing in the same way.

Of course there are occasions when we can justify our performance as being in accord with the rule. But, as we have repeatedly remarked, such justifications eventually give way and all we are left with is an ability to display one's unjustified use. And now the myth of the rule as rail to infinity is seen to be useless as well. For the point is that once the business of giving justifications has been exhausted, the pattern extending of itself to infinity can neither guide nor justify one's use; to do either it would have to be represented somehow; that is, it would be an interpretation. Thus the notion of a rule as rail collapses because, if it is to do any work at all, it resurrects the regress of interpretations.

Both the tactic of explaining a rule by illustrative uses and that of offering an interpretation exhaust themselves at a point that, if it is proof against misunderstanding, lies *within* the normative practice of rule-following – either because a notion of sameness is presupposed or because the interpretation presupposes certain meanings. There is thus no explanation of the rule that is both non-question-begging and proof against misunderstanding. One might construe this by thinking of one's understanding as transcending explanation and limited samples of use, but there is no *need* to do so and moreover doing so renders understanding a mysterious state, which ultimately cannot explain the phenomena that puzzle us.

What point is there, then, to remarks such as "All the steps are already taken"? Wittgenstein takes such a remark to be an affirmation that in obeying the rule one has no choice: one obeys the rule blindly. One's sense is that the rule leads the way on each occasion of its application: we do not choose what the rule dictates; it simply dictates. On the one hand this is a remark about the phenomenology of following a rule – this is how it seems to us when we follow a rule. And, on the other hand, it is a remark about the grammar of the term "rule": we would not call an activity that of following a rule were it the case that we felt free to choose what to do at each stage. A necessary condition for having a practice of rule-following is a felt constraint. What we should resist is the reification of the felt constraint into an obscure entity: the rule as rail.[1]

13.3 Consensualism

So we reject the myth of Platonic rules that reach out of themselves to fix a pattern of use. But we then seem to slip into the idea that the following of a rule is merely causally, not logically,[2] determined and that what counts as following the rule correctly is agreeing with one's fellows. As we have just learned, the following of a rule must go with a sense of having no choice about how one is to go on, if one is to accord with the rule. This is a prosaic enough demand but one that is apt to be interpreted as a metaphysical requirement on the nature of rules themselves. Instead, what it does is to set up certain requirements on the sort of situations that can give rise to rule-following. It would be impossible, for instance, for us to diverge radically in what we take to be accord with the rule; the divergence between practitioners would precisely throw into doubt one's inclination about how to go on and it is essential that, at a certain ultimate level, there be no such doubts.[3] So certain basic agreements between practitioners are a necessary condition for rule-following. And now, given that the rule itself is no standard of correct use, it seems that correctness collapses into agreement between speakers. The logical determination of a rule is thus sacrificed in favour of the mere causal determination of a rule and a surrogate of correctness is achieved by insisting on agreement in causal determination. Were this so, then whatever opinion was agreed on by practitioners would be beyond criticism and thus would perforce count as true.[4] Wittgenstein rejects the equation: "It is what human beings *say* that is true and false; and they agree in the *language* they use. That is not agreement in opinions but in form of life" (1958: 241).

13.4 Finding a way forward

The resolution of the problem of rule-following will, at least, require an account of how we can reject the idea of purely causal determination without subscribing to the mythological conception of rules. What Wittgenstein is outlining is a view of rule-following that repudiates both the view that the logical determination of how to go on should be sacrificed in favour of merely causal determination and the view which constructs a mythology of rules in order to hold on to a conception of logical determination. We have already seen one way in which we might achieve this. When we argued against the sceptical solution, we argued that a proper realization of the role of the policing practice would lead to a realistic view of rules. However, we also noted that this realism was quite different to Platonism or ultra-realism about rules. The point was that our conception of rules as making real demands on us is substantiated not by explicating the metaphysical basis of those demands but by revealing aspects of the way our concept of rules functions. In crude, but suggestive, terms, we legitimate realism about rules not by finding something external that constitutes the rule's demands but by seeing realism as demanded by the internal character of our practices. Scepticism is repudiated because it is seen as being incapable of permitting reason to be reconciled with itself; it is incapable, that is, of delivering a coherent reflection on the nature of our practices. This is not to beg the question against the sceptic. Of course she can tilt the table in her favour by saying that she wants an account of what constitutes the normative dictates of a rule but there is no reason why we should be prepared to sit down at such a table with her. Instead we might simply demand that we achieve a coherent understanding of ourselves as rule-followers. Now this need not be easy to accomplish – and the sceptic's arguments suffice to show at least that much – but one step in that direction might be to understand how reason demands that we take rules to be real. If we can show this much, then we can show not simply that we are bound to be under the *illusion* that we are following rules, but that a conception of ourselves as following rules is *rationally required.*[5] We can therefore feel rationally vindicated in the face of the sceptical challenge – that was the business of Chapter 12. But this is not to show where that challenge is irrational or mistaken. So our work is not done. I turn to that task now, partly because it simply remains left to us but, partly, too, because it will have important consequences for the publicity of meaning and the nature of our theory of meaning.

13.4.1 *Privacy and investigation independence*

A vast literature has been spawned by Wittgenstein's discussion of rule-following. Not all of it is directly relevant to our concerns here and not all of it can possibly be incorporated in this discussion. So I shall be very selective and attempt to work my way towards a view on what lesson we should learn by thinking about the debate between Crispin Wright and John McDowell.

On (the early[6]) Wright's view a prominent target of (the late) Wittgenstein's thought on rule-following is the idea that rules can be such as to make requirements of practitioners that exist in complete independence of the practice itself: Wittgenstein, in other words, rejects the idea that the dictates of a rule can be investigation independent – that is, independent of speakers' verdicts on whether or not the rule has been complied with. So on Wright's reading, Platonism about rules is the most serious casualty of the argument.

The passage to this conclusion runs roughly as follows. If the dictates of a rule are investigation independent, then grasp of a rule becomes essentially private. Grasp of a rule cannot be essentially private. So the dictates of a rule cannot be investigation independent. What we need to look at is the motivation for each premise. Let us begin with the major premise – the conditional. The reasoning for the second premise will obviously address our concerns about privacy and publicity of meaning.

If we suppose that the antecedent is true, then there is nothing a speaker can say or do to show that her grasp of a rule agrees with mine. She cannot *do* anything sufficient because any sample of agreed usage is always compatible with consistent extensions that diverge irresolvably. She cannot *say* anything sufficient because, no matter what she says, there will be an interpretation of that saying that brings whatever she goes on to do in accordance with the rule as captured by her saying. So, on this construal of a rule as making investigation-independent demands on its would-be adherents, there can be no knowledge that we share grasp of a rule. So such grasp of a rule is essentially private; that is, the character of each of our grasps of a rule is something that can be disclosed only to ourselves; our attempts to convey that grasp to another must always fall short.

It is clear, however, that Wittgenstein thinks that we have no privileged access to the character of our own grasp of a rule – the minor premise of the argument holds. He rejects the idea that, in attempting to communicate a rule, our illustrations of use and our offering of explanations somehow always fail to exhaust our own grasp of the rule, so that the would-be recipient of the instruction has "to guess the essential thing": "I shall teach the use of words by means of *examples* and by *practice*. – And when I do this I do not communicate less to him than I know myself" (1958: 208). Slightly further on he has his interlocutor ask the question: "But do you really explain to the other person what you yourself understand? Don't you get him to *guess* the essential thing? You give him examples, – but he has to guess their drift, to guess your intention" (1958: 210). And he responds, "Every explanation which I can give myself I can give to him too. – 'He guesses what I intend' would mean: various interpretations of my explanation come to mind, and he lights on one of them. So in this case he could ask; and I could and should answer him" (*ibid.*). Of course any explanation we give may go awry or may stand in need of further clarification. But in these cases we have language to fall back on: the learner can ask for further clarification and it can be provided.

But we are tempted to suppose that the evidence we give ourselves of our grasp of a rule is *not* subject to further interpretation. But what could this evidence consist in? Any sample of our own use can obviously be extended in indefinitely many ways and so requires an interpretation: we stand in relation to our own use just as the learner stands in relation to our illustrative use. How is the possibility of doubt removed in the first-personal case when it cannot be removed in the case of the learner? Could it be through the operation of intuition? Wittgenstein dismisses this notion: an intuition is mysterious, seems to require interpretation and is not guaranteed to guide correctly – so we need *something else* that assures us of what it is that the intuition dictates and that its dictates truly realize the dictates of the rule. As he says, intuition is an unnecessary shuffle (*ibid.*: §213). Nor can we appeal to the idea that what we mean is that we ought in the future to do the same as we are currently doing. As we have seen, the notion of sameness and of a rule are, as Wittgenstein points out, coordinate: what counts as the same will be determined by the nature of the rule and cannot determine it. (This point will crop up [yet] again below.) Any explanation one offers oneself of the rule can be reconciled with whatever, at that point, one is inclined to take as the correct implementation of the explanation – the terms of the explanation, of course, stand in need of interpretation and thus can be brought into accord with one's inclinations by adopting an appropriate interpretation. But that means that one's inclinations for use will proceed unchecked and thus will be under no normative constraint. The conclusion is that there is no relevant asymmetry between the private linguist and the learner in terms of their ability to display their grasp of a rule. But this is utterly destructive of the concept of a private linguist, for it means that she utterly fails to constrain her future use normatively. Thus the conception of a private linguist is mythical.

Wright's solution is to reject the conception of rules that imposes the private rule-follower on us, namely, the conception of rules that sees them as imposing investigation-independent demands on use; rather, we can make no sense of the dictates of a rule except in terms of a securable background of communal assent about the character of the rule's dictates.

McDowell (1984) responds to Wright by arguing that his rejection of investigation independence is not a minimal reaction to the incoherent privacy imposed by a philosophical overloading of the normative requirements of a rule; rather, Wright's reaction leaves us with nothing worth thinking of as a normative constraint. Investigation independence for McDowell is necessary for genuine normativity; we have to be able to think of ourselves as required to do such and such no matter what we might be inclined to do. Accordingly, rather than providing a way out of the sceptical paradox about rule-following, Wright offers a version of the sceptical position. What we need to do is to realize that the sceptical position is only mandatory under a false conception of what grasp of a rule consists in. Once we reject that premise, we need not be attracted by the sceptical train of thought. The premise to reject is the view that grasp of a rule is always an interpretation: "there is a way of grasping a rule which is not an interpretation" (Wittgenstein 1958: §201).

It is clear that Wittgenstein did reject the idea that grasp of a rule is always an interpretation. He says so, at the crucial §201. Moreover, the thought is crucial in his dissolution of the idea that one's grasp of a rule extends beyond what one can explain to a learner: "How can he *know* how he is to continue that pattern by himself – whatever instruction you give him? – Well, how do I know? – If that means 'Have I reasons?' the answer is: my reasons will soon give out. And then I shall act, without reasons" (*ibid.*: §211). My interpretation of a rule is a reason for going on thus and so but my reasons give out.

What is less clear is just where Wright errs by at least implicitly endorsing the problematic premise that grasp of a rule is always an interpretation. Part of the concern about Wright's account lies in the way he develops the objection to the private rule-follower. Recall that the points there depended on the private rule-follower's attempts to bind her practice by fixing on a particular way of going on. But she cannot seem to fix a pattern of use because she then launches a regress of interpretations, halted either by a spurious appeal to intuition or to an illusory notion of sameness that stands outside the nexus of rules. But as we have just seen, Wittgenstein's point is that this is misconceived: the rule-follower resolves – if it makes sense to speak of a resolution here – these hypothetical doubts not by reasons but by action in the absence of reasons. So, although Wright's points against the private rule-follower are well taken, they are not decisive. We shall return to this before too long. Our question then will be about what makes the notion of a private rule-follower so problematic and what difference the importation of the community makes.

13.4.2 The backdrop of custom and practice

In what follows I provide an account that is, in some measure, sympathetic to and suggested by aspects of McDowell's view,[7] but which is not intended as an exposition of McDowell.

Wittgenstein writes:

> But that is only a causal connection; to tell how it has come about that we now go by the sign-post; not what going-by-the-sign really consists in. On the contrary; I have further indicated that a person goes by a sign-post only in so far as there exists a regular use of sign-posts, a custom. (*Ibid.*: §195)

> ... if the pupil reacts to [the training] thus and thus; he possesses the rule inwardly.
> But *this* is important, namely that this reaction, which is our guarantee of understanding, presupposes as a surrounding particular circum-

stances, particular forms of life and speech. (As there is no such thing as a facial expression without a face.)

(This is an important movement of thought.)   (1978: VII 48)

What is Wittgenstein's point in these remarks? First, he is rejecting the idea that the way an expression of a rule determines those actions that accord with it is merely causal. The background of training, custom and practice is an *essential* aspect of taking a sign as the expression of a rule and not merely a matter of causal antecedents. A similar train of thought is apt in considering when a piece of behaviour betokens – can be taken as an expression of – understanding. The reaction is a guarantor of understanding only against the *essential* backdrop of a certain form of life, a certain set of linguistic practices.

We might apply these thoughts to Kripke's paradox in this way. Kripke finds himself unable to find the meaning-determining fact precisely because his methodology blinds himself to it. He asks his question in a distinctively first-personal mode: what in *my* previous use of an expression or *my* past mental history binds *my* present use, if *I* now intend that use to adhere to the meaning *I* had conferred on the expression in the past? If Wittgenstein's remarks are taken seriously, then it is no surprise that Kripke fails to find a satisfying answer to his question. Kripke finds himself able to focus on signs only in abstraction from their setting in a practice, on sets of use in ignorance of the practice those uses belong to. Conversely – and, arguably, this is the dialectical point of the sceptical train of thought – if the scepticism that ensues from an inability to answer Kripke's question is incoherent (and we have argued that it is – see Chapter 12), then this provides a reason for accepting a position of the form hinted at in the above quotations, a position that makes essential the location of signs and of use in a practice or custom.

So how do we respond to Kripke's paradox? Kripke asks whether I should plus now or quus now, if I intend to go on as before. The Wittgensteinian answer is that you ought to plus now, if your use of "+" has been part of a practice of plusing; quus if it has been part of a practice of quusing. Now there is no doubting that this answer is apt to seem unimpressive and it cannot be made more impressive by supposing that the communal practice has included a case of adding our disputed sum: "68 + 57" – just as in Kripke's case there will be many addition sums that the communal practice has not been extended to include. So have we made no progress? What difference is made by locating use in the setting of a communal practice?

Well, it might seem that this lame response is all that Wittgenstein is offering. He asks himself, "what has the expression of a rule – say a sign-post – got to do with my actions? What sort of connexion is there here?" (1958: §198). The dilemma we need to avoid is that of admitting either that it is connected with one's actions by means of an interpretation or that it is only connected causally. He answers his question thus: "Well, perhaps this one: I have been trained to react to the sign in a particular way, and now I do so react to it" (*ibid.*). The response seems as if it is the lame one because he seems to be saying that I have reacted to the sign in this way in the past and I now simply react in the *same* way. But this must be a bad reading of Wittgenstein since, as we have seen, he never tires of reminding his reader that we cannot presuppose a notion of sameness in finding a basis for rule-following; the notions of sameness and of rule are coordinate with one another.

So, once again, we have to ask: what is Wittgenstein's point? One plausible line of thought is this. One's reactions, one's use of a term, are guarantors of understanding when manifested to a competent co-practitioner; one's use displays one's understanding to someone who understands in the context of a practice. So the question of whether I ought to plus or to quus depends on whether competent co-practitioners have been plusing or quusing. But, once again, this cannot be a satisfying response for the obvious reason that it simply pushes the question from oneself on to one's co-practitioners.

13.4.3 Unjustified uses and measuring rods

However, there may be the glimmer of a response forming here. Recall that Kripke's question was about what *justifies* my present use as fulfilling my intention to carry on as before. Two points should be borne in mind. First, as Wittgenstein notes, it cannot always be in place to ask for a justification: "To use a word without a justification does not mean to use it wrongfully" (1978: VII 40). So, to start, the sceptic's wont to press us for a justification is not one we should be willing to pander to universally. But secondly, "The certainty with which I call the colour 'red' is the rigidity of my measuring-rod, it is the rigidity from which I start. When I give descriptions, *that* is not to be brought into doubt. This simply characterises what we call describing" (*ibid.*: VI 28). Here we need to be clear to distinguish what Wittgenstein is saying from like-sounding empiricist claims. Wittgenstein is not saying that there is a realm to which we have supremely reliable cognitive access such that our judgements about that realm are guaranteed to be reliable. Quite the reverse: his claim is that it makes no sense to raise a doubt here, to call for a justification, because there is nothing for these uses to be responsible to. We cannot ask whether it is right to apply the term in *these* circumstances (if we are to go on as before) because we would presuppose an ability to describe the relevant sorts of circumstance: how do we say what these circumstances are? To say that it would be right to apply "red" to red things is trivially true and it presupposes precisely what was meant to be explained – that is, conditions of application for the term "red". None of this denies that there may be some occasions when we can describe the relevant sorts of circumstance; doing so often provides a fine explanation of the meaning of a term. But we cannot *always* describe the relevant circumstances in any informative way and so we cannot meaningfully raise the question about whether this term ought to be applied in these circumstances. Thus Wittgenstein's point is that what finally establishes a mode of description is a propensity to use an expression with certainty; *that* use cannot be brought into doubt just because it cannot be questioned. It is only after we have established modes of description that we can sensibly ask for justifications.

Consider Wittgenstein's analogy with measuring rods. According to Wittgenstein it makes no sense to ask whether our system of measurement accurately reflects the phenomenon it is designed to measure – that is, to ask whether or not our measuring rod is rigid. The reason why such a question is meaningless is that our conception of the relevant phenomenon is a product of the system of measurement itself; our concept of length is connected to our means of measuring length. If we reject the system, we reject with it that concept. Analogously, we cannot both speak a language and question its adequacy for representation of the phenomena it talks about. Just as before, we have no conception of those phenomena but through our mastery of that language. We may, of course, adopt a different language, but that would be to change or modify our interests, not to find a better, more accurate way of representing the original phenomena.

Now, of course, we can acknowledge all of this without having to acknowledge that my confident use of a particular word on a particular occasion is not to be called into question. The reason is that all we have shown is that it makes no sense to question the system of measurement itself or the language itself. So we might, at any point, for instance, question whether a judgement about length results from a correct implementation of the criteria for measuring length. But Wittgenstein's point here is that in these cases we do not apply criteria ("What criteria do you use, then? None at all" [1978: VII 40]). Here we have reached the rigidity of our measuring rod. "'See here! If I follow the order I do *this*!' That is naturally not supposed to mean: if I follow the order I follow the order. So I must have a different identification for 'this'" (*ibid.*: VI 29).

Here the illustration of the order is trivial unless we can give an explanation of it – that is, can interpret it ("We ought to restrict the term 'interpretation' to the substitution of one expression of the rule for another" [1958: §201]). But triviality cannot always be avoided: our attempt to describe application of the rule calls on us to apply the rule itself. It is absurd in these cases to require a justification or explanation. The sceptic insists on this requirement, so her position is absurd.

It might strike one that following a rule at this basic level is dangerously like the private rule-follower's inability to distinguish between what is right and what seems right. However, there are these crucial differences. In the cases we are considering, the persistence of the practice depends on the condition that there is communal consensus. Without this the practice would fall apart. But recognizing this does not entail that the securing of communal assent constitutes correctness – as Wittgenstein points out, this is to supply a criterion for use when there is none. A second difference is that we are considering a speaker who has been brought to understand, say, the word "red". So crucially we can make sense in these cases of being inducted into the practice (see below).

The second point builds on the first. Kripke tries to force us to find a justification for current use that stands outside the practice. Justifications of this sort – what would be sceptic-proof justifications, that is – are supposed to ground our various uses of language and thus ground our practice. Our failure to provide such a grounding leads, in Kripke's view, to a general scepticism about meaning. But it can do so only *if* one grants that the original demand for a grounding is in place. And Wittgenstein thinks it is *not*. As we have seen, he offers at least three reasons for this position. First, he thinks that it cannot always be in order to ask for a justification, so that at a certain point one simply uses an expression without reason or justification and, at least, in certain circumstances so using an expression is not to use it without a right. Secondly, it is hard to conceive of what such a justification might consist in. The closest we seem to come is to think that my use of the rule is now justified (as implementing the rule I had grasped in the past) because, in a certain sense, I am doing the *same* thing, I am carrying on in the *same* way. But there is no notion of sameness that stands outside all rules. What counts as going on in the same way precisely depends on what rule one is supposed to be following. So we cannot appeal to a notion of sameness as justifying a course of action as in accord with the rule. Grasp of a rule and grasp of a notion of sameness are two sides of the very same coin. Thirdly – and this is largely a generalization of the second point – Wittgenstein thinks that the way we go on in these primitive cases determines what counts as description. There is no standard and nothing in the world that rule-following has to fit; rather, the way we go on determines what counts for us as description. One might think that the world has a character and that we need to develop appropriate modes of description – appropriate sets of rules – for representation of this character. But Wittgenstein's point is rather that our primitive ways of using signs characterize modes of description. Just as there is no sense to the notion of *same* except in terms of the rule, there is no sense to whether a certain situation warrants the application of a sign except in terms of our willingness to apply the sign with certainty. As he says, it is that certainty that provides our "measuring rod"; it is against that that the world is measured. The possibility of deploying a system of measurement *is* its own validation.

Clearly I ought to plus now if "68 + 57 = 125" is true; I ought to quus now if "68 + 57 = 5" is true. But whether 68 + 57 is 125 or whether 68 + 57 is 5 is a question to be settled from *within* the practice. In other words, we cannot look at the nature of the practice from the outside, as if we were radical interpreters – or, perhaps, philosophers – and determine features of it that determine whether the practice is one of plusing or quusing. Kripke tries to distinguish the question of whether 68 + 57 is 125 or 5 from the question of whether I ought to respond with "125" or "5" when asked for the answer to "57 + 68 = ?", if my intention is to accord with my past use. But if the latter question has any sense at all, it is the *same* question as the previous one: it is an arithmetic *not* a distinctively semantic question. One's intention to go on as before, to adhere to previously established meanings, is just a feature of one's participation in the practice. So making that intention explicit and making the question one about the use of signs in the practice does not conjure up a question that is *about* the practice, that is distinctively semantic; rather, what we have is a question that, since we are functioning in the practice, needs to be answered either by deploying mundane arithmetic criteria or without deploying criteria at all.

13.4.4 Bringing together ideas of practices and of measuring rods

It is important to realize from this the role played by the context of practice and custom. When Kripke's sceptic comes along and presses me for a justification for my response of "125" (if I am to accord with my past use) I shall not be able to say: I am justified because these features of my practice fix that these terms are to be used in such-and-such a way and, in combination, this means that here I should respond "125". In other words, I shall not be able to turn my context-bound justification into a sceptic-proof justification by making explicit the relevant features of context. Were one able to achieve this, one would be answering Kripke's distinctively semantic question; but the point was that because justifications are internal to a practice, there is no distinctively semantic question to answer. (More on this very soon.)

Now recall our question: in what sense does the notion of a community play an essential role here? What we have discovered is that the sceptic relentlessly and illegitimately searches for a justification of one's use. The search is illegitimate both because some uses are legitimate, although they are without justification, and because it presupposes the intelligibility of justifications of practices themselves. So we should admit that there is a way of grasping a rule that is a matter of having an ability to use an expression appropriately within the context of a communal practice. Thus our question might be put like this: why should the practice be communal rather than purely private? Or, once again, it seems that Wright gave an incomplete argument against privacy because he seems to assume that the private rule-follower must interpret her use or must offer herself an explanation of her meaning. That position cannot be complete since Wittgenstein accepts that we can use an expression legitimately in the absence of reasons. But such a use can count as demonstrating understanding only when it is situated in the context of a practice. So we are led back to our question: why need that practice be *communal*? We have, in essentials, already seen the answer to this question: training or, more broadly, displaying one's capacities to competent practitioners is an essential feature of Wittgenstein's notion of an apparently rule-governed practice. We need to be able to make sense of induction into the practice. The private rule-follower simply could not count as such because she cannot induct herself into the practice. To do so she would have to manifest her use to herself under the assumption that she was a competent practitioner. But of course there is no induction of an already competent practitioner.[8] Or, to put the point slightly differently, the private linguist cannot monitor her own practice. In essence, the point is that without these features such as training in and monitoring of a practice – features that are necessarily communal – the private rule-follower cannot distinguish between Kripkean use and a practice.

13.4.5 Rules and techniques

There is a potentially dangerous trap here – once again the horns of our dilemma beckon. For it would seem that either there are facts about correct use determined by the nature of the practice or there are not. If there are, then these facts will simply determine how one ought to go on and thus it is apt to seem that the distinction between legitimate questions raised within a practice and illegitimate attempts to ground the practice itself can be annulled. If there are not, then it is tempting to suppose that the rule cannot place any demands on *us*, the community of practitioners. We struggle to keep our middle position alive. So let us revisit the dilemma.

Let us consider the first horn of the dilemma before dismissing the hysterical recoil to its opposing horn. What we are naturally inclined to suppose is that when we set up a practice we establish rules that extend of themselves to indefinitely many novel cases. In other words, establishing the practice puts us in touch with – binds our use by – a set of rules each of which is associated with an indefinitely large set of facts about what constitutes compliance with it. For instance, the practice of arithmetic puts us in touch with the rule for addition that determines a fact about the sum of any pair of numbers. These facts are facts *about* the rule; they are facts that shape the practice; but they are objective facts, approachable independently of the practice. So, the thought would be, there is a fact of the matter about which rules we are put in touch with by our use, say, of "+" and these facts determine whether or not we are plusing or quusing; that is, there is a fact of the matter about the nature of our practice – which rule it aligns with – that can be approached from outside it, independently of the practice itself.

Wittgenstein sees the attraction of this view but sternly warns against this (Platonistic) construal of rules. He writes,

> What harm is done e.g. by saying that God knows all the irrational numbers? Or: that they are all there, even though we only know certain of them? Why are these pictures not harmless?
> For one thing, they hide certain problems. –   (1978: VII 42)

In explanation of the hidden problems he says, "We might put it like this: if the rule for the expansion has been given us, a *calculation* can tell us that there is a '2' at the fifth place. Could God have known this, without the calculation, purely from the rule of expansion? I want to say: No" (*ibid*.). If rules determine their compliance conditions independently of the practice, then these facts about compliance would be available to an omniscient being independently of the practice. But rules do not determine a range of (extra-practical) *facts*; rules determine a *technique*. "I give the rule an extension" (*ibid*.: VI 29). One cannot determine the characteristics of a rule but by employment of the technique it determines. (The implications of this for the business of semantics and for the philosophies of language, logic and mathematics promise to be profound.)

The consequence is that we cannot answer Kripke's question whether in the past I was plusing or quusing but by employment of the relevant technique. There are no facts *about* the practice that determine the nature of the technique, the character of the rule; rather, one can only persist with the technique *within* the practice. To ask whether the technique I employ now is the *same* as that employed in the past is, if not a question answerable within the practice (e.g. by explaining adding in terms of counting), to ask about the rigidity of one's measuring rod.

We seem, however, now to be saying that our employment of the rule is responsible only to *our implementation* of the technique it determines. And that seems to be saying that *our* employment of the rule is responsible to nothing. In other words, we seem to be embracing a position akin to consensualism and that McDowell attacks (as that advocated by Wright), namely, that Wittgenstein's discussion of rule-following contains a potent attack on the notion that there can be investigation-independent facts about correct use – that what counts as correct implementation will be what the community takes to be correct, and that the community is constrained by nothing.

But Wittgenstein is evidently equally hostile to this consensualist picture of rule-following:

> And does this mean e.g. that the definition of "same" would be: same is what all or most human beings with one voice take for the same? – Of course not.
>
> For of course I don't make use of the agreement of human beings to affirm identity. What criterion do you use then? None at all.
>
> To use the word without a justification does not mean to use it wrongfully. (*Ibid*.: VII 40)

Grasp of a rule is, as he says, "FUNDAMENTAL to our language-game" (*ibid*.: VI 29). Consensualism is false because it shares a crucial fault with Platonism:

215

both positions see there being a range of facts about compliance with the rule that are independent of the technique it determines. Unlike Platonism, consensualism does not dissociate those facts from the practitioners. But this is its *only* advantage over Platonism; the fact remains that, to define correctness in terms of agreement is to dissociate the rule from the technique it determines. To make this vivid, just imagine that determinism were true, then there would be indefinitely many facts about communal agreement in following a rule and thus, given consensualism, indefinitely many facts about what would count as following the rule and these facts would be accessible independently of applying the technique it determines. Of course, determinism may well be false but we do not want to rest our view of rule-following on that metaphysical commitment.

> Suppose that people go on and on calculating the expansion of π. So God, who knows everything, knows whether they will have reached "777" by the end of the world. [And so, if Consensualism were right, whether the rule for the expansion of π determines whether "777" occurs in it.] But can his omniscience decide whether they would have reached it after the end of the world? It cannot. I want to say: Even God can determine something mathematical only by mathematics. Even for him the mere rule of expansion cannot decide anything it does not decide for us. (*Ibid.*: VII 42)

Let us then reject either horn of the dilemma on the grounds that each ignores the absolute connection of the rule with the technique it determines. How though do we gain a fully satisfying middle position?

When we come to our new addition sum, there is no question but that we are bound by the meaning we have established for "+"; that is, we are bound by the technique for the proper use of the sign "+". But what our response should be in the particular case with which we are confronted cannot be answered except in terms of an implementation of arithmetic criteria within arithmetic practice. So, *of course*, we are constrained in how to answer the arithmetic question properly; what we must resist doing is to think of this constraint as a fact *about* the practice that can accessed from outside it.

13.4.6 In summary

We might characterize the position as follows. Contrast these positions about a range of facts:

- Ultra-realism: the facts in this area obtain in complete independence of our ability or methods of knowing them.

- Constructivism: the facts in this area are constituted by our recognition of them as obtaining.

Platonism about rules is a version of ultra-realism, while consensualism about rules is a version of constructivism.

But these two positions are not exhaustive and might be contrasted with a third:

- Modest realism: the facts in this area are not independent of our ability and methods used to disclose them.

What is being advocated is a modest realism about rules, which is all we need for rules to impose real constraints.

The resulting position is in many ways deflationary of some philosophical ambitions. There is no doubt that it reins in our urge to explain and, where it allows justifications, these *tend* to be mundane, rather than profoundly philosophical. But it is not simply a quietistic view; it arrives at a view about philosophical explanation/justification through a complex of philosophical arguments. And the philosophical position it adopts is no mere withdrawal from taking a philosophical stance.

I want to turn soon to draw out some (possible) implications the position may have for one's approach in the philosophy of language, but let us first pause to bring out some more direct implications. First, the position denies any content to the notion of an extra-linguistic reality with a determinate structure. Were we able to make sense of such a notion, we could make sense of justifying a practice itself in terms of its ability to portray the world as it is. We have renounced the possibility of any such genuine justification; so we renounce a conception of the world that would underwrite such a justification. Secondly, because a practice is, in this way, self-standing, it is guaranteed to fit, to be capable of describing reality. So there is in this sense an internal connection between the practice and the reality it represents, which is redolent of idealism. Thirdly, although we confer meanings on our terms by establishing rules for their use, the question of whether a certain action is a deployment of the technique that is determined by the rule is not up to us. That question possesses an objective answer. Fourthly, such a position, incorporating a notion of objectivity within an idealistic framework might well be seen as a form of transcendental idealism. The Kantian reverberations here are strong indeed: (i) realism is constituted not by a relation of the practice to something external to it but by its own internal richness, for instance, the necessity of an appropriate policing practice for any apparently rule-governed practice; (ii) the world we describe is conditioned by our means of describing it; (iii) the position is established by showing that it is the only position that coheres with our self-conception – here as beings capable of binding their use to a norm; (iv) although we cannot make sense of the idea in full detail, given the contingency we discover at the base of our practice, we must admit the possibility of alternative practices, alternatives based in different forms of life.

13.5 Back to the theory of meaning

And so we return finally to our question about how we should set about gaining a philosophical understanding of the phenomenon of language. I shall try to flesh out the position by translating an aspect of the pupil–teacher situation into a theoretical setting. The interesting position sketched by Wittgenstein was one in which the pupil reacts to a course of training in such a way that, given the particulars of that background of training, the reaction is rightly taken as a guarantor of understanding. Let us think first about the nature of this reaction, which is taken to display comprehension. Wittgenstein says little about how this reaction is to be described. His sympathetic commentator, McDowell, is rather more forthcoming. In his view, it is a cardinal mistake of the anti-realists – such as Wright and Dummett – to think that behaviour manifesting understanding can be described in terms that do not presuppose content. According to McDowell, one manifests one's understanding of, say, "The dog lies under the syringa tree" by using the sentence, among other things, *to assert that* the dog lies under the syringa tree. Dummett[9] (and Brandom [2008: ch. 1]) take issue with this because they rightly think that this means we cannot give an account of content or meaning in terms of what it is to grasp a content or meaning. For when we come to look at the latter, we explain it in terms that involve the deployment of a content, and thus that presuppose content. Far from objecting to this, McDowell concurs and takes this to show the hopelessness of Dummett's attempt to explain content from the point of view of a cosmic exile and thus to argue in favour of modest theories of meaning.[10] McDowell reinforces his position by noting that from an anti-realist conception of what speakers are able to do, we cannot achieve a conception of content. On Wright's account we conjure a consensualist surrogate of norms that, in fact, is merely the illusion of normativity. On the Dummettian view we are left with mere behaviouristic soundings-off from which content is indiscernible: Kripkean uses, if you will, that fail to bind future use.

McDowell's position thus has some independent plausibility, depressing as its consequences are for an ambitious philosopher of language. But I doubt whether it provides a good reading of Wittgenstein's remarks here. The reason is simple. Consider again Wittgenstein's comment:

> if the pupil reacts to [the training] thus and thus; he possesses the rule inwardly.
>
> But *this* is important, namely that this reaction, which is our guarantee of understanding, presupposes as a surrounding particular

circumstances, particular forms of life and speech. (As there is no such thing as a facial expression without a face.)

(This is an important movement of thought.)   (1978: VII 48)

If the pupil's reaction is to be described in McDowellian fashion, then there is no need for us to locate that reaction against a particular backdrop of training or custom. After all, uttering "the dog lies under the syringa tree" in order to *assert that* the dog lies under the syringa tree manifests an understanding of that sentence as bearing that content *irrespective* of other contextual features. It is clear that Wittgenstein, in contrast to this view, considers the context of practice and custom *essential* and considers too that it is important that it is essential.

So the suggestion is that McDowell's complaints against (his conception) of the anti-realists are plausible but fail to notice another way in which behaviour might manifest understanding; rather than addressing this problem by *enriching* the description of understanding, we might prefer to *situate* that behaviour properly. In sum, McDowell cannot find an acceptable role for the component in Wittgenstien's view of placing the behaviour in the context of custom and practice and so (i) fails to provide a good interpretation of Wittgenstein's insistence on that background of training and practice, and (ii) prematurely curtails what may well be perfectly respectable philosophical ambitions.

We shall look soon at the way we might set about fulfilling certain of our ambitions, but first we should note that we have, in the course of these discussions, developed some worries about radical interpretation as a methodology. Radical interpretation pretends to be able to discern a speaker's meanings from displays of use, which make no presupposition about custom and practice. Indeed, for the radical interpreter there is no such context – and this is precisely what makes her a *radical* interpreter; there is only a pattern of sentences held true in certain circumstances. So, whereas Wittgenstein seems to require only that a speaker make manifest her understanding to a co-practitioner, Davidson insists that she be able to do so to the radical interpreter. A consequence of this is that, although, as I have argued, Davidson should accept the normativity of meaning, he also concedes that meaning-rules fail to determine a determinate technique of application; instead, radical interpretation requires that use be conceived of simply in terms of holdings-true and consequently it entails the indeterminacy of reference, that terms do not have determinate application conditions. Thus meaning-rules are dissociated from use, from the technique they should be taken as determining. Davidson sees no context as relevant to meaning other than a speaker's own use of a term. But, unless this is described in rich McDowellian – and so question-begging – terms, it will not determine meaning.

A feature of the view sketched here is that we can make no sense of a determinate extra-linguistic reality. And it would seem that Davidson would concur; interpretation breathes meaning into our use of signs and sets up a relation between foreign and domestic signs. However, interpretation proceeds under the maxim of locating the content of a belief in (what the interpreter takes to be) the worldly cause of the belief and, since the interpreter may be omniscient, we could omit the bracketed qualification. So, in truth, radical interpretation is all about explaining the function of words by explaining their relation to things in the world. Precisely for this reason Davidson thinks that truth is a genuinely explanatory concept. But this was just the sort of justification of a practice that we had raised a suspicion about – the legitimacy of such a requirement draws us into Kripke's sceptical dialectic.

So let us concede the importance of the backdrop of custom and practice. The important point is that we cannot factor out this element – that is, we cannot attempt to account for the practice by explaining what use manifests understanding against an explicit account of the backdrop; we cannot make this explicit. This would be to explain or justify the practice itself. So we do need to restrain our philosophical ambitions. What we need to accept is that we are inalienably attempting to explain *our own* practices to *ourselves*. Dummett, for instance, conceives of the project of constructing a theory of meaning as an extension and systematization of our ordinary practice of providing explanations of meaning; the project is validated, in part, by its kinship with such practices and transcends them not in terms of penetrating to a more profound level but simply in terms of thoroughness and in being more extensive. Our explanatory programme thus proceeds against the very same backdrop of custom and practice as does our habit of providing mundane explanations. The capacities we take to constitute understanding are capacities that can be described *without presupposing content* but that can only be taken to be adequate descriptions of understanding when delivered against the backdrop of our practices and customs. The philosopher cannot ignore her own embedding in a complex of practices. The account of how language works will thus be inalienably *our* explanation of *our* language. There is no exiting our entire framework in an effort to make it available to a cosmic exile. But that is not the lucidity we seek; our aim is self-interested. Thus our approach is, in a certain sense, robust.

In sum, the notion of publicity, that is, the sense in which one's understanding is manifestable, is not that given by radical interpretation, nor that given by modesty, nor, indeed, that given by Dummett's conception of robustness. However, it is related to Dummett's notion: one manifests one's understanding by displaying behaviour describable in terms that do not presuppose content to competent speakers against a background of shared practices and customs. Because of the essential involvement of context, this is not the same as Dummettian robustness. But it mirrors that notion once we allow that our theorizing occurs within the very same context of practice and custom. A lesson of rule scepticism is that we need to appreciate the context of our own theorizing and once we fully recognize that we can turn our backs on the sceptical challenge, we do not need to respond to the sceptical possibilities, since these are excluded by the context of theorizing.

13.6 Privacy and first-personal authority

It is worth tying together the discussion of rules with the closing remarks of Chapter 11. There we had raised the question as to whether there are legitimate philosophically explanatory burdens that can be discharged only through a private conception of meaning; we might here be thinking that privacy is necessary as part of an account of first-personal authority over our own meanings or to explain the particular authority that we each display in relation to certain avowals about our own mental states. In this chapter we uncovered reasons for thinking that the private rule-follower cannot set up normative constraints over her use. So there appears to be a certain tension here and this apparent tension may well be the reason for Wittgenstein's long discussion of sensation talk, which immediately follows his discussion of following a rule. We might choose to sum things up like this. A consequence of the discussion of rule-following is that the notion of privacy supplies only the appearance of an explanation of such things as first-personal authority of our own meanings. For the private rule-follower can give no substance to the notion of purely private conferrals of meaning. So there is some work left to do: we need an alternative account of the epistemology of our own meanings. Here I want to look briefly at Wright's discussion of first-personal authority over our own meanings.

13.6.1 Wright's judgement-dependence account

In later work Wright argues that another way with the rule-following sceptic is to point out that she seems to require a reductive account of rule-following – what we called an external justification – and without more motivation for that assumption we can reject the rule-following sceptic as basing her argument on an assumption that we might choose to reject; we might choose to be non-reductionists about norms/meanings. However, he does not think that this is to dispose of the problem about rules. The problem is one not just of rejecting the sceptical train of thought but of making it comfortable to see ourselves as rule-followers, and there is an evident discomfort here: how do we see rules as being both the sort of thing that we have immediate, non-inferential and authoritative access to and the sort of thing that reaches beyond itself, classifying an indefinite number of potential moves as either in accord or in discord with it. Your judgement about your understanding of a word is not based on, is not justified by, anything else and is taken as being authoritative. That is, unless there is an accumulation of counter-evidence to your avowal of understanding, then that avowal is accepted as true. But how can it have this character, given that what constitutes your understanding is a feature of your linguistic behaviour in a multitude of cases, none of which you will have consciously considered? So the sceptical challenge is really just an insistence that we explain how knowledge of meaning can be subject to first-personal authority yet have this character of theoreticity. One way of responding to the challenge is to offer a reductive account of meaning. This, we have argued, fails. But the failure of the reductive approach does not entail that the challenge dissipates. Even if we are not going to attempt to explain knowledge of meaning in terms of some other states, we still need to explain how it is that in coming to know a meaning we occupy a state with the twin aspects just alluded to.

One way of proceeding here (see McGinn 1984) is just to question the need "to explain how it is that in coming to know a meaning we occupy a state with the twin aspects". One would simply attempt to defuse the felt need for a philosophical explanation by pointing out that such states are thoroughly mundane. My knowledge of my own intentions is likewise authoritative but also can be proved wrong – defeated – by what I go on to do. And surely our habit of forming and declaring our intentions is a common enough phenomenon. The response is surely bad – odd to think that multiplying a perplexity somehow resolves it. The familiarity of the phenomenon is not under question; rather, we have been given a reason for thinking that the familiar phenomenon is philosophically perplexing. We can eradicate our philosophical perplexity in one of three ways: (i) providing an explanation; (ii) demonstrating that the perplexity is based on a confusion; or (iii) arguing that we are simply unable to explain the phenomenon (in which case we just need to learn to accept our limitations). The response that has been offered denies the need for (i) but does not achieve either of the latter two. And thus it appears to be just a kind of intellectual laziness.

Wright's thought is that we can explain the relevant features of knowledge of meaning by returning to an old debate: the distinction between primary and secondary qualities (see Wright 2001: essays 5, 9). Recall that for Locke a primary quality is a quality that inheres in the object itself while a secondary quality is simply a power that a thing has to produce sensations in us. For Locke, colours are paradigm examples of secondary qualities. So an object is red only because it will look red to a suitable observer in suitable conditions; its *looking red* in these conditions is just what it is for it to *be red*. If we think about this in terms of judgements that an observer will make, the claim is that what the predicate "red" applies to is *determined by* observers' best judgements about what is red and thus the correctness of those judgements is not determined by the fact that "red" applies to it. In other words, observers' best judgements do not *reflect* the extension of the predicate "red"; rather, they *determine* that extension. And, in yet other words, the point is that observers' best judgements do not track states of affairs that exist independently of those judgements; rather, the facts about the application of "red" are constituted by observers' best judgements.

The suggestion now is that we should model the epistemology of meaning on the epistemology of secondary qualities. That is, when it comes to one's attribution of knowledge of meaning to oneself, one's best judgements do not track some prior fact about one's knowledge of meaning; rather, those judgements determine those facts. Provided your judgement about your own understanding is made in ideal conditions, then that judgement cannot be wrong because that judgement is not tracking some fact that exists independently of your judgement. So your judgement is authoritative, but it is not incorrigible because the judgement may have been made in conditions that are less than ideal. When I come to Kripke's addition sum "57 + 68", my judgement that I meant addition by "+" (in part) constitutes what I meant by "+" in the past and so dictates what I ought to do when faced with the addition sum, if I intend to accord with my previous understanding of "+". So the account makes sense both of first-personal authority and of the idea that my understanding of a word determines how it ought to be used on future occasions.

Let us call the ideal conditions for making a judgement about one's meaning C. Then what we might have is the following:

S means addition by "+" iff S judges that she means addition by "+" and conditions are C.

The worry with this proposal is that, if we think of it in terms, say, of colour, then bringing about C-conditions may well alter the colour of an object. So imagine a red chameleon sitting on a green baize in a darkened room (see Johnston 1993: appendix 2; Wright 1992: 117–18). We switch on a light, bringing about C-conditions for judgements about colour and the chameleon changes colour to green. We would thus be justified in saying that the red chameleon on the green baize in the darkened room is, in fact, green. So Wright prefers a different form of conditional, which he calls provisional equations:

If conditions were to be C, then S would judge that she means addition by "+" iff S means addition by "+".

And importantly we need also to consider significantly tensed versions of this:

If conditions were to be C, then S would judge that she *meant* addition by "+" iff S *meant* addition by "+".

For the proposal to be of any philosophical interest we need to ensure that the provisional equation has the right status and content. Thus we have (see among others Wright 2001: 196):

(i) The provisional equation holds true *a priori*;

223

(ii) The C-conditions are capable of being specified substantially – so, for instance, they cannot be simply whatever conditions it takes for S to get the judgement right;

(iii) Satisfaction of the C-conditions is logically independent of the extension of predicates attributing meaning and understanding;

(iv) There is no better explanation of the fact that (i)–(iii) hold than that such judgements are extension determining.

A problem for the proposal is this.[11] If we return to the case of "red", what we are saying is that the facts about an object's redness are constituted by facts about the way it appears to suitable observers in suitable conditions. That is, we explain the one sort of fact in terms of another sort of fact: an object's being red in terms of its looking red. In the case of meaning we explain what it is for X to mean plus by "+" in terms of X's belief that he means plus by "+". So we explain X's knowledge of meaning in terms of X's beliefs about her meanings. But that means we explain what it is to know a meaning in terms, taken for granted, of what it is to believe that a word has a given meaning. The worry here is that the account now becomes circular: we are trying to detail what constitutes facts about your meaning, say, plus by "+" and we do so in terms of your beliefs about meaning where we have to assume that your belief already has content. This is not an insistence on reductionism; it points to an incompleteness in the account. We were to be offered an explanation of the twin aspects of understanding, given a certain epistemology of understanding. But that account presupposes that certain judgements (judgements about one's own meaning) already have content. And this means that either those judgements are exempt from the account – in which case, we want an account of them – or they are somehow to be incorporated in the account – in which case we want to know how. Either way there is unfinished business.

Another cause for concern inhabits more general features of the approach. On the judgement-dependent view, a speaker's avowals of her meanings are authoritative because they have a constitutive status. But meaning is ascribed to speakers also on the basis of use, and now there are interesting questions as to how and why these two modes of accessing a speaker's meanings coincide, at least in general. On Wright's view it becomes a deep contingency that interpreting speakers so as to obey the *a priori* constraint of accepting their authoritative judgements about their own meanings is more successful than violating this constraint. So here explanation runs out.

13.6.2 An alternative view

There is no space here for the treatment that this issue deserves.[12] So I shall close this chapter with a brief sketch of an alternative to Wright's view. Once again we seem to be faced with a recoil from a strongly realist conception of the detec-tivist, extension-reflecting, view towards a constructive non-realist position in the extension-determining view. It might therefore occur to one that a modest realist position would provide a third, more congenial, alternative. The point of the modest realist position would be that we need to accept that facts about meaning and understanding are linked to practitioners' mastery of the relevant techniques – which was just Wittgenstein's point – but that this does not mean we need to relinquish a detectivist epistemology for them. If we find a way of retaining a detectivist view, then we need not get embroiled in the awkward business of constructing provisional equations.[13] The problem, though, is that linking the facts in an area to our epistemological access to them will not, in itself, explain first-personal authority. For example, we may argue that the facts of the mathematical matter depend on our access to those facts – so any math-ematical truth must be provably so[14] – but we shall not thereby have reason to think that any particular mathematician has any special authority with respect to mathematical truths. So we would have to say much more about the way facts about meaning and understanding are linked to our epistemological access to them for the proposal to carry any weight.

Perhaps there is progress to be made on that front, but perhaps not. There is anyway another way of attempting to explain authority. My claim that I am here now is bound to be correct and thus carries a certain authority. It carries that authority not because an extension-determining epistemology is in place – my judgements about where I am do not play a role in placing me in one spot rather than another – nor because I have a peculiarly secure method of detect-ing my position. The reason that my authority accrues is that the contextual features that determine the content of my utterance – here that determine the reference to a person and a place – ensure that the utterance is true; it is true just when the utterer is at a place occupied by the utterer. Now it may be that the relevant sorts of contextual features are in play in our judgements about our own present and past meanings.

Consider the case of the present-tensed provisional equation. Suppose too that S's judgement is trivial:

If conditions are C then S judges that S means that **snow is white** by "snow is white" iff S means that snow is white by "snow is white".

The content of S's judgement about her meaning will be fixed (partly) by her meaning for the sentence in bold, that is, it will be fixed by her meaning for the sentence "snow is white", which is given by the clause on the right-hand side of the biconditional. Thus her judgement about what she means by a term, when taking this trivial form, is bound to be right. Conversely, it would be hard to imagine S using a term but unprepared to use that very term in making a judge-ment about her meaning. Thus each element of the biconditional is guaranteed to covary in truth-value, so the biconditional will hold. The point is just that the speaker's judgement about the meaning of her term will, first, deploy that very meaning and thus will be guaranteed to be right and she will, secondly, always be prepared to make the judgement.

Perhaps this is labouring the point, but let us consider the matter by including the perspective of a third party, *T*. Consider these two judgements of *S*:

(i)   I mean that **snow is white** by "snow is white".
(ii) Snow is white.

For *S* to make the judgement that she reports in (i) she need not *identify* the meanings she deploys in using the sentence "snow is white" in such judgements as (ii); she simply needs to deploy those very same meanings and, in doing so, the judgement in (i) is rendered reliable. A third party *T may* have to identify *S*'s meanings in (i). But she determines the meaning of the emboldened "snow is white" and the meaning of the quoted "snow is white" in the *same* way: by reference to uses such as (ii). She obviously does so since these are the same sentence, on one occasion used and on the other mentioned. Thus *T* is bound to construe *S*'s judgement about her own meaning as reliable. So there is no miracle and no deep contingency in the meshing of the first-personal judgement based on no evidence with the third-personal judgement based on substantial evidence. And the reason is that the evidence that the third-personal perspective requires is structured in such a way that it is guaranteed to issue in agreement. Of course, this makes it seem that *S*'s knowledge that *S* means that snow is white by "snow is white" is somehow trivial whereas that of *T* is substantial: *T* has to identify this through *S*'s uses of (ii), whereas *S* does no such thing. And then the worry would be that we have not established first-personal authority over the right thing; we had wanted *substantial* first-personal authority, not its trivial surrogate. I shall return to this below.

As it happens, the proposal is not my invention but one I learned from Wright. He makes the point in his discussion of Putnam's proof that one is not a brain in vat. There Wright (1994: 225–6) reconstructs the argument by taking it as premised on the claim that one's language disquotes; that it does so is sufficient to give one authority in one's second-order judgements about the content of one's terms. His concern differs from the current one: it is to defend this authority in the face of worries raised by semantic externalism, the problem being that the fact that the meaning of one's terms depends on factors that are outside one's ken seems to threaten the reliability of one's second-order judgements or beliefs about one's meaning. Wright's point is that, whatever these factors are, they feed into the determination of the content of one's second-order judgements or beliefs. Thus the content of the second-order judgement about the meaning of a term is guaranteed to covary with that of the term concerned and authority is ensured. But the point is entirely general and it establishes that one's judgements about one's meanings, when they take the simple form of our example, are guaranteed to be correct. I fail to see why this is not sufficient authority in the current case.

Consider now a case in which S's judgement is made more informatively – we can suppose this holds with respect to our example of addition; so suppose that where the term "addition" occurs we replaced it with some informative account of the plus function.

> If conditions are C, then S judges that S means addition by "+' iff S means addition by "+".

Plausibly, if S judges that she means addition by "+", then, if asked for the meaning she attaches to "+", she will explain it in terms of addition. But we ascribe understanding, at least in part, on the basis of an ability to provide explanations. Thus one would be defeasibly entitled to take it that, in these circumstances, S means addition by "+". So the conditional from left to right has an *a priori* presumption of truth. Conversely, if S does mean addition by "+", then a criterion for her doing so will be her preparedness to offer such "core" explanations of her meaning. But if she is prepared to offer such an explanation, then she will be prepared to judge that that is her meaning. So there is an *a priori* presumption that the conditional holds from right to left. Thus there is a presumption that the biconditional holds, *modulo* certain conditions obtaining, which we may suppose are included in C.

The question of tensed versions of the conditional is more complex and oddly not sufficiently addressed in the literature. We shall soon see a possible reason for this. But we may be able to address it by noticing that one's present meanings are not the fabrication of the present moment but are the products of one's practice. So, unless there are reasons for thinking otherwise, one's current meaning cannot be detached from one's past meaning. Thus one's judgements about one's past meanings are guaranteed, *modulo* certain conditions, to be right, just in case one's judgements about one's present meanings are. But we have just seen reason for thinking that our present judgements enjoy this status.

The problem about first-personal authority appears not to be substantial.[15] It is solved, not by supplying a reliable epistemic route to identification of inner items, nor by denying that there is anything to be detected; rather, it is solved by noting that the circumstances in which such *judgements* are made – their situation within practices – and the conditions in which ascriptions of understanding are made ensure first-personal reliability. It is worth noting that extending the authoritative nature of such judgements away from judgements about one's current meanings made using the very terms whose meanings are the subject of the judgement entails that the account is not purely disquotational. So the triviality is not simply due to the form of the judgement. Rather, the triviality is due to the fact that such judgements acquire an authority due to their context and not because they depend on a privileged means of picking out one's meanings.

The underlying point seems to be this. Kripke puts the question as follows:

> [The primitive state of meaning addition by "plus"] is not supposed to be an introspectible state, yet we supposedly are aware of it with some fair degree of certainty whenever it occurs. For how else can each of us be confident that he does, at present, mean addition by "plus"?
>
> (Kripke 1982: 51)

Wright, focusing on intentions, writes in similar terms: "How is it possible to be, for the most part, effortlessly and reliably authoritative about, say, one's intentions if the identity of an intention is fugitive when sought in occurrent consciousness …?" (Wright 2001: 148). As I said, if we take this puzzle as a question about the reliability of one's *judgements* about one's own meanings, then it has an easy answer, which we gave in the last few paragraphs. But this is not the puzzle the Kripke and, it seems, Wright are trying to raise. The easy answer works *in part* because we simply notice that the second-order judgement about the meaning of a term deploys the meaning that we have conferred on it. So we secure the reliability of the judgement about meaning *on the basis of having conferred a meaning on our terms*. But that, it seems, is not the concern; the concern is with the conferral of meaning. How, Kripke wonders, can there be such a state of which we are reliably aware, and which thus can *guide* our use? How, Wright wonders, can we identify a mental state as being this or that intention?

We should note four things. First, if the concern is about how such an item guides my use, then the concern is one that relates purely to one's *current* use. Secondly, if this is the right way to take the worry, then Wright's concern with provisional equations and thus with the second-order judgements is not to the point; it is clear too that the judgement-dependent epistemology cannot help in explaining our immediate awareness of an item providing guidance; it precisely denies that conception. Thirdly, it is hard not to see the search for such an item as the search for a representation of the rule, and this is bound to launch the regress of interpretations. So there must be something wrong with Kripke's question. Fourthly, Wittgenstein denies that there is anything *by which* we are guided in primitive cases of rule-following: we are constrained without being guided.

One might attempt to rebut the insubstantial response by claiming that to mean something by a term is to intend to use it thus-and-so. Thus a judgement about one's meaning will be a judgement about one's intentions; and now we need an explanation of one's authority in judging one's own intentions. But this is not so: it may follow from the fact that I mean that snow is white by "snow is white" that I intend to use it thus-and-so; but the two judgements are distinct.

There is, of course, a residual question about the first-personal authority one has over the *intention* to use an expression thus-and-so. However, that is probably a more general question about one's authority over one's avowals of intention. I do not propose to address that here, since I do not think it is a question about language in particular. My – very restricted – aim has been to reconcile the first-personal authority exhibited by speakers in judgements about their own meanings with a conception of rule-following.[16]

14. Truth-conditions versus use-conditions

Thus far we have argued that we should pursue the philosophy of language by attempting to construct a theory of meaning for a natural language. We have rejected radical interpretation as the stance to adopt in constructing such a theory and have instead recommended a modified robust approach. According to the latter, we shall be aiming to provide an informative account of the meanings of expressions in our own language. In other words, we are attempting to make the workings of our own language perspicuous to ourselves. Because we are constructing the account against the backdrop of our own facility with our language, the account will not explain the workings of our language from a completely external point of view. One consequence of limiting our explanatory ambitions in this way is that we need not do any work to exclude sceptical possibilities; these are excluded by our context of theorizing rather than by anything explicit in the theory itself.

In this last chapter I want to turn to the question of the form of the theory of meaning. The only theory that we have looked at in any detail is the truth-conditional theory advocated by Davidson (among others). We shall first consider attacks on truth-conditional theories of meaning and then go on to sketch possible alternatives.

14.1 Dummett's attack on truth-conditional theories

Dummett[1] gives three related arguments against truth-conditional accounts of meaning: one focuses on the social role of language; one on knowledge of meaning; and one on acquisition of language. The arguments are distinct but each develops an aspect of the publicity of meaning, which is the fundamental idea motivating each argument. We shall turn to the arguments in a moment, but first we should draw out some features of the truth-conditional account of meaning.

For Dummett, a theory of meaning is (or should deliver) a theory of understanding: the meaning of a term is what someone who understands the term knows. Thus, either a theory of meaning is directly a theory of understanding – it is a theory stating those capacities that constitute understanding – or it is a theory that characterizes what speakers know (and should then be supplemented with an account of what possession of that knowledge consists in). When we move to a truth-conditional account of meaning, the claim must thus be that in understanding a sentence, a speaker knows what condition the world must fulfil for that sentence to be true (in a given context of utterance). Traditionally one views truth-conditions as conditions that the world determinately either fulfils or fails to fulfil independently of our ability to tell which is the case. Although it is not our concern here, Dummett argues that this traditional conception constitutes an important strand in the realist metaphysical conception of the world. The reason for this, in brief, is that the conception requires us to see the world as having a determinate structure such as to confer a determinate truth-value – either true or false – on every potential statement of our language. Since the world's possessing that structure owes nothing to us in particular, since it is thought of as obtaining independently of our ability to know it, the conception incorporates a strong sense in which the world is as it is *objectively*. Now if Dummett is right that this conception of truth is an integral feature of realism and if he is also right that this feature cannot be sustained, then he provides a very general argument against realism. So much for background; let us now turn to Dummett's arguments.

First let us consider the social role of language. The social role of language is as an instrument of communication. Although language may have uses that are not directly related to communicating – for example one may think through a problem by using language – the meaning of an expression cannot include elements that are not involved in its role in communication. For this reason, if two speakers agree in the use of an expression, then they agree about its meaning; to suppose otherwise is to suppose that they might diverge in their meanings in a way that cannot be brought to light, and that, in turn, is to suppose that there is an ingredient of meaning that is purely private, that can play no role in communication. Let us suppose now that in understanding, say, the sentence "There is intelligent life elsewhere in the universe" we claim that the speaker grasps its truth-conditions as traditionally conceived. Dummett's challenge is to ask what, in the speaker's use of that sentence, demonstrates that this is the right account of her understanding of the sentence. His point then is that, in using the sentence, the speaker demonstrates a capacity to recognize whether or not such-and-such circumstances warrant assertion of the sentence. In other words, the speaker has a capacity to categorize one or another evidential situation as one that either warrants assertion of the sentence or fails to do so. Thus her capacities relate purely to the use of the sentence – being either prepared or not prepared to assert the sentence – in response to situations *that she can recognize*. We cannot therefore infer anything about whether or not the sentence is true or false in relation to situations that lie outside what the speaker is able to recognize. We cannot, for instance, say that the world must provide a state of affairs that either makes our sentence true or makes it false. Since we do not know whether or not there is intelligent life elsewhere in the universe and have no definitive way of finding out, to say either that there is a state of affairs that makes the sentence true or that there is a state of affairs that makes it false is to say that there is a way of using the sentence in response to that state of affairs, which our speaker may be incapable of performing. That is, we suppose that the meaning of our sentence transcends any use of it that our speaker may be capable of making. However, we had rejected that notion as being alien to the social character of language, so it is not correct to describe speakers' grasp of that sentence as grasp of truth-conditions, as traditionally conceived.

Let us move on to think about knowledge of meaning. If it makes sense to ascribe knowledge, then we must be able to say what manifests possession of that knowledge; we cannot ascribe knowledge except on the basis of what a would-be possessor of that knowledge is able to do. Our knowledge of language is often explicit knowledge in the sense that it is knowledge of which the possessor is able to give an account. For instance, I display my knowledge of the meaning of the term "square" by explaining that a square is a four-sided figure whose sides are equal in length and whose internal angles are also equal. Provided I understand the terms of my explanation, I understand the meaning of "square". It is obvious that, for this reason, one's knowledge of language cannot be purely explicit knowledge; otherwise our ability to speak a language would presuppose grasp of a language. So at certain points our understanding of language will consist in implicit knowledge, that is, knowledge that is ascribed on the basis of what a speaker is able to *do*. As we remarked above, our use of a sentence will consist in being able to tell whether or not a given epistemic situation is one that warrants or fails to warrant assertion of the sentence. And again nothing in that capacity for use shows that the sentence is either true or false, even though we cannot tell which. Thus we can have no grounds for attributing knowledge of truth-conditions, as traditionally conceived.

And finally we have the acquisition argument. We learn language through exposure to the use of language made by competent speakers. We cannot learn more than is made available in that use and that use, as we have mentioned, consists in willingness or refusal to assert the sentence in response to evidential situations. Nothing in that use warrants the assumption that the sentence is true or false independently of our ability to know which. Thus the meanings of sentences cannot be taught and learned if they are construed as traditional truth-conditions.

Wright has recast the argument once again in terms of normativity. If we think of meaning as given by traditional truth-conditions, then we are thinking of ourselves as having conferred a normative standard for the use of some sentences that outruns anything we may be able to police. So if the sentence "There is intelligent life elsewhere in the universe" is determinately either true or false, then it is, in an objective sense, either right now to assert the sentence or wrong now to do so. But we have no way of determining whether it is right or wrong, and so no way of policing such a use. Rather, all we can do is to say that it is wrong now to make the assertion *given our evidential situation*. Thus the traditional conception of truth-conditions runs up against the interpretation of rule-following according to which there could be no sense in there being standards of correctness that outrun our ability to police by implementation of the technique determined by the rule.

There are, of course, a host of responses to Dummett's arguments. I shall not rehearse these here except to anticipate their broad shape. A very basic assumption of all the arguments is that, when we consider the understanding of a sentence, we should be able to think of that understanding as consisting in a set of capacities that relate to that particular sentence without bringing in similar capacities relating to a whole host of other sentences or that relate to an ability to speak the language as a whole. This is Dummett's molecularity requirement. Essentially it is a way of unpacking the idea that in order to understand a given sentence one needs only an understanding of a range of other sentences that are no more complex than the sentence we are considering. The assumption plays a role in the argument because we limit the uses of our sentence to assertions of it and exclude, for instance, using it as part of a more complex sentence. The motivations for insisting on molecularity have to do with an attempt to explain our progressive acquisition of language, our ability to understand novel sentences (linguistic creativity) and a requirement that meanings are surveyable and so can figure in our rational use of language; speakers need to be aware of the meanings of their terms – those meanings must be surveyable – if those meanings can figure in their reasons for using language. In my view, the telling consideration here is the last. Linguistic creativity and the progressive acquisition of language each require a conception of linguistic competence as the overlaying of capacities on more fundamental capacities. But there is no reason why we should think of these capacities as grasp of meaning. To be sure, the end result is grasp of meaning but, in Wittgenstein's memorable phrase, we might think of that as "light dawning gradually over the whole" (cf. 1969: §141); the gradual dawning would consist in the building up of capacities, not the progressive understanding of the meaning of elements of language. So each of these considerations fails to motivate molecularity because it fails to focus the requirement on grasp of meaning. The third consideration mends this lack because one rationalizes linguistic behaviour in terms of grasp of meanings. If this is so, then meanings must be surveyable: in some sense, speakers must be aware of the meanings of their terms. Holism, in characterizing the meaning of an expression only by reference to the meanings of expressions in the rest of the language, renders meanings unsurveyable. So if language use should be seen as rational, meanings must be surveyable and holism is therefore false.² Despite this, holism still finds no shortage of adherents.

Another assumption of the argument relates to Dummett's insistence on robustness. If one were McDowell, for instance, one would say simply that the terms in which Dummett is willing to describe use are excessively impoverished. If one is permitted to consider the use of "There is intelligent life elsewhere in the universe" to assert that there is intelligent life elsewhere in the universe, where the that-clause specifies a truth-condition traditionally conceived, then the argument clearly fails.

I have argued for a conception of the publicity of meaning that accords with a version of Dummettian robustness and here I shall simply recommend molecularity as a methodological position that is well motivated. So, conceding the main assumptions of the arguments, we shall soon turn to the question of what alternatives there are to traditional truth-conditional conceptions of meaning. Dummett's thought is that we need to think of meaning as captured by use- rather than truth-conditions.³ However, before we add any detail to that thought I want to look at Brandom's quite different reasons for favouring use- over truth-conditional accounts.

14.2 Brandom on inferentialism versus representationalism

Brandom frames his discussion in terms of a clash between two approaches to semantics: representationalism versus inferentialism (see Brandom 1994: ch. 2; 2000: esp. ch. 1). On the representationalist approach one explains meaning in terms of the semantic relations of expressions to items in the world. So notions of truth, reference and satisfaction take explanatory priority. On the inferentialist view we think of the meaning of a sentence as determined by its inferential relations with other sentences. So notions of entailment, of compatibility and of incompatibility take explanatory priority. Brandom argues in favour of the inferentialist approach. Whichever approach we adopt, we shall need to explain the terms taken as basic by the other approach: an inferentialist will have to explain semantic notions in terms of their inferential (for Brandom, that is expressive) potential; a representationalist will have to give an account of good inference in terms of semantic concepts.⁴ Brandom bases his belief in inferentialism partly on concerns about representationalism and partly on a belief in the efficacy of the inferentialist order of explanation, the latter belief being justified by the detail and power of the inferentialist programme that he undertakes. However, we shall look only at his concerns about representationalism.

We might begin this way. Ask yourself what it takes for someone to deploy concepts. Clearly it will not do simply to say that one has, say, the concept *red* just in case one reliably responds differentially to red and to non-red things. Parrots can be trained to utter the word "red" in response only to red items but this does not mean that they have mastery of the concept. What the parrot lacks is an ability to judge that such and such is red and she lacks that ability because she cannot incorporate her response in a network of inferences. A speaker precisely has the concept of red because she can, *inter alia*, move by inference from her judgement that Fred is red to the judgements that Fred is coloured, that Fred is not green and from the judgement that Mildred is crimson to the judgement that Mildred is red and so on. In other words, it is *inference* that forms the essential mark of conceptual expertise rather than representation.

Now this, of course, is not enough to establish an inferentialist order of explanation over a representational one because a representationalist will want to provide an account of inference. What it does establish is the essential role played by inference. We can bring out the point of this role by noting the following levels of explaining the function of representings. On the one hand we have representational *success*: a name succeeds in referring to an object; a sentence in being true. On the other hand we have representational *purport*: use of a name aims to refer to an object; assertion of a sentence aims at truth. Although the distinction is more general, we could think of it in terms of one of its possible manifestations: Frege's distinction between sense and reference. Representational success concerns the referential properties of a sign; representational purport concerns the semantic content, the sense *expressed* by a sign. Brandom warns us to beware of losing sight of this distinction, and this warning carries with it an important lesson. For to hold on to the distinction between referential purport and referential success – to be able to explain the content of the distinction – we need to explain what it is *to take a representing as a representing* – more simply, what it is to understand the representing.

Although the parrot's utterance of "red" in some way *represents* the presence of red – we can certainly take it to indicate such a presence – it has no representational purport and it has none because the utterance is not *taken by the parrot as such*. What would be needed for it to have representational purport is for the parrot to take the utterance as one that could be caught up in the game of giving and asking for reasons; that is, we need to bring in the inferential role of the utterance.

Accepting these points, how might the representationalist respond? A first concern is that if the primitive state of the parrot can be taken to have representational properties, then these properties are insufficient to explain the function of language, the function of a system of representation in which the representings are taken as such. So the account requires serious supplementation; we need some account of the inferential properties of representings. One might hope to make progress here by offering a representationalist account of the relation of entailment. Since Tarski's work in formal semantics, we have such accounts available. A problem, though, is that these accounts supply only a ready account of relations of *formal* entailment but, as Brandom points out, and as our example above illustrates, the sorts of inference concerned will not be merely *formally* valid inferences but will include some that are only *materially* valid (such as that from "*X* is scarlet" to "*X* is red"). Thus the representationalist is faced with the difficult task of giving a representationalist account of materially good inferences – essentially of reducing material goodness of inference to formal goodness of inference. Brandom is pessimistic about the prospects here and is correspondingly optimistic about the prospects of providing an account of formal goodness of inference in terms of the notion of material goodness of inference. If we can pick out logical vocabulary – which Brandom attempts to do by means of its expressive role – then a formally valid inference is one that cannot be transformed from a good material inference into a bad one by substitution of non-logical vocabulary for non-logical vocabulary. So the recommendation is to jettison the representationalist order of explanation in favour of that of the inferentialist. But, as was foreshadowed, the supremacy of the latter can emerge finally only from the success of the resulting programme.

14.3 Use-conditional accounts of meaning

14.3.1 Dummett's account

The aim in this final section is simply to outline some of the main features of these under-explored theories of meaning. Again Dummett and Brandom will occupy the limelight. We shall start with Dummett's attempt to generalize intuitionistic accounts of mathematics[5] and use this to lead into Brandom's rather different approach.

One positive thing we can take from Dummett's negative critique of truth-conditional accounts of meaning is that understanding a sentence is a capacity to use it appropriately in response to one's evidential situation. Evidence in the mathematical realm consists in proof. Thus, if we think about what capacity a speaker has when she understands a mathematical sentence, it is likely to consist in an ability to tell whether or not a given mathematical construction constitutes a proof of a given sentence. So we shall aim to give an account of the meaning of such a sentence by determining what constitutes a proof of it, in terms of what constitutes a proof of its components. In mathematics, this approach has been well studied; it gives rise to the following explanations of the meanings of the (intuitionistic) logical connectives (as given originally by Heyting):

- A proof of "$A \,\&\, B$" is a proof of A and a proof of B.
- A proof of "$A \vee B$" is any construction of which it can be recognized that it yields a proof of A or a proof of B.
- A proof of "$A \rightarrow B$" is any construction of which it can be recognized that, applied to a proof of A it yields a proof of B.

- A proof of "$\neg A$" is any construction of which it can be recognized that, applied to a proof of A, it yields a proof of an absurdity.
- A proof of "$(\exists x)Fx$" is a proof of "Fa" for some a in the domain.
- A proof of "$(\forall x)Fx$" is any construction of which it can be recognized that, applied to any a in the domain, it yields a proof of "Fa".

There is a good deal to be said about these explications of the logical connectives. However, we shall restrict ourselves to the following few points. First, note the overtly epistemic caste to many of the explanations: a proof is *a construction of which it can be recognized* and so on. Secondly, a proof of the conditional is seen as a function from *proofs* of the antecedent to *proofs* of the consequent. So here we are incorporating into the meaning of the conditional a particular conception of the truth of sentences; we are thinking of a sentence as being true only if there is a proof of it available. For that reason, when we think of the conditional as acting on situations in which A is true, we take these to be situations in which a proof of A is available. So we can think of the conditional as a function taking such proofs as arguments. Thirdly, negation is also taken as a function from proofs to proofs. Thus we can think of it as a conditional: "$\neg A$" is "$A \rightarrow \Lambda$", where "Λ" stands for an absurdity. So negation is explained in terms of the notion of an absurdity, which had better then be explained independently of negation. Fourthly, consider the sentence "$A \vee \neg A$". To have a proof of this sentence is to have a construction that yields a proof of "A" or that, applied to a proof of "A", yields an absurdity. It is quite consistent to hold that we may be in an evidential situation in which we do not possess a construction fulfilling either of these functions; that is, we might be in a situation in which we can neither prove nor refute "A". In these situations "$A \vee \neg A$" is not assertible and thus the law of excluded middle is not a valid law of intuitionistic logic.[6]

The question we should focus on here is how we should generalize this account to empirical discourse. In order to do so we need to find an analogue for proof in the empirical realm. Dummett's suggestion is that the relevant notion is that of warrant for assertion; proof provides warrant for assertion of a mathematical sentence and, in the empirical realm, certain evidence warrants assertion of the sentence. Dummett's thought is that we can characterize the meaning of a sentence in terms of the conditions that warrant its assertion; we can characterize understanding in terms of grasp of such conditions; and we can develop this into a systematic account, characterizing the assertion-conditions of complex sentences in terms of those of its components.

As we mentioned, the proposal is to characterize the meaning of a sentence in terms of its assertion-conditions. So the meaning must be a function of assertion-conditions; that is if two sentences share assertion-conditions, they must be alike in meaning. The problem with the proposal is very direct; there are many pairs of sentences that differ in meaning, one from the other, yet that share assertion-conditions. Take the following sentence pairs, for example:[7]

(a) The moon is made of green cheese.
    I know the moon is made of green cheese.
(b) Maromokotro is the highest peak in Madagascar.
    It is assertible that Maromokotro is the highest peak in Madagascar.
(c) I shall die before I am fifty.
    I foresee that I shall die before I am fifty.

The problem here is that in each of these pairs the first sentence – the objective member of the pair – has certain assertion-conditions and the second sentence is about one's epistemic situation, effectively stating that those assertion-conditions obtain. So plausibly each shares its assertion-conditions with the other. This is problematic for two reasons. First, the use-conditional theorist needs to distinguish each member from its partner in order to gain a notion of objectivity. If the first member cannot be distinguished from the second, then, it seems, all we ever talk about is our own epistemic position and the world threatens to vanish. Secondly, it is quite clear that each differs in meaning from the other. They function very differently with respect to negation, to tensed formations and embedding in conditionals: "The moon is not made of green cheese" may be false (I think, as it happens, it is true), yet "I do not know the moon is made of green cheese" may be true; "If I shall die before I am fifty, then I shall be the fourth member of my family to die prematurely" may be true, yet "If I foresee that I shall die before I am fifty, then I shall be the fourth member of my family to die prematurely" is likely to be false. "Maromokotro is the highest peak in Madagascar" is true, yet "It was assertible that Maromokotro is the highest peak in Madagascar" is not true, if we are referring to a time before there was much geographical knowledge of the island. So we either have to reject the idea that the meaning of a sentence is a function of its assertion-conditions or we have to reject the idea that the meaning of complex sentences such as negations and conditionals is a function of the meanings of their components. The latter seems a desperate remedy, so it appears we ought to give up on the hope of characterizing meaning in terms of assertion-conditions.

The underlying problem is caused by a disanalogy between the notion of proof and the notion of warrant for assertion. Proof constitutes a very special warrant for assertion: proofs provide *indefeasible* warrants for assertion. If what we have is genuinely a proof of a statement, then nothing can arise that deprives it of its warrant-conferring status. In contrast, in the empirical realm anything worth thinking of as a warrant for assertion will be defeasible. Let me first explain what we mean by this and then let me explain why it is true. What we mean by saying that the warrant is defeasible is that a certain piece of evidence may be deprived of its warrant-conferring status without our having to revise our view about the obtaining of that evidence or our view of whether evidence of this sort in general provides warrant for assertion of such sentences. Consider an example. Let us say that we take an episode of behaviour by X (rolling the eyes, drumming of the finger-tips, looking purposefully away from the speaker) to warrant the assertion that X is irritated by the speaker. Say we come to learn that in X's culture rolling the eyes is a gesture of agreement, looking away from the speaker indicates respect and drumming of the finger-tips often accompanies concentration. We would then revise our view that X is irritated by the speaker yet we would not revise our view that X was drumming her finger-tips and so on, nor would we revise our practice of, in general, taking such behaviour to warrant assertions about irritation (unless, perhaps, we were living with X's people). So the warrant would be deprived of its status as a warrant by our discoveries about X's culture, without that impugning the statements about behaviour that constitute the warrant. Nothing analogous occurs in the mathematical realm: if a proof ceases to provide a warrant, then this must be because we cease to see it as a correct proof.

Why is it true that warrants in the empirical realm will be defeasible? On the one hand, it is plausible to suppose that the best evidence we can access for many sorts of claim – for example those about the past and future; about other minds; about unsurveyable regions – is short of conclusive. This is one way to explain the difference between appearance and reality in these cases. We make judgements about the way things are on the basis of the way things seem and the way things seem may differ from the way things are because the way things seem provides only defeasible evidence for the way things are.[8] On the other hand, suppose that we do have a notion of indefeasible warrants for empirical statements. Such a warrant would conclusively confer truth on the statement and would be such as to be epistemically accessible; otherwise it would not be a *warrant*. But that entails that we would have given an explanation of an anti-realist conception of truth.[9] So really, settling for defeasible warrants for assertion is a way of distinguishing our approach as use-conditional rather than truth-conditional.

What this reveals, arguably, is that the source of the difference between one member of the pairs and the other is that although each agrees in assertion-conditions with its partner, the statements that we effect by uttering them have different defeating-conditions. The statements made by uttering "The moon is made of green cheese" and "I know the moon is made of green cheese" may come to be defeated in different ways: imagine that my warrant for both is defeated but that I uncover alternative evidence that the moon was made of green cheese. In that case my best judgement now is that I did not know that the moon is made of green cheese, yet it was; the former statement is now defeated, the latter not. The moral of this story is that we seem to need to consider more than just assertion-conditions in order to characterize the meanings of empirical statements.

Dummett notes that there are two aspects to making an assertion with a given content: the grounds on which the assertion is properly made and the consequences that flow therefrom (see Dummett 1991b: ch. 5; 1993: essay 2, §5). Up until now we have been focusing on warrants for assertion, that is, the grounds for assertion, and thus have been focusing exclusively on a single aspect of the use of a sentence in assertion. We could therefore supplement the account and thereby make it more refined by factoring in the other aspect of assertion, the consequences of assertion. Although he considers meaning-theories that take this form, Dummett is sceptical about them because he thinks that unless we ensure that there is a matching between grounds and consequences, then we contravene his requirement of molecularity. The argument for this conclusion proceeds as follows. Molecularity requires that the meanings of more simple regions of language are unaffected by the introduction of more complex regions of language. In other words, the extension of a language must be *conservative* relative to the meanings in the language prior to the extension. If this were not so, then we could not think of those meanings as having been finally established in relation to some proper fragment of language. Let us suppose that the meaning of a sentence is captured in its assertion-conditions (meaning both its grounds and consequences). Now suppose that we introduce a sentence, S, whose grounds and consequences do not match – by which we mean simply that they are independent of one another. It is also plausible to suppose that since the new sentence extends the old language, its use will be based on the old language. So its grounds will be specifiable by sentences in the old language, G_S, and its consequences will be or will include sentences in the old language, C_S. If G_S obtains, then S is assertible and thus C_S is assertible. The question then is: is this warrant for asserting C_S novel or was it already included among its assertion-conditions? If it is novel, then the assertion-conditions and hence the meaning of C_S has changed, which compromises the requirement that the extension be conservative relative to C_S's meaning. If it is already included, then that, in itself, displays a matching between S's grounds and consequences: its consequences are already consequences of its grounds.[10] Thus, if we want to be molecularists we had better insist on a matching between grounds and consequences. What is this matching? Dummett calls it "harmony" and its character is implicit in the argument we have just sketched: a sentence's grounds and consequences are in harmony when its consequences are consequences of its grounds and are the strongest consequences. Dummett thus insists that we should be able to *derive* the consequences of a sentence from its grounds (or vice versa). Therefore a meaning-theory will focus on a single aspect of a sentence's use in assertion, providing a general means of deriving the other aspect from that one.[11]

This insistence provides Dummett with another complaint against classical logic. For the rules governing the use of classical negation enable the derivation of sentences that do not involve negation, that could not have been derived before the introduction of classical negation. Thus the introduction of classical negation is not a conservative extension of language.

The problem with Dummett's position here is that in restricting his focus to single-aspect accounts of meaning he seems impotent in the face of our problematic pairs. These appear precisely to show that single-aspect accounts are inadequate: each member of the pair shares its grounds with its partner but each differs in meaning from its partner.

There is, however, a clear gap in Dummett's argument. Granted that it is implausible to suppose that an acceptable linguistic practice can accept just any matching of grounds and consequences, and granted too that accepting G_S as new grounds for C_S would contravene molecularity, we still do not need to accept that we should be able to *derive* C_S from G_S. Why not? Well, because we can allow that it is a *presupposition* of the practice that the grounds for C_S provided by G_S will coincide with its original grounds. There is no need to justify this presupposition by providing a derivation and, indeed, the presupposition may not be derivable because it may hold only as a matter of empirical fact. All we need require is that practitioners be prepared to reject this aspect of their practice if the presupposition can be shown to be false.[12] We have good grounds therefore for investigating double-aspect accounts of meaning. Let us therefore turn to Brandom's account, which differs from that of Dummett importantly in focusing on two aspects of assertion rather than one.

14.3.2 Brandom's account

Brandom constructs his account against the background of a normative practice in which practitioners keep track of one another's normative status. He calls this a deontic score-keeping practice. The main point is that practitioners will monitor one another's moves in the practice as being either correct or incorrect. A correct performance is constituted by doing *only* what one is *entitled* to and *whatever* one is *committed* to. So one practitioner will keep track of another by monitoring the propriety of her moves against an assessment of her commitments and her entitlements. We can then think of the semantic content of asserting a sentence as determined by what would entitle the assertion and by what commitments would follow from having made it. So the semantic content of a sentence is determined by the normative status of the move of asserting it, which is, in turn, determined by the normative status that this move has in the business of assessing practitioners' normative statuses. This last point is important. Since a practitioner's entitlement to a particular move will be a matter of what else she is committed to, the focus on practitioners imposes a kind of holism: an assessment of entitlement is made against a slew of attributed commitments and there need be no way of circumscribing in advance just which commitments will figure in the assessment of entitlement.

Taking the notions of commitment and entitlement as primitive, we can then define inferential relations and logical concepts such as the conditional. We have the following:

Inference$_m$: If one is committed to $P_1 \ldots P_n$, then one is committed to C.

Inference$_n$: If one is entitled to commitment to $P_1 \ldots P_n$, then one is entitled to commitment to C.

Incompatibility: Commitment to P precludes entitlement to Q (and vice versa).

The first notion of inference coincides with deductive or monotonic inferences; the second with ampliative or non-monotonic inferences[13] (hence the subscripts); while incompatibility sponsors a third notion of inference that is modal and counterfactual-supporting. Among the non-monotonic inferences we have in view here are inductive inferences, but presumably also included are non-deductive inferences that are also not inductive. Thus the inference from "John is howling and writhing" to "John is in pain'" might well not strike one as inductive but is not monotonic. It will be of a piece with other inferences of the form inference$_n$: If one is entitled to commitment to "John is howling and writhing", then one is entitled to commitment to "John is in pain". We might then define two conditionals as follows:

$P \to_m C$ iff if one is committed to P, then one is committed to C.

$P \to_n C$ iff if one is entitled to commitment to P, then one is entitled to commitment to C.

Thus the notion of a practitioner's entitlements and commitments sets up a notion of the entitlements and commitments to asserting a sentence, which, in turn, establish inferential relations for that sentence.

It is tempting to identify the entitlement associated with a sentence with its grounds and the commitments with its consequences: tempting, but wrong. The two distinctions combine to yield a fourfold set of distinctions. We have grounds that entitle, grounds that commit, consequences that are entitled and consequences that are commitments.

Because the inferential relations are set up *jointly* by the commitments *and* entitlements associated with asserting the sentence, those inferential relations need not be purely formally valid. Thus the account yields an appreciation of the meaning of a sentence in terms of its *material* inferential relations, just as we had advertised Brandom as advocating. Any assessment of the details of this project would be a vast undertaking in its own right (see Wanderer 2008). I shall not attempt anything of that sort here. I want to consider how the account deals with our problematic pairs and then to look at Quine's attack on the analytic–synthetic distinction through the perspective it provides.

14.4 The problematic pairs

Consider the pair:

(c′) I shall die before I am fifty.

(c″) I foresee that I shall die before I am fifty.

We know that these have distinct contents because, for instance, the conditional "If I shall die before I am fifty, then I shall die before I am fifty" is trivially true; while "If I foresee that I shall die before I am fifty, then I shall die before I am fifty" is probably false and probably only to be endorsed given collateral information about my reliability as a seer. Our task is to explain this difference in terms of the properties of the sentences (c′) and (c″), commitment to which, it is conceded, is entitled in the same circumstances. Brandom's explanation is that the consequences of the two claims differ. (c′) has as a consequence that I shall die before I am fifty; (c″) does not. The first conditional makes explicit this consequence and hence is entitled; nothing analogous applies to the second conditional. In slightly different terms, (c′) is incompatible with the claim, (d), that I am alive at an age of fifty or more; (c″) is not. So the two claims sustain different incompatibility relations and thus are different. Of course the incompatibility would distinguish our problematic partners but we need to explain the incompatibility in terms of commitments and entitlements. Now two claims are incompatible just in case commitment to the one precludes entitlement to the other. So we have:

(I) (c*) is incompatible with (d) iff commitment to (c*) is precluded by entitlement to (d).

And then the claim would be that (I) holds when we replace "(c*)" by "(c′)" but fails to hold when we replace it by "(c″)".

The response has been questioned by Wright and Hale (forthcoming), who notice that since incompatibility is symmetric we will also have:

(I′) (c*) is incompatible with (d) iff commitment to (d) is precluded by entitlement to (c*).

And now, since (c′) and (c″) are, by hypothesis, co-entitled, it becomes mysterious as to why the one sustains an incompatibility relation that the other fails to sustain; either that or the account appears to be incoherent.

Brandom's response is to say that the two claims are not co-entitled but that they are only provisionally co-entitled. The attribution of commitments and entitlements is a complicated three-stage business. A score-keeper begins by making provisional attributions of commitment given a speaker's new assertion (including, of course, any commitment derivable from these by a commitment-preserving inference); she then attributes provisional entitlement to those commitments she takes her to be entitled to (including, of course, any entitlement derivable from these by an entitlement-preserving inference); finally she subtracts entitlement to those claims that are incompatible with commitments the speaker already has. It is only entitlements that survive through to the final stage that are to be included in a claim's final entitlements. On this account, although (c′) and (c″) share *provisional*, they do not share *final* entitlements.

This defence cannot, however, be a good strategy. If we know that the two claims differ in final entitlement, then that, in itself, provides reason for distinguishing them. There is no need to proceed through the detour of incompatibility relations. And more, we want an explanation for the origin of the difference in final entitlements. A good place to look, since the claims share provisional entitlements, is to incompatibility relations. But this will not help us because Brandom informs us that when we attempt to understand them we need to do so in terms of final entitlements. No progress is made.

There is a different strategy available; it is provided by Wright (1993: essay 14: §4). The use-conditional theorist may have overplayed her hand. To be sure, we want to move away from an account that helps itself to a semantic notion such as truth and then explains meaning in terms of it. So we want to take some notion that relates closely to use as fundamentally explanatory. And thus we fix on conditions of assertion and attempt to explain meaning in terms of such conditions. But the final step is too quick. We can maintain a use-conditional approach not by using use-conditions to explain meaning but by using them to explain truth and then to use this in an account of meaning. Or, to put the point another way, let us suppose that we can characterize a certain sort of use-conditions for assertions; call these superassertibility-conditions. We might then notice that these superassertibility-conditions can be used in explaining meaning because they do not suffer from the same defect as ordinary assertion-conditions. We might also note that because of this we can see superassertion-conditions as truth-conditions that are bona fide use-conditional since they have been explained purely in terms of use-conditions.

What defects need we free superassertion-conditions from? The crucial defect in assertion-conditions is their defeasibility; none of the current problems affects our account of the meaning of mathematical statements in terms of their proof-conditions, precisely because proof-conditions are indefeasible. So Wright's strategy is to try to emulate this property of proof-conditions in the empirical realm. Thus, just as satisfaction of proof-conditions provides an enduring warrant, we seek a certain sort of assertion-condition whose satisfaction provides an enduring warrant. Wright (forthcoming in Wanderer and Weiss) offers the following: "a content is *superassertible* if and only if it is, or can be, warranted, and some warrant for it would survive arbitrarily close scrutiny of its pedigree and arbitrarily extensive increments to or other forms of improvement of our state of information".

Some comments on this somewhat complex notion are called for. Superassertibility is a complex modal notion making reference to possible and actual situations. What it claims is that a content is superassertible just in case there is a warrant available for its assertion and some such warrant will not be defeated by further investigation, no matter how thorough. So a claim is superassertible just in case we *can* possess a warrant for it that is, *in fact*, indefeasible. There is no implication that a warrant of this sort will in general be indefeasible for claims of this sort; contents have superassertion-conditions; types of sentence do not. Nor is there any implication that such a condition that is a superassertion-condition for a given content will continue to be so in alternative possible situations. An occasion of Jones's writhing may provide a superassertion-condition for his being in pain – he may genuinely be in pain and writhing because of it – but in another such situation it may not – he may be simulating.[14]

Wright, like the truth-conditional theorist (because he is a truth-conditional theorist), has little difficulty in distinguishing members of our problematic pairs (see Wright 1993: essay 14; Wright & Hale forthcoming). Each member has different truth-, that is, superassertion-conditions. The content expressed by my use of (c′) may fail to be superassertible because there is good evidence available that my mild heart complaint is easily controlled; but the content expressed by my use (c″) may nonetheless be superassertible in these circumstances.

There is another fairly obvious strategy here and it will help to understand Wright's approach if we have it before us. Why not focus simply on conditions warranting an assertion and their defeating conditions? That is, why not deploy both of these notions in our account of meaning? We could then quite straightforwardly say that (c′) and (c″) differ because their defeating conditions differ, despite sharing conditions-warranted assertion. There are two problems with such a proposal, which Wright's account is aimed at avoiding. The first is redolent of Dummett's queasiness about dual-aspect accounts of meaning, namely, that we cannot allow just any pairing of grounds with consequences. Wright concurs but makes the point in rather different fashion. If there are no constraints on the way aspects of assertion are paired, it seems there would be nothing amiss in a situation in which speakers make assertions only to find that in all or in very many cases they then have to withdraw the assertion. They would be following the rules of the practice perfectly, so on what grounds could it be criticized? On Wright's view, accepting such a situation would do violence to our concept of assertion since when we make an assertion we are not indifferent to its defeat; we aim to make warranted assertions and when we assert, we set ourselves against defeat of the assertion.[15] We can capture this in the content of assertion. A truth-conditionalist will say that in asserting we put forward our assertion as true; in echo, Wright says that in asserting we put forward our assertion as enduringly assertible, that is, as superassertible.

The second problem is this. We cannot simply say that the two *sentences* (c′) and (c″) share assertion-conditions but differ in defeating conditions because, in any situation, any warrant for the one will provide a warrant for the other and if a warrant for the one is defeated, likewise is the warrant it had provided for the other. In the above scenario involving my heart complaint what is defeated is that *statement* effected in uttering (c′) while what fails to be defeated is the *statement* effected in uttering (c″). In other words we need to appeal to the notion of a statement made by use of a sentence and we cannot do this if we are in the business of constructing a theory of meaning since, after all, the statement made is or is determined by the meaning of the sentence.

However, Wright's account is not itself free of these concerns. We noted above that what is superassertible is not a sentence but a content or a statement; thus his account lends itself to a similar complaint. Furthermore, if we set aside this worry, it is doubtful that using superassertibility to characterize the content of the act of assertion will help matters. For if that is the content of asserting then it goes with both our assertion of "*P*" and of "*P* is assertible"; that is, we claim that each is enduringly assertible. But, if either is assertible so is the other, so in claiming that the one is enduringly assertible one is doing no more than claiming that the other is. So we fail to distinguish the two claims.

The account focusing on assertion and defeating conditions can be amended. To be sure, we cannot think of these in terms of assertion- *and* defeating-conditions attaching to sentences. But we can characterize the meaning of a sentence in terms of conditions that would warrant its assertion and conditions in which *that assertion* would be defeated. Thus (c′) and (c″) are both assertible in the same circumstances but my assertion of (c′) is defeated by the welcome news on the medical front; my assertion of (c″) is not.

The question clearly calls for much more investigation but the availability of possible responses should dispel any sense that the problem is a knock-down blow against the use-conditional theorist. However, coming up with the form of a solution is only the first stage; we then have to develop this into a systematic account of meaning. Dummett continues to think of linguistic practices that lack harmony as being flawed, but concedes that such practices are likely to be common and that their flaw is likely to be difficult to discern. So descriptive accounts of meaning should, in all likelihood, focus on two aspects of assertion – but development of such theories is likely to be a formidable task. He writes revealingly of his philosophical temperament:

> My ground for doubting the strategy of specifying sense in terms of just one of the two features of use is that we are not entitled to assume that harmony and stability obtain in the linguistic practice in which we – or others – grow up to participate. In some cases, for instance that of unwarrantedly pejorative terms, they blatantly do not obtain, but we can easily eliminate from our vocabulary the expressions to whose

use this is due. But harmony may fail for subtler reasons, without our detecting the failure; outside formal logic, it is not an easy matter to decide whether or not harmony prevails. If we are to describe linguistic practice as it actually is, perhaps we need a theory of meaning in which the justification and consequences of assertions are specified independently of one another. That would be quite a complicated theory to have to construct; I do not much want to contemplate it.

(Dummett, forthcoming)

14.5 The analytic–synthetic distinction

I mentioned that I want to use Brandom's perspective to reflect on Quine's attack on the analytic–synthetic distinction. Although there is a good lesson to be learned by focusing on Brandom, the lesson should apply to other developments of the double-aspect approach.

As we said, according to Brandom (1994: ch. 2, §§IV–VI), the meaning of a sentence can be seen in terms of its material inferential role. In other words, we can see its content as determined by the inferences it spawns, particularly those from the grounds for its application to the consequences of having applied it. These material inferences may be substantial and, indeed, may be inferences that, on reflection, are seen as bad. Thus, for instance, the sentence "Klaus is Boche" is asserted on the grounds that Klaus is German and has the consequence that Klaus is cruel. So anyone prepared to assert the sentence is committed to the inference from its grounds, "Klaus is German", to its consequence, "Klaus is cruel"; and commitment to the goodness of that inference is part of the sentence's meaning. Thus anyone prepared to employ the concept *Boche* is committed to the conditional "If Klaus is German, then Klaus is cruel"; for such a speaker, commitment to the antecedent entails commitment to the conclusion. Because we reject the inference from grounds to consequences here as being materially bad (we may be committed to the truth of "Klaus is German"; "Klaus is compassionate" and "Whoever is compassionate is not cruel"), we would reject the concept of *Boche*. There are, however, many other concepts that facilitate analogously substantial inferences, but which we take to be good material inferences.

Recall that Quine (1961: ch. 2, §§5–6) had raised suspicions about the concept of analyticity and thus of meaning because he argued that there are no sentences whose truth is guaranteed by meaning and *thus* that are exempt from revision in the light of experience. In brief we could summarize the argument as follows:

Premise 1: If there are sentences that are true in virtue of meaning, then there are sentences that are immune to revision in light of experience.
Premise 2: No sentence is immune to revision in light of experience.

Sub-conclusion: So no sentence is true in virtue of meaning.
Conclusion: Thus the notion of meaning is otiose.

But if the foregoing account is right, then it suggests that rather than focus on the notion of *true in virtue of meaning* we do better to focus on the notion of sentences *to whose truth we are committed in virtue of meaning*. Clearly if such a notion is coherent and substantial, then we cannot claim that the notion of meaning is otiose. So the question is whether a version of Quine's argument can be mounted when framed in terms of this notion. However, we immediately encounter a problem with the first premise, which becomes:

Premise 1': If there are sentences to whose truth speakers are committed in virtue of meaning, then there are sentences that are immune to revision in light of experience.

There is no reason to accept that this claim is true. As we have just discovered, employers of the concept *Boche* will be committed to the truth of the sentence "If Klaus is German, then Klaus is cruel" purely in virtue of the meaning they have assigned to "Boche". Despite this, the sentence is clearly revisable in light of experience. So Premise 1' is probably false. Quine's mistake is to think that meanings must be sanitized of any presupposition about the way the world is – a dogma that informs both classical empiricist and rationalist thinking about meaning, but which is exorcized in Kant's thought (see Sellars 1953) and in much pragmatist thinking. The character of our language is not immune to its worldly embedding – quite the reverse: it is constructed by a community that is shaped and influenced in innumerable ways by its worldly context. Of course the analytic–synthetic distinction is then suspect, but for rather different reasons. If it is read as imposing a dichotomy between truths holding purely in virtue of meaning and truths that are substantial, then, according to this conception of meaning, it is simply a false dichotomy: these categories, we discover, are not mutually exclusive.[16]

Notes

1. The puzzles of language

1. But see Chapter 13, where some of these issues will emerge again.

2. The starting-point for analysis

1. The comparison is suggested by Dummett (1993: 1).
2. I say "seem" because some philosophers have dismissed this surface form as deceptive, for example Russell (1992), who thought instead that the knower was multiply related to the constituents of what he had previously taken to be the proposition.
3. We should not confuse these two claims. (i) The meaning of e is m iff e refers to m; and (ii) the meaning of e is given by the fact that e refers to m. (i) is the claim in the text; (ii) is a claim of quite a different sort that we shall come to discuss only in Chapter 6.
4. There is an unfortunate lack of agreement among commentators about how to translate Frege's German term "*Bedeutung*". It is variously translated as: "denotation", "nominatum", "meaning" and "reference". I shall use "reference" and "denotation" pretty much interchangeably as translations; "meaning" will not be used in this way at all. And "nominatum" will not be used at all.
5. See Russell, "On Denoting" (1905); reprinted in Russell (1956, 1972).
6. See Chapter 11 for more.
7. This assumption contradicts Kripke's view of the necessity of origin, but that does not matter: if you do not want to question Kripke's view, then change the example – suppose that "Red Rum" is synonymous with the three-times winner of the Grand National.

3. Analysing sentence-meaning

1. Reprinted in Harnish (1994) among others.
2. This is a point made by Schiffer (1972: 162); he attributes it to Loar.
3. Carroll seems to think the problem lies in the fact that the meaning-determining whim would then have to be communicated to the hearer in language, presumably launching a regress. The truth in this is surely that there is an irresolvable epistemological problem in a hearer divining a speaker's communicative intentions unless those intentions are not merely whimsical, that is, are in some way constrained – see below.
4. Grice shows evidence of being aware of this point, as the main text points out. However, there is another pertinent example worth recording. He asks himself whether a grunt could

mean that you should incur a malady, if I utter the grunt with the appropriate intentions. He answers negatively, and the reason he gives is that "the intended effect must be something which in some sense is in the control of the audience". He goes on to explain this in terms of the recognition of the intention being a reason and not merely a cause in bringing about the appropriate effect. But we might just as well fix on the speaker – after all it is the speaker's intentions that will be meaning-determining irrespective of what effect the utterance actually has on its audience – and insist that the speaker's intentions be reasonable. Since reasonableness will depend upon the circumstances, including the nature of one's audience, this implicitly appeals to the nature of the audience, at least to the extent of constraining what it is reasonable to expect of one's audience. See the discussion of Searle below for further restrictions on the nature of the communicative intentions.

5. A coordination problem is one in which two or more agents each need to make a choice about what to do in a given situation and where each one's choice will be affected by how the other chooses to act.

6. This term derives from Dummett (1978: 194).

7. For more discussion see Schiffer (1972: §II.3).

8. We could think of the relevant procedures as those of an individual speaker but there is no reason why we should not think of them as being associated with a particular community of speakers.

9. Note that in this case, unlike that of the hapless American soldier, there is no attempt to deceive – so Jack may intend that none of his intentions is concealed. This meets Blackburn's requirement of full openness (1984: 115), which therefore does not yield sufficiency.

10. One might find Searle's counter-example perplexing on the following grounds. We know that in quite mundane cases of sarcasm, irony and so on the speaker's meaning will differ from the conventional sentence-meaning. So why see Searle's counter-example where the speaker- and sentence-meaning come apart as any more worrying than this? There is this difference between the cases. Arguably, in cases of sarcasm the speaker-meaning is effected on the basis of the literal meaning of the sentence uttered; in Searle's example the speaker-meaning is entirely unrelated to the meaning of the sentence uttered. One way of explaining this might be to say that in uttering a sentence of a particular language there is a level of description where speaker-meaning and sentence-meaning always coincide. So in uttering "You look great!" in circumstances where you clearly look anything but great, I have the intention to announce that you look great and the other associated Gricean intentions. So the speaker-meaning and sentence-meaning coincide. However, the question would then be why I would announce such an obvious falsity and the reason might be: simply in order to draw attention to its falsity, that is, to express my belief in the opposite. So a distinct speaker-meaning would be generated. In Searle's case we cannot generate a speaker-meaning that coincides with the sentence-meaning; arguably it is thus better to say that because the speaker fails to intend to conform to the conventions governing utterance of that sentence, his act is not communicative, although it is aimed at manipulating his audience into forming a certain belief.

11. Or that he is announcing that he is a German officer – but let us ignore this complication.

12. $B_S P$ = S believes that P; $K_S P$ = S knows that P.

13. For the point at issue it matters not whether we focus on Lewis's or Schiffer's account. I focus on the former not because I think it is more plausible – quite the reverse – but simply because it is more familiar.

14. Using Schiffer's "mutual knowledge" in place of Lewis's "common knowledge" simply for uniformity; our task is not to decide between these related conceptions.

15. $K^*_{SA} p$ = S and A mutually know that p.

16. Cf. Schiffer (1972: 164). Instead of saying "is T" says "meets C", but I cannot see that anything important hangs on this.

4. Analysing synonymy

1. One might, I suppose, focus on analysing the notion of meaningfulness, which would seem to have these virtues also. But this would not be a wise strategy. Arguably "*x* is meaningful" means the same as "There is some *y* such that *x* means the same as *y*"; so we would be back to the notion of *meaning the same as*. And otherwise it is hard to see how the notion will be informative about linguistic meaning. If we characterize a general notion of meaningfulness (see Shope [1999] for just such an attempt) and then somehow restrict this to linguistic items, then the latter part of the programme would satisfy our interests: being an element of a language is necessary and sufficient for possessing linguistic meaning. And the prospects look dim for coming up with a more interesting characterization of linguistic meaningfulness: what is shared by each of the diverse range of simple and complex expressions that have meaning? In contrast it does not appear far-fetched to think that there is something interesting shared by those pairs of expressions that are synonymous with one another.

2. See Wright (1983) for argument to this effect.

3. We can explain the notion of one–one match using second-order logic and identity thus:

$$F1\text{–}1G \text{ iff } (\exists R)((x)(\exists y)(Fx \supset Rxy \bullet Gy \bullet (z)(Rxz \bullet Gz \supset z = y) \bullet$$
$$(x)(\exists y)(Gx \supset Ryx \bullet Fy \bullet (z)(Rzx \bullet Fz \supset z = y))$$

4. However, one might question this. Does this not amount to saying that an analytically true sentence is a sentence *correctly* accorded the value true in any *possible* circumstance? And, in Quinean fashion, we should now wonder how we are to explain the notions of correctness and of *possibility*.

5. See the closing pages of the book, where I offer a conception of meaning that is hostile to the idea that a sentence held true in virtue of meaning is vacuous in content.

6. For discouraging discussion of Quine's view here see Grice & Strawson (1956) and Dummett (1978: ch. 22).

5. Radical translation

1. Note the punctuation. The capitalization and the period indicate that we treat the utterance as an utterance of a sentence – so we are tempted to translate the *sentence* "Gavagai." by the *sentence* "Rabbit."

2. See the close of Chapter 4.

3. See Chapter 6 for more detailed discussion of theories of meaning.

4. The example of the gavagese sentence is borrowed from Miller (2007: 147ff.).

5. The clauses are for illustrative purposes only – the use of italics stands in for a more interesting characterization of meaning (it is not one in itself). Such an account might be given in the bracketed clause, which would then replace the italicized clause – see Chapter 6 for an explanation of why such a clause does not contravene Frege's distinction between sense and reference. But no suggestion that we ought to adopt such an account is intended.

6. For discussion of these points see Hookway (1988: 146–54) and Miller's exposition (2007: 149–55).

7. Choosing here to translate "*x*" and "*y*" as terms for rabbits.

8. The principle can take many forms, but whatever form it takes it is an insistence that meanings are, in some sense, public. We shall have much more to say on this topic in the following chapters.

9. "[O]ne may protest that a distinction of meaning unreflected in the totality of dispositions to verbal behaviour is a distinction without a difference" (Quine 1960: 26), quoted above.

10. In fact this scheme follows Hookway (1988: 154–5) more closely.

11. "Fi ... neht ..." is the native conditional, which we are supposed to be able to translate.

6. The structure of a theory of meaning

1. However, just how unthinkable is a moot point: is this a contingent feature of human languages or of anything we can imagine calling a language?
2. But is this mode of dissection mandatory for a systematic theorist? No, see Lewis (1970).
3. Computer languages are another possible example, but note that these are not complete languages.
4. Some philosophers claim that what appear to be assertions in a given area are merely sham assertions, for example, expressivists about ethics. Setting aside internal difficulties with these claims, the claim should not be read as saying that here we have a content that cannot be asserted. Rather the claim is merely that the surface form of these speech acts is deceptive: they are not assertions but, say, expressions of attitude. And we can still assert that we take such-and-such an attitude to such-and-such an act.
5. See many of the essays in Davidson (1984), but especially essay 2.
6. For good introductions to Tarski's work see Tarski (1969), Platts (1979) and Miller (2007).
7. The point goes through equally well if we focus on the other facets of making an assertion.
8. Where, it is hoped, there is a more interesting account of what pain behaviour consists in.
9. See Chapter 14 for elaboration of these issues.

7. Radical interpretation

1. Cf. the discussion of the context principle in Chapter 5.
2. And, of course, if she could make these distinctions she would have additional information about what sentences a speaker does and does not hold true.
3. Other writers making this point include Ramberg (1989: ch. 6), Evnine (1991: §6.3) and Glüer (2006).
4. It is worth being clear that systematicity is not the only constraint; simplicity, for instance, will also play a role. If not, then we could construe speakers systematically and as exceptionlessly right just by allowing ambiguities to be rampant.
5. Grandy's interest is, in fact, translation since Quine rather than Davidson is his focus. But this does not alter the appropriateness of the point.
6. See Ramberg (1989: ch. 6) for trenchant argument to this effect.
7. See the discussion of Quine's views about this in Chapter 6. These views are labelled linguistic pragmatism by Brandom. Linguistic pragmatism comes in a variety of strengths, from those who conceive of meanings as constituted by use to those who think that meanings earn their place in our view of language through being explicative of use.
8. Of course this raises questions about how those beliefs succeed in being about clouds, and Davidson would have to give a holistic answer here: those beliefs mutually support one another; the collection of true beliefs manages to be simply a collection of beliefs about clouds. Or, put in Davidsonian terminology, *given that these beliefs are agreed to be true* (so we are not presupposing the Principle of Charity), an interpretative T-theory will interpret them as beliefs about clouds.
9. See McGinn (1977) for examination of the descriptivist assumptions about reference in play in Davidson's argument.
10. See Dummett's attack on this element in Dummett (1978: 140–44).
11. Of course, some of this knowledge is knowledge that philosophers will deploy in justifying an interpretative principle. But we should not distance too greatly the philosopher's role from that of Davidson's fiction, the radical interpreter. The radical interpreter needs not only to have a means of constructing an interpretative scheme; she needs to be able to justify her methodology to herself. (See the discussion of Foster below.)

12. My suspicion is that Wittgenstein allows that we might say either thing because he takes it that the case is underdescribed and that a range factors might play a role in pushing us in either direction.

13. We shall look at indeterminacy in the context of Davidson's project – the indeterminacy of reference – in Chapter 10.

14. The discussion draws on Dummett (1993: essay 1).

15. Note that the precise operation of the Principle of Charity is not at issue here. That is, we are not concerned with what we do with the relevant sentences but with their status: are they external to the theory and its content or integral to the theory and its content?

16. Again, the precise nature of the constraint is not to the point; what matters is that it applies holistically – that is, to the evidence of speakers' use taken as a whole.

8. Linguistic norms, communication and radical interpretation

1. See Chapter 9 for an explanation of why this might be thought to be so.

2. See LePore (1986: 445), where he does not distinguish between the ability to use language to communicate and linguistic ability.

3. I am using an asterisk here and shall continue to do so for a while. The reason is that norms* have not been shown to be fully fledged norms. So far they cannot be distinguished from mere regularities.

4. Here "history" is meant in a loose sense as that of actual and/or *potential* uses.

5. Note that we only say "*a* theory"; there is no assumption of uniqueness.

6. Davidson could supplant radical interpretation by holding that the unregularized methods provide an epistemically reliable route to convergence but (i) this would make it hard for him to exploit radical interpretation as the means of illuminating the nature of meaning – why then suppose the radical interpreter will have any access to meanings? – and (ii) it is utterly mysterious why these methods should lead to *knowing* convergence. Note that if speaker and hearer cannot know that they have converged on interpretation schemes, then meaning will fail to be public; meanings need to be not merely shareable but capable of being known to be shared.

7. In a sense then we could think of this merely in terms of possession of a set of dispositions to use language. The only problem with that way of putting things is that we also want to think of the interpreter as a speaker, in which case she must intend to display the relevant dispositions, or, as it comes more naturally to say, she must intend to uphold a pattern of use (see below for much more discussion of this).

8. As I said (note 6) we might think of the consequent in terms of intending to have certain dispositions to use, but surely to intend to be disposed to use a term thus and so is just to intend to use it thus and so.

9. There may be such cases: see the literature on pejoratives (e.g. Brandom 1994: 125–30; Dummett 1981: 454; Hornsby 2001; Williamson 2003: §2).

10. *Modulo* the reservations already aired.

11. The challenge here is that if we choose to think of meaning in terms of subjectively correct patterns of use, then how do the objectively correct patterns so much as emerge? See Chapter 14 for more on what is essentially this problem tackled from within the very different perspective of use-conditional accounts of meaning.

12. It was there left undetermined whether a malapropism is the result of a slip or of an idiosyncratic understanding.

13. See Parsons (1973) for a good discussion of truth-theories and ambiguity.

14. We seem obliged, however, to interpret on the basis of evidence that includes the slip as a bona fide use, since it is only after interpretation that the slip is diagnosed as a slip.

15. See Glüer (2001), Ramberg (1989: ch. 8) and Bilgrami (1993) for claims to this effect.

16. I have only sketched the possible link between the two chapters here.

9. Linguistic normativity

1. Miller (2006, forthcoming), Wikforss (2001), Glüer & Pagin (1998) and Horwich (1998) could be added to this list.
2. Pronounced to rhyme with "la-di-da".
3. If points are regarded as already steeped in normativity, suppose that one has to give one's opponent a cookie when she wins a point. The question is then whether I ought to give her a cookie – in the circumstances and given that one is playing this version of tennis, one surely ought.
4. See Hattiangadi (2006: 225 n.4), where she comments on this scope distinction. I see no reason why we should not also consider *oughts* that arise from norms expressed with the following antecedent: "*S* intends to speak *L*", where *L* is some language – English or that of one's parents, say.
5. To use a terminology borrowed from Brandom (1994).
6. It is, of course, likely that one will want to explain linguistic norms and obligations for use of sentences in terms of such norms and obligations relative to the components of the sentence. But laudable as that enterprise undoubtedly is, it is not necessary for me to make my point here.
7. Where "*c*" is a variable ranging over contexts of use – specified in your favoured manner.
8. Presumably we could also argue for: S does not mean that F by $s \to (c)$ (S ought not (to assert s in c if S intends to assert that F, in c)).
9. We could identify this with Millar's notion of use that respects the conditions of true application, use in accordance with meaning (see Millar 2002: 63).
10. Of course, we (legitimately) assume here that one does not have *another* intention that would render (PA″) reasonable.
11. We might have instead (CR): ψing counts as φing.
12. Its general form is: I intend to φ G; F is R to G; So I intend to ψ F. This, formally, is hopeless.
13. See Austin ([1962] 1975: 92–3), §9.3, where these distinctions are exploited again, and the discussion of Searle in Chapter 2, §5.4.
14. Whether meanings are, in addition, constituted by those normative consequences is a further question.
15. It is worth noting that sticking with the premise (R′) does not detract from the *sui generis* nature of the inference. This is because, as Glüer and Pagin correctly point out, the role of the correctness-condition stated by (R′) is to determine a content for *s*.
16. For example, comparativists about metaphor, that is, those who treat the metaphorical statement as equivalent to a non-metaphorical comparative.
17. For example, speaker-meaning theorists about the non-literal, in general, and about metaphor, in particular. Note that there is no assumption that one ought to follow one or another strategy uniformly with respect to all non-literal uses.
18. I take it too that saying need not be distinctively verbal. See Austin ([1962] 1975: 92–3): a phatic act is making an utterance of words "belonging to *and as* belonging to a certain vocabulary"; a rhetic act is uttering words "with a more or less definite 'sense' and a more of less definite 'reference'". Theorists might take different views here; Alston's illocutionary analysis (2000) would reject purely rhetic acts. That is fine; on such an account there must be some illocutionary act performed in using the sentence. We can then think of intending to say that as intending to perform some illocutionary act.
19. Clearly, though, there is no need for it; the revised prescription would cohere with a meaning-shifting approach too.

10. Radical or robust?

1. For now we are taking this as a requirement; we shall examine the basis for the requirement in the next three chapters.
2. Of course being radical is not incompatible with being robust. Indeed, when construed appropriately, it is one way of being robust – but only one way.
3. One's information may well include empirical findings about language.
4. Where p strictly implies q just in case q is true in every possible world in which p is true.
5. "φ^{-1}" stands for the inverse of φ: $\varphi x = y$ iff $x = \varphi^{-1}y$.
6. As Putnam (1981: ch. 2) shows, the example can easily be extended to allow deviant schemes even if we fix assignments of truth-conditions across possible worlds.
7. Not only are there the papers by Davidson but there is Putnam's use of the arguments (1981: ch. 2; 1983: introduction, ch. 1) and various responses (Wallace 1977; Lewis 1984).
8. Note that the relations of CAUSE and CAUSE* will both be complex causal relations, and we cannot prefer one over the other on the basis of being, for instance, naturalistically accept-able. If the relation of CAUSE between "Wilma" and Wilma is naturalistic, then the relation of CAUSE* between "Wilma" and the mother of Wilma is equally naturalistically acceptable (all we need is to ensure that the relation "x is the mother of y" is naturalistic).
9. Note that McDowell would not accept acquisition as we have stated it. Rather, he would claim that its provenance stems from a misplaced empiricist epistemology. Thus I do not think the claim made in the text is controversial. Whatever controversy there is lies one step further back, namely, in the epistemology of understanding.
10. This is not Price's aim. He is interested in naturalistic accounts of what one is able to do by using terms that express concepts that are not themselves susceptible of naturalistic reduction.

11. Language and community

1. Wiggins (1994) pursues what might be a similar strategy, arguing that a Fregean might try to incorporate the lesson of Putnam's examples by employing a notion of sense according to which to form a conception of the relevant concept (in the Fregean sense of that term) the speaker must have encountered instances of the concept.
2. McGinn (1982a,b) argues for such a notion of sense and then uses this to buttress realism by claiming that such a notion of sense shows the manifestation requirement to be misplaced.

12. Rules and privacy: the problem

1. This has become a controversial claim. Some writers now claim that Kripke's sceptical solu-tion is a variety of *factualism* and thus read him as conceding meaning-facts. Whatever the merits of such positions as philosophical views, I find it impossible to treat them as exposi-tions of Kripke. Interested readers should consult Byrne (1996) and Wilson (1998).
2. In Chapter 14 we shall return to assertibility-conditional accounts of meaning. However, that conception of assertion-conditions will be normative: it will encapsulate permissions for the use of a sentence.
3. For more on this see Miller (2007) and Wright (2001: essay 4).
4. It might well seem that this architecture of practices is immediately problematic in that it sets off a regress of policing practices. Although in the text I stick with talk of a practice and its policing practice – so that the crucial feature of rule-following seems to be a matter of the way practices interlock – I do not think that anything crucial depends on this. We could instead talk of a practice of a certain degree of complexity, one that includes judgements about correctness. I thank David Martens for raising this issue.
5. Note that we do not say that the factuality of the policing practice *explains* the internal connec-tion it bears to the practice itself; rather, the claim is that there is no *incoherence* in supposing

that there is such an internal connection, given that the policing practice is factual – although see the next section, where I argue that there is an incoherence on a certain view of what that factuality consists in. Claims of this sort are philosophically familiar; for example take Sellars's (1997) claim that talk of the way things seem presupposes talk of the way things are.

6. See McGinn (1984, 2002) for argument in favour of non-reductionism and Wright (2001: essay 6; reprinted Wright 2002) for a critique of his view as not offering a sufficient response.

13. Rules and privacy: the solution?

1. Others argue that this remark is *not* an observation about the phenomenology of rule-following but about its very nature – that justifications in the end give out. Although obviously I agree that Wittgenstein holds the latter point, my claim here is that Wittgenstein *is* making an observation about the phenomenology of rule-following and is warning us not to provide it with a metaphysical underpinning in terms of the rule as rail.

2. The idea of logical determination is derived from the *Tractatus*. There one thinks of a proposition as determining a division in the totality of facts, of logical space. And so here, by analogy, we think of the rule as detemining similar division among possible moves. In effect the term is a label to contrast with mere causal determination, which, for our purposes, is unproblematic.

3. See, for instance, McDowell (2002: 60–61) and Pettit (2002: 200).

4. The argument in the text is, it must be admitted, too quick. Implementation of a rule will, in most, cases depend on one's beliefs about the relevant situation. Thus it is possible that practitioners may diverge in their actual practice yet adhere to the same rule; agreement in implementation of the rule does not lead directly to agreement in practice. The problem with this thought is that it helps itself to the notion of beliefs, that is, of certain states possessing semantic content. Wittgenstein is, however, concerned with the idea that meaning and contentful states generally exert a normative sway over action. In other words, he would be thinking of having a belief in terms of rule-following. Thus ultimately what we are concerned with is the following of what may be a complex of rules. Now if what counts as correctness in this endeavour is coinciding with one's fellows, then whatever is agreed by the community will be beyond reproach; shared opinions will be true opinions.

5. My thanks to Pedro Tabensky and Ward Jones for pressing this point.

6. Wright's views undergo a significant shift in more recent work. For the early view see Wright (1980) and for the later view see the essays in Wright (2001), in particular, essays 5, 7 and 9.

7. See McDowell (1984, 1991, 1992, 1998b), and especially his "Response to Wright" (1998a).

8. McDowell (1984) has a rather different take on the need for community. In his view the terms in which we need to describe use will have to presuppose content. So we shall, for example, describe a speaker's use of an expression in terms of her ability to use it to assert that such and such. And now his point is that such use requires a community of speakers who make their meanings available to one another in their use of language. See below for my worries about McDowell's position here.

9. See McDowell's papers and Dummett's responses in Taylor (1987) and Heck (1997).

10. We have already noted that this may not be the best way of understanding Dummett's robust approach – see Chapter 10.

11. This problem is raised by Johnston (1993: 124).

12. For a very good survey and prognosis see Smith (1998).

13. See Miller's insightful paper (1998), which advances a view sympathetic to that just sketched. Miller's point is that we can retain Wright's provisional equation without having to face the problems of filling these out in order to substantiate an extension-determining epistemology, for example, by demonstrating substantiality, *a prioricity* and so on. That is fine, but then we still require an explanation of why the equations hold.

14. See Chapter 14 for discussion of this and related issues.
15. To stress, I am discussing only a very limited case of first-personal authority: knowledge of one's meanings. I have not discussed knowledge of grammar nor avowals of one's intentions, beliefs, desires and the like. See Smith (1998) for some hostile commentary about the insubstantial solution offered here and Higginbotham's (1998) response in the same volume for some support. Note, however, that Smith is concerned with recruiting knowledge of one's own meanings in explanation of other avowable knowledge. I would agree with him that the current proposal is likely to be as useful in that enterprise as is a sieve for collecting water.
16. This is not to adopt McGinn's strategy. McGinn claimed that the relevant phenomena relating to language were not unusual and thus called for no explanation. I claim to have given an explanation of the phenomena as they relate to judgements of one's own meanings. True, the linguistic case is embroiled with that of intention; so more needs to be said. But what needs to be said is part of a more general philosophical understanding of intention and that I cannot hope to address here.

14. Truth-conditions versus use-conditions

1. The arguments crop up again and again in Dummett's writings on realism but a good, short account is the early exposition in *Truth and Other Enigmas* (1978: essay 14; see also *ibid.*, preface, and essays 1 and 10; 1993: essay 11).
2. For elaboration of the issues here see Weiss (2007b).
3. Actually, it is not clear whether the right response is to reject truth- in favour of use-conditional accounts. One might instead simply reject the traditional or realist conception of truth-conditions in favour of an anti-realist alternative. The issues here are interesting but technical. For a positive prognosis on such a proposal see Wright (1993: essay 14; 2000); for a negative prognosis see Weiss (2007a). My concern is that: (i) forming a conception of the anti-realist truth-conditions of a sentence will require a conception of the meaning of the sentence, so we cannot, without circularity, then explain meaning in terms of truth-conditions; and (ii) we do not know how to explain these truth-conditions for complex sentences. But see below for more discussion of this aproach.
4. It is not obvious that we face a dilemma here: representationalism or inferentialism. It may be that we can elucidate each set of concepts only by means of relations it bears to concepts in the other set, without being able to reduce the one set to the other. Perhaps, too, the reduction can be run in both directions. See Kremer (forthcoming).
5. See his extended treatment in Dummett (1991b; 1993: essays 2, 4, 6).
6. Note that if Dummett is right to think that he has given a philosophical argument in favour of use-conditional accounts, then he seems to have given a philosophical argument in favour of revising our logic from classical to intuitionistic.
7. To my knowledge, the first to raise the problem was Brandom (1976); for his more recent discussion see *Articulating Reasons* (2000: ch. 6).
8. But see McDowell (1994) for strong disputation of this contention.
9. Wright's approach is precisely this: to explain a notion of indefeasible warrant that constitutes an anti-realist conception of truth (Wright 1993: essay 14). And in mathematics provability is truth for an intuitionist.
10. We could run a similar argument by focusing on the grounds: are these consequences of G_s, that is, C_s, novel or not? If novel, then its meaning has changed; if not, then S's grounds and consequences match. See Dummett (1991b: chs 9–13) for his development of these ideas in terms of the notions of conservative extension, harmony and stability.
11. The seminal source of these discussion lies in a debate between Prior (1960) and Belnap (1962) about how the meanings of logical constants might be specified by means of rules for their use: introduction rules and elimination rules.

12. The content of the presupposition is captured in the conditional claim: If G_s, then C_s. What the text argues is that we do not need to justify the presupposition by deriving the conditional. Nor do we have to verify the truth of the conditional in advance of adopting the practice. Rather, we shall reject or modify the practice if the conditional can be shown to be false. But that raises other issues since the content of the conditional claim needs to be settled. It is far from obvious that occasional instances of the truth of G_s combined with the falsity of C_s will suffice to unsettle the presupposition: it may be sufficient that there be some reliable inference from G_s to C_s.

13. Inferences that are not guaranteed to be truth-preserving.

14. Brandom questions the notion of superassertibility. Either extensions of an investigator's states of information can include the introduction of false beliefs or they cannot. If they cannot, then the exclusion of false beliefs presupposes a concept of truth. If they can, then a false content may be superassertible because it remains assertible as a consequence of the inclusion of the false belief. I do not think that this is a good criticism. We are entitled to restrict the extensions to include only warranted beliefs. Brandom thus argues that a content may be superassertible because some other false belief might be warranted and included in our state of information no matter how it is extended. Thus the false belief he considers must be enduringly warranted, which is to say that it is superassertible. So he demonstrates simply that a false content is superassertible if a false content is superassertible.

15. This observation is the basis of Wright's attack on the notion of criteria (see Wright 1993: essays 12, 13). Criteria are supposed both to be defeasible and to be necessarily good evidence for a claim. Wright shows that this conjunction is incoherent since a prevalence of defeat will undermine a criterion's status as necessarily good evidence.

16. One might take Quine's conclusion to be intolerable and thus treat the argument as a *reductio ad absurdum* of either premise 1 or 2. If one accepts premise 2, then obviously the force of the argument will be focused on premise 1. Now if, in contrast to the use-conditionalist just described, a truth-conditionalist cannot reject premise 1 – how, on a truth-conditional view, do we account for speakers' commitments to the truth of a sentence in virtue of its meaning, without supposing that the sentence is true in virtue of meaning? – then we have another argument against truth- and in favour of use-conditional accounts of meaning.

Bibliography

Alston, W. 2000. *Illocutionary Acts and Sentence Meaning*. Ithaca, NY: Cornell University Press.

Austin, J. L. [1962] 1975. *How to do Things with Words*, 2nd edn, J. O. Urmson & Marina Sbisà (eds). Oxford: Clarendon Press.

Auxier, R. E. & L. E. Hahn (eds) 2007. *The Philosophy of Michael Dummett*. Chicago, IL: Open Court.

Belnap, N. D. 1962. "Tonk, Plonk and Plink". *Analysis* **22**(6): 130–34.

Bilgrami, A. 1993. "Norms and Meaning". In *Reflecting Davidson*, R. Stoecker (ed.), 121–44. Berlin: de Gruyter.

Blackburn, S. 1984. *Spreading the Word: Groundings in the Philosophy of Language*. Oxford: Clarendon Press.

Boghossian, P. 2003. "Blind Reasoning". *Aristotelian Society: Supplementary Volume* Supp. **77**(1): 225–48.

Boghossian, P. 2005. "Is Meaning Normative?" In *Philosophy – Science – Scientific Philosophy*, A. Beckerman & C. Nimtz (eds), 205–18. Paderborn: Mentis.

Brandom, R. 1976. "Truth and Assertibility". *Journal of Philosophy* **73**(6): 137–49.

Brandom, R. 1994. *Making it Explicit: Reasoning, Representing, and Discursive Commitment*. Cambridge, MA: Harvard University Press.

Brandom, R. 2000. *Articulating Reasons: An Introduction to Inferentialism*. Cambridge, MA: Harvard University Press.

Brandom, R. 2008. *Between Saying and Doing: Towards an Analytic Pragmatism*. Oxford: Oxford University Press.

Byrne, A. 1996. "On Misinterpreting Kripke's Wittgenstein". *Philosophy and Phenomenological Research* **56**(2): 339–43.

Carnap, R. 1934. *The Unity of Science*. London: Kegan Paul.

Carroll, L. 1982. *The Complete Illustrated Works of Lewis Carroll*. London: Chancellor Press.

Clark, P. & B. Hale (eds) 1994. *Reading Putnam*. Oxford: Blackwell.

Davidson, D. 1984. *Inquiries into Truth and Interpretation*. Oxford: Clarendon Press.

Davidson, D. 2001a. *Essays on Actions and Events*, 2nd edn. Oxford: Clarendon Press.

Davidson, D. 2001b. *Subjective, Intersubjective, Objective*. Oxford: Clarendon Press.

Davidson, D. 2005a. *Truth, Language and History*. Oxford: Clarendon Press.

Davidson, D. 2005b. *Truth and Predication*. Cambridge, MA: Harvard University Press.

Devitt, M. & R. Hanley (eds) 2006. *The Blackwell Guide to the Philosophy of Language*. Oxford: Blackwell.

Dummett, M. A. E. 1978. *Truth and Other Enigmas*. London: Duckworth.

Dummett, M. A. E. 1981. *Frege: Philosophy of Language*, 2nd edn. London: Duckworth.

Dummett, M. A. E. 1991a. *Frege and Other Philosophers*. Oxford: Clarendon Press.

Dummett, M. A. E. 1991b. *The Logical Basis of Metaphysics*. London: Duckworth.

Dummett, M. A. E. 1993. *The Seas of Language*. Oxford: Clarendon Press.

Dummett, M. A. E. 2000. *Elements of Intuitionism*, 2nd edn. Oxford: Clarendon Press.

Dummett, M. A. E. forthcoming. "Should Semantics be Deflated?" In *Reading Brandom: Making it Explicit*, J. Wanderer & B. Weiss (eds). London: Routledge.

Evans, G. 1985. *Collected Papers*. Oxford: Clarendon Press.

Evans, G. & J. McDowell (eds) 1999. *Truth and Meaning: Essays in Semantics*. Oxford: Clarendon Press.

Evnine, S. 1991. *Donald Davidson*. Cambridge: Polity.

Foster, J. A. 1999. "Meaning and Truth Theory". In *Truth and Meaning: Essays in Semantics*, G. Evans & J. McDowell (eds), 1–32. Oxford: Clarendon Press.

Frege, G. 1953. *The Foundations of Arithmetic: A Logicomathematical Enquiry into the Concept of Number*, 2nd edn. Oxford: Blackwell.

Frege, G. 1977. *Logical Investigations*, P. Geach & B. Stoothoff (eds). Oxford: Blackwell.

Frege, G. 1979. *Posthumous Writings of Gottlob Frege*, H. Hermes, F. Kambartel & F. Kaulbach (eds). Oxford: Blackwell.

Frege, Gottlob. 1980a. *Philosophical and Mathematical Correspondence*, G. Gabriel & B. McGuinness (eds). Oxford: Blackwell.

Frege, G. 1980b. *Translations from the Philosophical Writings of Gottlob Frege*, 3rd edn, P. T. Geach & Max Black (eds). Oxford: Blackwell.

Glüer, K. 2001. "Dreams and Nightmare: Conventions, Norms and Meaning in Davidson's Philosophy of Language". In *Interpreting Davidson*, P. Kotatko, P. Pagin & G. Segal (eds), 57–74. CSLI lecture notes no. 129. London: CSLI Publications.

Glüer, K. 2006. "The Status of Charity I: Conceptual Truth or *A Posteriori* Necessity?" *International Journal of Philosophical Studies* **14**(3): 337–59.

Glüer, K. & P. Pagin 1998. "Rules of Meaning and Practical Reasoning". *Synthese* **117**(2): 207–27.

Goldfarb, W. 2002. "Kripke on Wittgenstein on Rules". In *Rule-following and Meaning*, A. Miller & C. Wright (eds), 92–107. Chesham: Acumen. Originally published as "Kripke on Wittgenstein on Rules", *Journal of Philosophy* **82**(9) (1985), 471–88.

Grandy, R. 1973. "Reference, Meaning, and Belief". *Journal of Philosophy* **70**: 439–52.

Grice, H. P. 1957. "Meaning". *Philosophical Review* **66**: 377–88.

Grice, H. P. 1968. "Utterer's Meaning, Sentence-meaning, and Word-meaning". *Foundations of Language* **4**: 225–42.

Grice, H. P. 1969. "Utterer's Meaning and Intentions". *Philosophical Review* **78**: 147–77.

Grice, H. P. 1989. *Studies in the Way of Words*. Cambridge, MA: Harvard University Press.

Grice, H. P. & P. F. Strawson 1956. "In Defense of a Dogma". *Philosophical Review* **65**(2): 141–58.

Haldane, J. & C. Wright (eds) 1993. *Reality, Representation and Projection*. Oxford: Oxford University Press.

Hale, B. & C. Wright (eds) 1997. *A Companion to the Philosophy of Language*. Oxford: Blackwell.

Harnish, R. M. (ed.) 1994. *Basic Topics in the Philosophy of Language*. London: Harvester Wheatsheaf.

Hattiangadi, A. 2006. "Is Meaning Normative?" *Mind and Language* **21**(2): 220–40.

Heck, R. G. (ed.) 1997. *Language, Thought, and Logic: Essays in Honour of Michael Dummett*. Oxford: Oxford University Press.

Higginbotham, J. 1998. "On Knowing One's Own Language". In *Knowing Our Own Minds*, C. Wright, B. C. Smith & C. MacDonald (eds), 429–42. Oxford: Oxford University Press.

Hookway, C. 1988. *Quine : Language, Experience and Reality*. Cambridge: Polity.

Hornsby, J. 2001. "Meaning and Uselessness: How to Think about Derogatory Words". *Midwest Studies in Philosophy* **25**: 128–41.

Horwich, P. 1998. *Meaning*. Oxford: Oxford University Press.

Johnston, M. 1993. "Objectivity Refigured: Pragmatism Without Verificationism". In *Reality, Representation and Projection*, J. Haldane & C. Wright (eds), 85–130. Oxford: Oxford University Press.

Kölbel, M. 2002. *Truth without Objectivity*. London: Routledge.

Kölbel, M. & B. Weiss (eds) 2004. *Wittgenstein's Lasting Significance*. London: Routledge.

Kotatko, P., P. Pagin & G. Segal (eds) 2001. *Interpreting Davidson*, CSLI lecture notes no. 129. London: CSLI Publications.

Kremer, M. forthcoming. "Representation or Inference: Must we Choose? Should we?" In *Reading Brandom: Making it Explicit*, J. Wanderer & B. Weiss (eds). London: Routledge.

Kripke, S. A. 1980. *Naming and Necessity*, rev. & enlarged edn. Oxford: Blackwell.

Kripke, S. A. 1982. *Wittgenstein on Rules and Private Language: An Elementary Exposition*. Oxford: Blackwell.

LePore, E. (ed.) 1986. *Truth and Interpretation: Perspectives on the Philosophy of Donald Davidson*. Oxford: Blackwell.

LePore, E. & K. Ludwig 2005. *Donald Davidson: Meaning, Truth, Language, and Reality*. Oxford: Clarendon Press.

LePore, E. & B. C. Smith (eds) 2006. *The Oxford Handbook of the Philosophy of Language*. Oxford: Oxford University Press.

Lewis, D. 1969. *Convention: A Philosophical Study*. Cambridge, MA: Harvard University Press.

Lewis, D. 1970. "General Semantics". *Synthese* **22**: 18–67.

Lewis, D. 1983. *Philosophical Papers*, vol. 1. Oxford: Oxford University Press.

Lewis, D. 1984. "Putnam's Paradox". *Australasian Journal of Philosophy* **62**: 221–36.

Lycan, W. G. 2000. *Philosophy of Language: A Contemporary Introduction*. London: Routledge.

McCulloch, G. 1989. *The Game of the Name: Introducing Logic, Language and Mind*. Oxford: Clarendon Press.

McDowell, J. 1976. "Truth Conditions, Bivalence and Verificationism". In *Truth and Meaning*, G. Evans & J. McDowell (eds), 42–66. Oxford: Clarendon Press.

McDowell, J. 1981. "Anti-realism and the Epistemology of Understanding". In *Meaning and Understanding*, H. Parret & J. Bouveresse (eds), 225–48. Berlin: de Gruyter.

McDowell, J. 1982. "Criteria, Defeasibility, and Knowledge". In *Proceedings of the British Academy* **68**: 455–79. Oxford: Oxford University Press.

McDowell, J. 1984. "Wittgenstein on Following a Rule". *Synthese* **58**: 325–64.

McDowell, J. 1987. "In Defence of Modesty". In *Michael Dummett: Contributions to Philosophy*, B. Taylor (ed.), 59–80. Dordrecht: Nijhoff.

McDowell, J. 1991. "Intentionality and Interiority in Wittgenstein: Comment on Crispin Wright". In *Meaning Scepticism*, K. Puhl (ed.), 148–69. Berlin: de Gruyter.

McDowell, J. 1992. "Meaning and Intentionality in Wittgenstein's Later Philosophy". *Midwest Studies in Philosophy* **17**: 40–52.

McDowell, J. 1994. *Mind and World*. Cambridge, MA: Harvard University Press.

McDowell, J. 1997. "Another Plea for Modesty". In *Language, Thought, and Logic: Essays in Honour of Michael Dummett*, R. Heck (ed.). Oxford: Oxford University Press.

McDowell, J. 1998a. "Response to Crispin Wright". In *Knowing our own Minds*, C. Wright, B. C. Smith & C. MacDonald (eds), 47–62. Oxford: Clarendon Press.

McDowell, J. 1998b. "Meaning and Intentionality in Wittgenstein's Later Philosophy". In his *Mind, Value, and Reality*, 263–322. Cambridge, MA: Harvard University Press.

McDowell, J. 2002. "Wittgenstein on Following a Rule". In *Rule-following and Meaning*, A. Miller & C. Wright (eds), 81–91. Chesham: Acumen.

McGinn, C. 1977. "Charity, Interpretation, and Belief". *Journal of Philosophy* **74**: 521–35.

McGinn, C. 1982a. "Realist Semantics and Content Ascription". *Synthese* **52**: 113–34.

McGinn, C. 1982b. "The Structure of Content". In *Thought and Object: Essays on Intentionality*, A. Woodfield (ed.), 207–58. Oxford: Clarendon Press.

McGinn, C. 1984. *Wittgenstein on Meaning: An Interpretation and Evaluation*. Oxford: Blackwell.

McGinn, M. 1997. *Routledge Philosophy Guidebook to Wittgenstein and the Philosophical Investigations*. London: Routledge.

McGinn, C. 2002. "Wittgenstein, Kripke and Non-Reductionism about Meaning". In *Rule-following and Meaning*, A. Miller & C. Wright (eds), 129–40. Chesham: Acumen.

Millar, A. 2002. "The Normativity of Meaning". In *Logic, Thought and Language* (Royal Institute of Philosophy Supplement 51), A. O'Hear (ed.), 57–73. Cambridge: Cambridge University Press.

Millar, A. 2004. *Understanding People: Normativity and Rationalizing Explanation*. Oxford: Clarendon Press.

Miller, A. 1998. "Rule-following, Response-dependence, and McDowell's Debate with Anti-realism". In *European Review of Philosophy, Volume 3: Response-Dependence*, R. Casati & C. Tappolet (eds), 75–97. Stanford, CA: CSLI Publications.

Miller, A. 2006. "Meaning Scepticism". In *The Blackwell Guide to the Philosophy of Language*, M. Devitt & R. Hanley (eds), 91–113. Oxford: Blackwell.

Miller, A. 2007. *Philosophy of Language*, 2nd edn. London: Routledge.

Miller, A. forthcoming. "The Argument from Queerness and the Normativity of Meaning". In *Truth, Existence and Realism*, M. Grajner & A. Rami (eds). Paderborn: Mentis.

Miller, A. & C. Wright (eds) 2002 *Rule-following and Meaning*. Chesham: Acumen.

Parsons, K. P. 1973. "Ambiguity and the Truth Definition". *Noûs* **7**: 379–93.

Pettit, P. 2002. "The Reality of Rule Following". In *Rule-following and Meaning*, A. Miller & C. Wright (eds), 188–208. Chesham: Acumen. Originally published as "The Reality of Rule Following", *Mind* **99** (1990), 1–21.

Platts, M. de Bretton. 1979. *Ways of Meaning: An Introduction to a Philosophy of Language*. London: Routledge & Kegan Paul.

Price, H. 2004. "Immodesty without Mirrors: Making Sense of Wittgenstein's Linguistic Pluralism". In *Wittgenstein's Lasting Significance*, M. Kölbel & B Weiss (eds), 179–205. London: Routledge.

Prior, A. N. 1960. "The Runabout Inference-ticket. *Analysis* **21**: 38–9.

Puhl, K. (ed.) 1991. *Meaning Scepticism*. Berlin: de Gruyter.

Putnam, H. 1975. *Mind, Language and Reality. Philosophical Papers*, vol. 2. Cambridge: Cambridge University Press.

Putnam, H. 1978. *Meaning and the Moral Sciences*. London: Routledge & Kegan Paul.

Putnam, H. 1981. *Reason, Truth and History*. Cambridge: Cambridge University Press.

Putnam, H. 1983. *Realism and Reason: Philosophical Papers*, vol. 3. Cambridge: Cambridge University Press.

Quine, W. V. 1960. *Word and Object*. Cambridge, MA: MIT Press.

Quine, W. V. 1961. *From a Logical Point of View: Logico-philosophical Essays*, 2nd edn. Cambridge, MA: Harvard University Press.

Quine, W. V. 1962. *Methods of Logic*, 2nd edn. London: Routledge & Kegan Paul.

Quine, W. V. 1970. "On Reasons for the Indeterminacy of Translation". *Journal of Philosophy* **67**: 178–83.

Ramberg, B. T. 1989. *Donald Davidson's Philosophy of Language: An Introduction*. Oxford: Blackwell.

Russell, B. 1903. *The Principles of Mathematics*, London: Allen & Unwin.

Russell, B. 1956. *Logic and Knowledge. Essays, 1901–1950*, R. Charles Marsh (ed.). London: Allen & Unwin.

Russell, B. 1973. *Essays in Analysis*, D. Lackey (ed.). London: Allen & Unwin.

Russell, B. 1992. *Theory of Knowledge: The 1913 Manuscript*, E. Ramsden Eames & K. Blackwell (eds). London: Routledge.

Schiffer, S. R. 1972. *Meaning*. Oxford: Clarendon Press.

Searle, J. R. 1958. "Proper Names". *Mind: A Quarterly Review of Philosophy* **67**: 166–73.

Searle, J. R. 1969. *Speech Acts: An Essay in the Philosophy of Language*. Cambridge: Cambridge University Press.

Sellars, W. 1953. "Is There a Synthetic *A Priori*?" *Philosophy of Science* **20**: 121–38.

Sellars, W. 1997. *Empiricism and the Philosophy of Mind*. Cambridge, MA: Harvard University Press.

Shope, R. K. 1999 *The Nature of Meaningfulness*. Lanham, MD: Rowman & Littlefield.

Smith, B. C. 1998. "On Knowing one's own Language". In *Knowing Our Own Minds*, C. Wright, B. C. Smith & C. MacDonald (eds), 391–428. Oxford: Oxford University Press.

Stoecker, R. (ed.) 1993. *Reflecting Davidson: Donald Davidson Responding to an International Forum of Philosophers*. Berlin: de Gruyter.

Strawson, P. F. 1971. *Logico-linguistic Papers*. London: Methuen.

Tarski, A. 1944. "The Semantic Conception of Truth and the Foundations of Semantics". *Philosophy and Phenomenological Research* **4**: 341–76.

Tarski, A. 1969. "Truth and Proof". *Scientific American* **220**: 63–77.

Taylor, B. (ed.) 1987. *Michael Dummett: Contributions to Philosophy*. Dordrecht: Nijhoff.

Thayer, H. S. (ed.) 1970. *Pragmatism: The Classic Writings*. New York: New American Library.

Wallace, J. 1977. "Only in the Context of a Sentence do Words have any Meaning". *Midwest Studies in Philosophy* **2**: 144–64.

Wanderer, J. 2008. *Robert Brandom*. Stocksfield: Acumen.

Wanderer, J. & B. Weiss (eds) forthcoming. *Reading Brandom: Making it Explicit*. London: Routledge.

Weiss, B. 1996. "Anti-realism, Truth-value Links and Tensed Truth Predicates". *Mind: A Quarterly Review of Philosophy* **105**(420): 577–602.

Weiss, B. 2002. *Michael Dummett*. Chesham: Acumen.

Weiss, B. 2004. "Knowledge of Meaning". *Proceedings of the Aristotelian Society* **104**: 75–94.

Weiss, B. 2007a. "Anti-realist Truth and Anti-realist Meaning". *American Philosophical Quarterly* **44**(3) (July): 213–28.

Weiss, B. 2007b. "Molecularity and Revisionism". In *The Philosophy of Michael Dummett*, R. E. Auxier & L. E. Hahn (eds), 601–16. Chicago, IL: Open Court.

Weiss, B. 2007c. "Truth and the Enigma of Knowability". *Dialectica* **61**(4): 521–37.

Wiggins, D. 1994. "Putnam's Doctrine of Natural Kind Words and Frege's Doctrines of Sense, Reference, and Extension: Can They Cohere?". In *Reading Putnam*, P. Clark & B. Hale (eds), 201–15. Oxford: Blackwell.

Wikforss, A. M. 2001. "Semantic Normativity". *Philosophical Studies* **102**(2): 203–26.

Williamson, T. 2003. "Blind Reasoning: Understanding and Inference". *Aristotelian Society: Supplementary Volume* **77**: 249–93.

Wilson, G. M. 1998. "Semantic Realism and Kripke's Wittgenstein". *Philosophy and Phenomenological Research* **58**(1): 99–122.

Wilson, N. L. 1959. "Substances Without Substrata". *Review of Metaphysics* **12**: 521–39.

Wittgenstein, L. 1922. *Tractatus Logico-philosophicus*. London: Routledge & Kegan Paul.

Wittgenstein, L. 1958. *Philosophical Investigations*, 2nd edn. Oxford: Blackwell.

Wittgenstein, L. 1969. *On Certainty*, G. E. M. Anscombe & G. H. von Wright (eds), D. Paul & G. E. M. Anscombe (trans.). Oxford: Blackwell.

Wittgenstein, L. 1978. *Remarks on the Foundations of Mathematics*, G. H. von Wright, R. Rhees & G. E. M. Anscombe (eds), 3rd edn. Oxford: Blackwell.

Wittgenstein, L. 1979. *Notebooks, 1914–1916 [of] Ludwig Wittgenstein*, 2nd edn, G. H. von Wright & G. E. M. Anscombe (eds). Oxford: Blackwell.

Wright, C. 1980. *Wittgenstein on the Foundations of Mathematics*. Cambridge, MA: Harvard University Press.

Wright, C. 1983. *Frege's Conception of Numbers as Objects*. Aberdeen: Aberdeen University Press.

Wright, C. 1992. *Truth and Objectivity*. Cambridge, MA: Harvard University Press.

Wright, C. 1993. *Realism, Meaning and Truth*, 2nd edn. Oxford: Blackwell.

Wright, C. 1994. "On Putnam's Proof that we are not Brains in a Vat". In *Reading Putnam*, P. Clark & B. Hale (eds), 216–41. Oxford: Blackwell.

Wright, C. 2000. "Truth as Sort of Epistemic: Putnam's Peregrinations". *Journal of Philosophy* **97**(6): 335–64.

Wright, C. 2001. *Rails to Infinity: Essays on Themes from Wittgenstein's Philosophical Investigations*. Cambridge, MA: Harvard University Press.

Wright, C. 2002. "Meaning and Intention as Judgement Dependent". In *Rule-following and Meaning*, A. Miller & C. Wright (eds), 129–40. Chesham: Acumen.

Wright, C. 2003. *Saving the Differences: Essays on Themes from Truth and Objectivity*. Cambridge, MA: Harvard University Press.

Wright, C. & B. Hale forthcoming. "Assertibilist Truth and Objective Content: Still Inexplicit?" In *Reading Brandom: Making it Explicit*, J. Wanderer & B. Weiss (eds). London: Routledge.

Wright, C., B. C. Smith & C. MacDonald (eds) 1998. *Knowing our own Minds*. Oxford: Clarendon Press.

Zalabardo, J. L. 1997. "Kripke's Normativity Argument". *Canadian Journal of Philosophy* **27**(4): 467–88.

Zalabardo, J. L. 2000. "Realism Detranscendentalized". *European Journal of Philosophy* **8**(1): 63–88.

Zalabardo, J. L. 2003. "Wittgenstein on Accord". *Pacific Philosophical Quarterly* **84**(3): 311–29.

Index

worlds, possible   30, 257n.4 (ch. 10), 257n.6
Wright, Crispin   233, 244, 253n.2 (ch. 4),
    258n.6 (ch. 12), 258n.6 (ch. 13), 258n.13,
    260n.15

on rules   205–8, 213, 215, 218, 257n.3 (ch.
    12)
on judgement dependence   221–9
on superassertibility   245–7, 259n.3, 259n. 9